Walk with the Wind

The Endless Circle

by

Thomas W Savage

Edited by

Thomas W. Savage

Copyright and Disclaimer

Acknowledgements

This story came to me in unspoken words, words heard in the hearts of those who sit quietly listening high atop the mountains as they view the wonders of nature. I would be remiss, however, were I not to recognize the help of my family and the friends with which I am blessed in my life.

To my wife Pat, who toiled endlessly beside me and supported me during the writing of this book, I give you my heartfelt thanks.

To Steve who guided and advised me often, and to my daughters who were a wonderful soundboard for my ideas, I say thank you.

To Marjorie, who first edited this text and worked with the tenacity of a badger, I say again, you were exactly the person I needed for this book, Thank you, Marjorie.

My best friend's life journey ended as I completed this book. Together, my dog and I walked untold miles in the mountains as this story grew in my mind, and he lay at my feet as I brought it to life on paper. Thank you, Reno, for your tracks before me, in the trail.

Tommy.

For comment or discussion, I can be reached at tommys@3rivers.net. I thank you in advance for your reviews. Post your thoughts about *Walk with the Wind* at *amazonbooks.com.*

Table of Contents

Pronunciation

Written form and spoken form

Tateh = Tăh-těh'

Wahketa = Wăh-Kē'-tuh

Woslolkia = Wō-slō'l-kē-ŭh

Ksapa = Kŭh-să'-pŭh

Wicala = Wĭh-căh'-lŭh

Zomika = Zōh-mē'-kŭ

Kasota = Kŭh-sōh'-tăh

Glossary

1. *All that is* = All of Creation
2. *Changleska* = The hoop; the circle of life
3. *Creeping crawlers* = Insects
4. *Great water birds* = Geese
5. *The four-legged ones* = All four-legged animals including deer, elk, bear, and others
6. *The great circle of life* = A person's journey from the time of his/her birth to the time of his/her death
7. *The rooted ones* = All plants and trees
8. *The two-legged ones* = Man
9. *Ones who carry thunder* = ones who hunt with rifles.

10. *The safe place* = The thicket of trees in which a calf elk stays after birth until strong enough to travel with its mother
11. *The season of ducks returning* = Spring
12. *The season of growing grass* = Summer
13. *The season of falling leaves* = Fall
14. *The season of renewal* = Winter
15. *The season of ripening berries* = Late summer
16. *The season of yellowing leaves* = Early fall
17. *The season of killing* = Hunting season
18. *The Wakia*; Also known as, The Thunder beings = Spirits, believed by the Native Americans, to travel cloaked in the clouds of thunderstorms; spirits that hurl lightning to the earth, purifying both air and earth in the process.

Chapter One

The nearly impenetrable fog through which I now walked had descended suddenly. It had come floating mysteriously down the canyon sides and quickly consumed this ancient tree-filled canyon that was my mountain home. The sun was hidden somewhere above, and all had become bathed in a translucent whiteness of churning clouds and swirling wisps that floated silently through the forest around me.

It was a warm mist, though, and it embraced me in a curiously reassuring way. I felt protected and concealed, safely hidden from all things threatening. A wonderful, warm light emanated through the murk, and I felt as if I could see as plainly in this blinding fog as I ever had on the clearest of days. Tiny beads of water clung to lush, green blades of grass and from the moss hanging on the limbs of the great rooted ones around me. The droplets captured this strange light and released it in small bursts of glimmering color as I moved by. Until now, I had only seen these shimmering colors in the rainbows above my mountain home.

As I walked through the woods this day, it was as though I was feeling the soft earth and plants beneath my feet and seeing the shapes of this bizarre new forest for the first time. I stared in awe at the shapes of this once familiar woodland that now seemed to float past me in the haze as I moved slowly along. The ghostly forms of huge trees with twisted, reaching branches seemed to spring suddenly forward as I approached, then vanish again into the fog as I passed, hiding as if with a life their own. The menacing silhouettes of great bears towered suddenly from the fog in the trail ahead. They faded slowly into huge, moss-covered rocks as I neared, then sank quietly into the gloom behind me as I walked on. Gnarly, twisted roots, pulled from the forest floor by the crashing fall of an ancient giant, would appear suddenly from the murk as I approached. They would strain frightfully forward as if to seize and hold me, but then disappear harmlessly in the mist as I moved on.

This strange fog heightened my senses, though. I was certain that the alluring smells about which I was suddenly aware, came to my nose for the first time. The steam rising from the trail before me, held a rich fullness. Captured in the scent of the moist soil was the story of relatives who had long ago passed to the earth upon which I now walked. My senses were filled with their fleeting words, but one my age could not hope to understand the meaning of their ancient message. The tangy smell of fir and pine trees hidden in the white mist was intoxicating, tempered only by the musky aroma of awakening aspen. Nearly overwhelming was the smell of the rich, abundant grass underfoot, mingled with the sweet scent of newly formed buds on the bushes around me. Buds, that would soon be brightly colored berries.

Through the blinding haze came the whispering voice of the forest in a way that only one without sight could hear. I felt as though the sounds I had heard here in the past were but a distant dream. It seemed the sounds that now echoed through this wonderful mist came to my ears for the first time. I became aware

8

of a soft breeze that played quietly through branches, and gently rattled leaves hidden in the fog around me.

Soooooon, the mysterious voice seemed to say to me as it pushed the billowing clouds of mist along.

As I listened more closely, I realized that many voices spoke from the shrouded forest around me. The wind passing over the rough, weathered surfaces of rocks both large and small, and through the twisted branches and leaves of the trees gave to each a voice of its own. They now shared their secrets with all who listened. From somewhere overhead, surely in the clear blue sky far above this hidden world, came the whistling screech of a great winged one. The eagle's echoing voice told of the huge circles it flew in the sky above.

'What a wondrous sight this fog-cloaked land must be from so far above,' I thought.

From another direction came the deep, reverberating voice of *owl,* a voice heard normally only at night.

'The strange near-darkness caused by this blinding murk,' I reasoned, 'must have deceived even this wise one.'

The ever-quickening thump, thump, thump sound from the drumming wings of mating grouse echoed softly from the forest around me. I could hear the raucous call of raven as it flew through the forest somewhere far away. It searched carefully, I knew, for those animals who had passed in the night, and upon which he would feast today. From all directions came the voice of squirrel as

9

they gathered pinecones in preparation for the next snowy *season of renewal*. Their chattering call told their mates of their ever-changing locations as they worked. Their tiny claws made scratching noises on the bark of the great rooted ones hidden in the whiteness as they scurried quickly along on their relentless quest.

Alongside my trail, a small brook barely one step wide, gently stroked flowing lines of water plants that grew beneath its surface. From the tiny creek came a cheerful, gurgling sound as it coursed between lichen-covered rocks, and splashed over moss covered logs. A sense of joy and belonging rushed suddenly over me. I realized that like all that I beheld around me, I, too, was a part of this wondrous place.

Here in the mountains, it was now the season of *ducks returning*. The heavy snows from *the time of renewal* had receded finally, and waking rooted ones now grew tall and green as the sunny days became longer. Winged ones and small animals were everywhere, flying or scurrying this way and that, preparing for the season of *growing grass*, during which each would bring new life to the forest. So intent were they on their private missions, they did not seem to notice this wonderful fog or my passing.

Behind me, walked my most trusted friend and teacher, Woslolkia. Woslolkia was an enormous bull elk who stood tall and burly. His chest was broad and deep. Muscles rippled beneath the sleek tan hair on his shoulders and hips as he walked. Dark, thick antlers grew from his head, reaching far beyond his sides. They towered above him to such a height, that when he tipped his head to look upward, his great white-tipped antlers reached well behind his rump. Woslolkia was certainly the most magnificent bull our kind ever comes to be.

"The first people who shared this land with us," he had told me, "called certain ones of our kind, *Woslolkia, ones who know.*" This name, he said, had been passed down through generations of our kind, to him.

"These first two-legged ones," he said, "were wise and lived in harmony with the land and respected all things that existed here." Woslolkia called me "Tateh," the ancient two-legged-ones' word for *wind.* "This," he said, "was because, the wind touches all in the mountains and knows all the secret places there," as I would someday.

Woslolkia, from my earliest memory had always been with me. Guiding, and prodding me patiently along, he taught me that which I would need to know to live and survive in our mountains. I wanted desperately to someday be as big, as strong, and as magnificent and wise as was Woslolkia.

We traveled this trail today to a secret destination only Woslolkia knew. The steady crunching sound made by his heavy feet behind me was especially comforting in this blinding fog. His presence filled me with confidence as he prodded me on to this mysterious place where he said, "we must soon be."

The fog became thicker, and now I could barely see the grass and small plants growing at the trail's edge.

"Woslolkia," I said nervously, "are you still there?" as the fear of hidden enemies settled over me.

"Yes," said Woslolkia calmly, "I am here, Tateh." "Do not fear this fog that blinds your eyes and shrouds from view that which surrounds you. And have no fear either, when the sun rests below the mountains, and you are engulfed in darkness, blinded as you are now. It is during these special times when you will learn to see with eyes that see always, regardless of blinding fog or darkness of night. You will learn to see, Tateh, with the eyes of your heart. When you become able finally to see with your heart, and trust what you feel there, you will no longer fear the unseen. You will walk with strong, firm steps on your chosen path in darkness or fog."

"Know this, Tateh," continued Woslolkia, "we, the four-legged ones, the two-legged ones, all the rooted ones, flying ones, swimming ones, and creeping crawlers, come from one Mother, our Mother, the Earth. When our journeys here are done, our mortal bodies will return to Her. All things here come from, depend on, and return finally to the same Mother. All things in our world, both living and not, are related. Indeed, Tateh, we are all *one*," said Woslolkia.

"Feel the soil and rock that is beneath your feet. Though they do not live," he continued, "hear them speak to you in the sound of your hooves as you walk. Hear the voice of the rooted ones that brush your sides as you move past. Look at your countless relatives of every shape and size, that surround you now.

12

Remember the great *oneness* that you share with each of them. We are all a small part of our Mother Earth. This new awareness will ground and center you as your path leads you through times of darkness on your great journey. Knowing that all things around you are brothers and sisters, you will walk fearlessly forward. Your steps will be strong and firm on that from which you came, your Mother, the Earth."

"Thank you, Woslolkia," I said quietly, "your words comfort me and give me strength. I will now carry a feeling of oneness with that which I cannot see. With this knowledge you have given me, I now have the courage to walk this foggy trail in wonder instead of fear."

"Yes, Tateh," said Woslolkia, "think often about this oneness you share with your relatives. As you travel through this ancient land that is our home," he continued, "understand that in this great oneness, each of us walks a special journey. This is true from the largest of us four-legged ones, to the smallest of animals and rooted ones. We are dependent on one another for our survival and existence. No one's life is more important than another's, regardless of how large or small the animal or rooted one. The life of the mouse is as important to it as your life is to you, Tateh. Indeed, the little rodent's life is as important to the great circle, as is yours. The first two-legged ones who long ago lived among us called this great harmony of oneness, *changleska.* It was their word for the *circle of life.* They knew that when all here lived in harmony in this great oneness, what they knew as *the great tree of life* would bloom and grow strong, and life would be good for all."

Puzzled, I stood thinking silently. "Woslolkia," I said finally, "I know what you say is true, but I struggle to understand how ones as large as we, could possibly be dependent on the smallest of animals for our existence."

"Well," said Woslolkia, "remember the grassy meadows where we eat. Do you remember the soft mounds of freshly dug earth, and the tiny lines of soil on the meadow's surface in which your feet sank easily?" he asked. "These freshly dug spots and telltale lines of dirt, tell of the presence of the small four-legged one, the meadow vole, who lives there beneath the surface. As the vole churns the earth, digging tunnels through which it then passes secretly, he not only loosens the soil, but unwittingly buries seeds that have fallen to the earth. The seeds of the many rooted ones that share our land are covered in this layer of loose dirt by the little vole. They grow quickly when the sun first warms the soil in the season of the ducks returning. They become the countless rooted ones you now see all around us. With the grass the little vole has planted, we strengthen and sustains ourselves through all the seasons. So, Tateh, aren't we, the largest of the four-legged ones, dependent then, on this smallest of all, the meadow vole, for the grass we eat?"

I stood quietly listening as the great bull continued. "The highest flying and most magnificent of all our winged brothers is dependent on one of the smallest four-legged ones not only for food, but for the great trees in which eagle builds its nest. The tiny squirrel, Tateh, gathers pine cones from high in the limbs of the great rooted ones. It is meant to be that squirrel gathers and stores

14

more than it needs to sustain itself. These hidden caches are sometimes found by the keen nose of bear and feasted on by it. Is not the great bear, then, like eagle, dependent also, on the small four-legged one for its existence? Many of the pinecones hidden by squirrel are eaten during the snowy months of renewal as it hibernates, but many are left uneaten. In time, they sprout from the earth to become yet another great tree like those you see all around us. So, like bear and eagle, Tateh, even the great rooted ones are dependent on squirrel for their existence, as is squirrel dependent on the trees for his. Small flying ones who live among the concealing branches of the rooted ones sustain their kind by eating the creeping crawlers they find there. These bugs, if left unchecked would kill the great trees. Are these small birds and tree, not then dependent on one another? Is not the little winged one dependent on the tiniest of all, the creeping crawlers?"

"The great rooted ones," continued Woslolkia, "are home too, for the winged sentinels, magpie, and stellar jay. The calls of these birds, I know, you have heard echo through our forest as they voiced their objection to the stalking presence of the great predators here. Their noisy outbursts warn all who live here of these unseen dangerous ones. Tateh," said Woslolkia, "are we not all then, in some way dependent on one another, from the largest of the four-legged ones, to the tiniest of the creeping crawlers, for our well-being and existence in this great oneness?"

I stood silently looking at all that grew around us as the meaning of Woslolkia's words grew within me. In a whisper I said finally, "The balance and harmony in our world is incredible, Woslolkia. It seems so complex and yet is so simple."

Woslolkia nodded his head in silent confirmation. After a moment of quiet thought, he drew a deep breath, and as he slowly exhaled, he continued.

"The trees and plants that give us the air that we breathe and the food that we eat, draw their nourishment from the earth in which their roots are deeply sunk. The life-giving water that sustains all our lives, both rooted one and animal, is a gift from our Mother, the Earth. Tateh," said the great bull, "above all else, remember this. The great circle of life for all living things begins and ends with the Earth."

The great bull turned slowly then, and started into the fog. Woslolkia led the way now, as we continued on through the misty whiteness.

We crossed a grassy opening in a flat-bottomed canyon, where a small stream had been blocked by beavers to make a pond. Ducks rose noisily from the water as we approached, then circled in the sky above us, quacking excitedly.

"They are nesting somewhere in the tall grass near the water's edge," said Woslolkia as we moved on. We crossed the little canyon and climbed through a stand of twisted, weathered trees to the top of its far side and entered a heavily timbered basin beyond.

The trees here were huge and towering, but the forest floor was covered completely with small bushes of all kinds, and the ground upon which we walked was soft and spongy.

"The water is not far below the surface here," said Woslolkia, stopping to gaze at the beauty around us. "Tateh," he said finally, staring now at the large trees standing before us, "within the *hoop*, the great circle of life, as I have told you, no one is more important than another, regardless of how large or small. But understand also, Tateh, there is no end to that degree of largeness or smallness in our world."

Following his gaze, I looked upward to that place where the tops of the great rooted ones before us disappeared into the foggy ceiling above. "Beyond this mountain on which we stand, lies another, and beyond that one, still another. On and on it goes, Tateh, forever and ever. And," he continued, lowering his head to peek beneath the leaves of the small plants growing at our feet, "there is no end either, to the smallness of our existence."

Lowering my head now, we peered together beneath the small rooted ones that carpeted this magic land. There, hidden beneath the green canopy of grass and leaves were more rooted ones, smaller still, and beneath them moved a miniature world of colorful little creeping crawlers. Bugs that could barely be seen moved slowly among tiny pebbles and twigs. They climbed everywhere on the tiny stalks of plants, and hair-like blades of grass. Some moved slowly, others darted this way and that, while still others sprang mysteriously in and out of view. Beetles crept silently in all directions, their shapes, and the strange designs on their backs making them nearly invisible. Tiny green caterpillars clung on the undersides of leaves, and on the stalks of some of the small bushes, multicolored ones were busy making what Woslolkia told me would be a *cocoon.*

"From this small brown pod," he said, "will emerge a colorful little flying one, like ones now floating on the breezes of the forest."

'What magic,' I thought!

On the hairy underside of still other leaves and blades of grass clung small eggs. Some were single eggs wrapped in strange, silken thread, while others hung in clusters. They all waited patiently to perform their small miracles of coming to be. Nearly hidden in the tiny branches of miniature bushes were colorful spiders. These were much smaller than the ones I had seen before in the trees of the forest. Some were busy making their silken webs, others sat motionless in the center of theirs, waiting to entrap one of the tiny flying ones upon which it would then feast. All of the mysterious members of this miniature world were very busy. They were focused only on the importance of their own mission in life. They were unaware of a larger presence watching from above.

Nearby on the forest floor, the hulking trunk of a great rooted one that had fallen long ago lay nearly hidden in the tall grass. Only its greying roots now stood above the canopy of greenness that was everywhere. From tiny holes in the rotting tree sawdust occasionally fell, telling of some unseen bug boring deeper on its journey into the log. Piled over the trunk at its rooted end were pine needles teeming with ants in numbers I could not imagine. Ants scurried this way and that, each with its own purpose. Upon meeting, the ants would pause nearly touching, then move the two hairs protruding from each one's head. As their "feelers" gently touched, they spoke a language known only to them. So intent was I on this miniature world before me, that I was startled when Woslolkia suddenly spoke.

"Hidden somewhere safely in the soil below, is a queen ant," he said. "She gives life to the ants you see by laying the eggs from which they all come."

"This is incredible, Woslolkia," I said. "These little worlds hidden beneath the rooted ones at our feet, with worlds smaller yet within those worlds. How fragile it all seems," I said.

"As I have told you, Tateh, as with the largeness of our world, there is no end either, to the smallness," said Woslolkia. "Even the smallest of these creeping crawlers knows of worlds smaller yet, where they peer down on animals unaware of their larger presence. There is no end to it," said Woslolkia. Looking intently into my eyes now, he said in almost a whisper, "Our existence, Tateh is without end." He turned then, and started quietly up the trail.

'Worlds within worlds, and no end to their largeness or smallness. And our existence…there is no end,' I pondered silently as I followed Woslolkia into the radiant whiteness. The big bull walked now at a more insistent pace than before.

Our trail continued across the flat basin beneath immense rooted ones, then turned up a rocky, winding canyon covered with tall green bushes.

"These bushes will be thick with huckleberries in the season of *ripening berries*," said Woslolkia. "The great bears will dine here often at that time, as the irresistible aroma of the ripe berries will draw them from afar. It is wise that we stay far from this canyon at that time, Tateh. The bears that will surely be here mean certain death to the young ones of our kind."

At the top of the canyon, the bushes and trees gave way to a large flat area where stood blackened rooted ones of all sizes. As far as I could see, the ghostly black trunks of a dead forest floated mysteriously in and out of view between swirling fingers of fog. Some trees were broken halfway up, their tops lay on the forest floor beneath them. Others, ominously blackened, stood as if alive with charred branches reaching in all directions. It seemed as if they were straining to escape the mysterious force that had consumed them.

"Fire swept through the forest here, Tateh," said Woslolkia.

"What is fire, Woslolkia?" I asked.

"Fire, Tateh, is the most powerful thing on our earth. It happens in our mountains when the mysterious ones known by our kind as *thunder beings,* come cloaked in the towering clouds of great storms. From these storms come what we call *lightning*, streaking lines of terrifying light that shoot downward from the clouds to our Mother Earth. Crackling and sizzling, the great lines of light purify all that they touch. The lightning strikes the Earth with a terrible roar that causes even the bravest of our kind to shudder. The light cast from these dreadful lines of light is so bright, that for an instant, it makes the darkest night as light as day. The lightning strikes the tallest of the rooted ones. If the tree is dead or very dry, Tateh, the amazing energy of the streaking light will cause the tree to burst into flame. If the forest is very old with many trees that are standing dead, the fire will quickly spread and consume all in its path. That is what happened here. The smoke from these fires can be seen and smelled for miles and often becomes so thick that it hides the sun. All animals, large and small, must flee for their lives. Fire almost always climbs uphill as it burns, Tateh," continued Woslolkia. "If ever you are faced with the terrible specter of fire, seek escape from below the blaze. Never try to climb above it, for it will almost certainly overtake you," he said ominously. "Many lives are lost in the great fires, Tateh, but most do escape and for them, life goes on as before."

"It is sad, Woslolkia, to think of so many small animals losing their homes and dying in these fires. The rooted ones here are all dead and blackened," I said, shaking my head sadly.

"Fire is a very important part of our lives here in the mountains, Tateh," said Woslolkia. "When a forest becomes old, many rooted ones begin to die and fall to the forest floor. Soon the forest becomes a tangle of fallen trees that no longer provides passage or food or a good home for the animals there, and they are forced to move on. Fire comes to these old forests then, removing the old rooted ones and readying the land for a new, healthy forest. The great heat of the fire enriches and prepares the soil for new and rapid growth of a whole new array of young rooted ones. This heat," continued Woslolkia, "opens the seeds and starts the growth of plants that grew here before the fire came. It starts some seeds growing that have waited patiently in the ground for generations, Tateh. Plants appear that were thought to have been gone from our land forever. Pine cones hidden in squirrel caches are opened by the heat of the fire and drop their seeds into the soil and soon become growing young trees again."

As I looked again more closely between the charred trunks of the blackened forest, I saw that there were many little sprouts of green poking through the blackened forest floor. 'Another mystery,' I thought, as we moved through the last of the ghostly trees and entered a forest untouched by fire. As we entered the green woodland, I was struck by an amazing realization. Between all living things, and that which could easily destroy them, there existed a mysterious bond. I understood suddenly, that the frightful relationship that we share with fire, the most powerful force of all, was much the same as the relationship shared by the great rooted one and tiny creeping crawler. This strange harmony and balance, this great oneness, I realized, is what ensures a land lush with greenness and life. A world that promises the survival of both animals and rooted ones for all of time. 'Not all things in these mountains are easily understood,' I thought, as I walked on.

Ahead of me, my great friend moved more purposely now, his great antlers swaying side to side as we walked through a vibrant green forest. The bright colors and sweet pine scent seemed even more alluring after having walked through the ghostly, blackened forest that lay behind us.

We moved silently through the growing mist, weaving between towering trees as we made our way across a flat bench of dense forest. We came finally to the base of a broad mountain where the forest climbed steeply upward on the concaved face of its rocky slope.

From near its summit, hidden high above in the fog, dropped tiny canyons, each with a surging flood of water in its bottom that tumbled boisterously downward from melting snow far above. The towering draws converged before a flat apron of rock over which their combined waters tumbled freely through the air. The boiling cascade of water splashed noisily to the earth and formed a large, shimmering pool at the mountain's base. The mysterious pond was surrounded by looming trees with trunks covered in reddish-brown bark. The bark was gnarled and grooved by their many years of growth. Beneath these giant rooted ones grew a thick wall of bushes that rimmed the pond completely. In places, huge trees had fallen and lay in the pond. They protruded from the bushes at the pond's edge, their tips disappearing finally below the pond's surface near its middle. Twisted branches reached from their sunken trunks and stood in the mist above the water as if they grew from the pond's surface. Some of the trees were so large that in falling, they spanned completely across the pond's surface and were now natural bridges used by the small residents of the basin. Huge, moss-covered rocks that had long ago thundered down the mountain rested now beneath the trees surrounding the pond. The rocks seemed like moss-covered mountains themselves, peering half-hidden from the fog. From a small canyon below the pond came the soft rumble of water, telling of its continuing journey downward through the forest below.

Woslolkia stood silently before me, slowly turning his great head as he viewed the beauty before us.

"Tateh," he said finally, "this is a special place. All that is our untamed mountains lies before you. Here, Tateh, in these secret places, I will live forever. When you wish to talk to me, come here. You will find me in this magnificent pool, and in the rocks and ancient trees that surround it. If you listen carefully with your heart, you will hear me call from the water below, and you will hear my voice in the wind, Tateh…. and we will talk. Come," said Woslolkia, excitement growing in his voice, "your time is soon, we must move quickly now."

We climbed upward on a vague trail that angled across the mountain, crossing its many draws as we went. We topped a large ridge finally, then wove back and forth along its rocky spine as we climbed higher into the deepening murk.

'What did Woslolkia mean?' I wondered, as I scrambled up the steep hog back behind him. 'Why would I have to go to the special places to talk to him? Couldn't we always talk as we do now? And what about this mysterious place at which we must arrive soon?' I puzzled.

We climbed to the place where the ridge hit the main mountain and then walked into a small, fog-choked saddle. Here, Woslolkia stopped and slowly turned to me. His huge body and antlers were outlined clearly by the glowing white mist beyond him as he stood quietly facing me. His eyes were filled with knowing as he looked into mine.

"Tateh," he said finally, "you must now begin the first of two journeys which you must walk alone in your lifetime. Remember," he continued, "as you walk your path in life, look at your feet as often as you do the sky and savor each step. It is in the experience of each step you take on your life's journey, not in your destination, that you will find joy. Our chosen destinations merely cause our journeys to be. With strong, firm steps, walk always forward, and go fearlessly to that place where your heart leads you. Though I will no longer walk beside you, Tateh, I will be with you always. From here, your journey must be alone. Go now, Tateh, it is at last your time. Go, and do not look back."

I held the big bull's gaze for a long moment. Looking into Woslolkia's eyes, I suddenly felt the pride and love known between a father and son. With an unspoken goodbye, my emotions clutching at my throat, I turned slowly from him and walked upward into a churning wall of fog.

Walking alone now, engulfed entirely in opaque whiteness, the many things Woslolkia had said, rang through my mind. I had always trusted him completely, so although I did not understand why it was necessary, I knew I must climb this foggy mountain alone.

The fog became so thick that the trail immediately in front of me was at times difficult to see, and the settling mist made the trail increasingly soft and muddy. I slipped often as I made my way cautiously upward, sending rocks tumbling into the fog. Their noisy, downward ramble ended each time in an echoing collision with a forest hidden in the murk far below. I continued up the ridge carefully following the narrow trail as it led me onto the face of the mountain. Moving anxiously forward, I began to cross above the heads of roaring ravines. They held the cascading water, I was sure, that filled the mysterious pond at the mountain's base. As I worked my way cautiously along, the terrain became increasingly steep and rocky. There were no trees along the trail now to guide me through the fog, and at times it seemed as if I were floating in the whiteness that boiled around me.

'What is this journey I must make, Woslolkia,' I wondered aloud, 'and why must I walk it alone?'

"Fearlessly, Tateh, walk fearlessly," I whispered with a trembling voice, as I remembered Woslolkia's words.

As I crossed above the head of yet another steep gulley, my journey suddenly ended. The water-soaked trail gave way beneath me with a loud, shuddering crack, and terrible grating noise. Horror stricken, I slid downward amidst tumbling boulders and mud into the steep ravine and blinding fog below.

Still on my feet, I clawed furiously at the earth with all my might to stop my sliding fall, but the rocky soil was loose and water-soaked. I could not stop, or even slow my descent. The pitch of the tiny canyon quickly steepened, and I rapidly gained downward momentum. I dug frantically at the mountain's side with my hooves leaving deep furrows in the mud as I slid. My desperate battle served only to loosen more rocks and debris that now tumbled around me as I skidded ever downward. It occurred to me suddenly that the short life I had known would now end in this terrible fall through this awful fog. No one would even know. Strangely, though, an unexplained excitement and an odd anticipation grew within me as this frightful reality unfolded.

"Woslolkia, where are you?" I begged.

Time seemed suddenly to slow. In this strange slow-motion world, it seemed as if my tumbling fall had halted. It was as though I lie unmoving as I curiously watched rocks and brush tumble uphill past me in a groggy, muffled rumble. I became slowly aware of a deafening roar in my ears. It matched the terrible pounding thump that I felt deep within my chest.

Woslolkia appeared suddenly from the fog and stood silently before me.

"Have no fear, Tateh," I heard him say with unspoken words, "this is but the beginning of your grand journey."

"Woslolkia!" I heard myself cry hoarsely, as the great bull vanished into the fog.

A shocking collision with the earth snapped me suddenly back to reality. My death plunge had not ended.

My world was filled with my painful outcries, and grunts of exertion. I felt the dull thud of rocks as I struck them, and heard the terrible scraping sound of brush as it tore at my flesh. Oddly, above the sound of my frightful fall, I heard moans and cries, not my own, as I tumbled downward.

My unrelenting slide had become a series of bone-jarring cartwheels as I tumbled uncontrollably toward a band of rock that lay in the bottom of the ever-narrowing ravine. Twisting and turning, I flew over the cliff. Wrenching helplessly through the air, I plunged unimpeded through the terrible sea of fog. I knew that unseen rocks below meant my certain death. I struck the earth with a painful, sickening thud, my dreadful fall had ended at last. Certainly, I was dead.

As I lay quietly on the ground in a world of blackness, I realized slowly that somehow, I clung still, to life. Though my heart beat wildly in my chest, my terrible impact with the earth had rendered me unable to breathe. In vain I drew desperately at the air around me to fill my aching lungs. As darkness began slowly to consume me, I felt my lungs swell at last with one tiny breath. And then a larger one. Soon I lay gasping, sucking hoarsely at the air as its wonderful coolness soothed the burning ache in my lungs. My breathing at last began to slow, as did the terrible pounding in my chest. Feeling began to return again to my battered body. My hips and shoulders throbbed with pain, and my head spun dizzily

28

from my terrible fall. I was afraid to move my trembling legs. They lay folded awkwardly beneath me, I was certain they were broken.

Wet and cold, with eyes squeezed tightly shut, I lie quivering in the grass afraid of what I would see if I opened them. Desperately I tried to gather my senses.

Suddenly, I heard movement in the grass near me. Startled by the unexpected noise, I opened my eyes. Strangely, the world around me was no longer cloaked in thick fog but was now bathed in bright sunlight. A beautiful blue sky shown above. I had miraculously avoided landing among sharp rocks. I had landed instead, in a clump of tall, soft grass surrounded by a small thicket of bushy trees.

Suddenly, I heard movement again, and a large shadow passed over me. Instinctively, I squeezed my eyes tightly shut and held my breath. Totally exhausted, I lay shaking helplessly in surrender, my heart pounding in my ears. I waited for the crashing attack of eagle, the great winged one whose shadow had passed over me. His piercing talons would now penetrate my chest and finish the killing that my great fall had started. Was this then, the journey Woslolkia knew I must make alone?

I heard soft breathing, and then something touched me. Fearfully, I opened my eyes. As the world around me focused once more, I realized I was looking into two dark eyes, mere inches away. Above these large, dark eyes were two soft, brown ears, and these sat on either side of the chocolate brown head of a large cow elk. In these eyes shone love, and an unspoken bond that transcended all of time. It told of a special love and devotion known only between a mother and her newborn one.

"Welcome, little one, my son, I have long been awaiting your arrival," said my Mother.

My first journey was complete.

I had come to be.

Chapter Two

Foggy trails winding steeply upward in precarious rock draws, and muffled words spoken by a mysterious bull elk were swept suddenly away into the darkness. Gentle nuzzling beckoned me again, into consciousness.

As my eyes opened slowly, I emerged from my troubled sleep. Again, I looked into a pair of soft, dark eyes. The love that shone in these eyes seemed even warmer than the fondness I had seen in the eyes of the mysterious cow elk in my dream.

As I became fully awake, a feeling of love and security settled over me as I realized that it was my mother who nudged me gently. "Come, little one," she said softly, "it's time to try those little legs of yours. Stand up and have a look at this wonderful place that is now your world!"

'No problem,' I thought, as I remembered the miles I had walked in these mountains before my mysterious arrival here. Strangely though, as I extended my legs beneath me, I quickly realized the strength I had known had somehow vanished. My legs shaking uncontrollably, failed me as I sought to rise. First, my rear would stand as my front collapsed, then my front would stand as my rear legs sagged weakly. With a mighty effort I extended all four legs at once. Teetering on wobbly legs, I stood successfully erect finally, looking proudly at my mother. In wonder, I looked beyond her then, at this strange new place in which I now was. My mother

31

lowered her head and with her strong, broad neck steadied me and held me close to her chest.

She then said quietly, "I will call you "Tateh," my son, for you will travel freely and with knowing. You will touch all parts of this land as does the wind, after which I now name you."

My mother held me against her chest until my trembling legs steadied. Then, with a gentle push of her nose, she sent me forward on the first tentative steps of my life's journey. The steps I now took were much more difficult than the many strong paces I had known in my dream, but were nonetheless exhilarating as I walked shakily about on the forest floor.

In the forest around us grew trees of every size. Grass mingled with small bushes grew everywhere beneath the trees forming a green carpet that stretched as far as I could see. Everywhere, there were small animals. Some scrambled through the limbs of trees around me, others floated gracefully through the sky. Though I now heard their excited calls for the first time, their voices seemed strangely familiar. A curious gurgling sound beckoned from somewhere in the forest beyond my sight, and the soothing sound of moving air seemed to come from everywhere around me.

"That sound," said my mother, "is called 'breeze.'"

From the rooted ones that surrounded us, and from the rich earth in which they grew, floated an aroma, again, vaguely familiar. I stood with eyes closed, drawing the tantalizing scent of my new home to my nose, concentrating intently on these alluring new smells. Above, through the limbs of the trees that grew around us, stretched a boundless blue sky. The bright sun cast shadows of these rooted ones and their reaching branches across the forest floor, creating a cascade of light and color everywhere around me.

As I stood looking in silent awe at all that was my new home, a strange new emptiness gripped my stomach. My mother, seeming immediately to sense my hunger, guided me beneath her where I instinctively sought to suckle. After a few fumbling tries, I fed greedily at last.

In a short time, with my craving satisfied, a warm, sleepy feeling settled slowly over me, and I laid down in the soft grass at my mother's feet. My mother lowered herself to the ground behind me, forming a warm, soft cushion against which I then comfortably rested. My eyes closed, and soon I traveled again through ancient forests. I climbed up steep, craggy ridges where I crossed quietly through fog-choked saddles. Now, though, in this shadowy dream world, the words of the great antlered one with whom I walked became strangely muffled. I could no longer understand the words that he shared.

I was awakened by the gentle prodding of my mother. I had slept the remainder of that day and night, and it was now early morning of the next day. I quickly stood, my legs much stronger already, and fed greedily again beneath my mother.

When I was finished at last, my mother looked down at me and said "Come, Tateh, follow me closely."

With me trailing carefully at her feet, she led me slowly from the small grassy thicket of my birth. Not yet entirely in control of my shaking legs, I wobbled nervously along. We proceeded through the brush that surrounded the thicket and turned onto a lightly traveled trail where we walked in the direction of the rising sun.

In a short distance, our trail crossed a noisy stream. 'The source of the gurgling, rushing noise I heard yesterday,' I reasoned silently.

"This is water, Tateh, a stream," explained my mother as she lowered her head to its surface. She made the same sucking sounds I made when I fed beneath her as she drank.

Her thirst quenched finally, my mother raised her head from the water and splashed across the small stream. She stopped and looked beckoningly back at me from the opposite bank. Filled with apprehension, I stared nervously at this gurgling specter before me. I knew nothing about this water stuff and fully expected to walk 'on' it, as I started forward to join my mother on the far bank.

To my great surprise, though, as I entered the little stream, my feet disappeared into the cold murk beneath the water's surface. In terror, I tried to pull them from this watery trap into which they had vanished before I lost them forever. The unseen rocks in the bottom of the stream were slick with moss, and I slipped and slid on my quivering legs. Desperately I tried to free myself from this splashing monster that had attacked me from beneath the stream's surface. My wobbly legs soon tired from my fruitless attempts to free myself, and I fell headlong into the water.

34

My eyes were instantly blinded by the terrible wetness of the stream and with my ears, I could hear only curious, gurgling sounds as I fought to free myself from its depths.

Suddenly, I felt strong jaws clamp at the base of my head. I hung helplessly as my mother lifted me upward, freeing me from the terrible water monster that had entrapped me. She laid me gently on the far side of the stream in a gasping wet heap. With a twinkle in her eye that I instinctively knew to be amusement, she said, "That was a good crossing Tateh, but in time you will do even better."

After a brief rest and with renewed confidence, I happily followed my mother once again as we made our way through the forest. I had already forgotten the stream, and the frightful beast that lurked beneath its surface.

We came at last to a small knoll. Thick brush stood guard amongst rocks and short, bushy trees at its top. There was no trail here, so my mother picked her way carefully upward through the maze of trees so that I could follow her to its top. Once there, we lay down in a tiny opening hidden in the trees and gazed at the dense forest that lay below us.

We were surrounded by rocks nearly as tall as me, and the bushy trees and thick brush formed a concealing wall of green around us. We were completely hidden as we lay there, but by peering carefully between the rocks and brush, we were able to see a short way through the forest below.

My mother looked at me for a moment with eyes holding a message of love and devotion. Then, with a very serious voice, said ominously, "Tateh, you must listen very carefully to what I now tell you. You must trust what I say to be so, and do exactly what I say. Your life depends on it. This spot in which we now lay," she continued, "is your *safe spot*. Upon my warning, or your sensing danger, you must lie here with your head to the ground, motionless, among these concealing rooted ones and rocks. No matter how close the danger comes, Tateh, do not move or even blink an eye. It is so, that for a time after birth, newborn calf elk are scent free. The dangerous ones here, even the keen nose of bear, the greatest hunter of all, cannot detect your presence. The light-colored spots on your brown coat make your motionless form in the grass nearly invisible to their eyes. It takes great courage, Tateh," continued my mother, "for one so young as you to do this when faced with what seems like certain death, but you must trust what I say. Do not move, and they will not detect you. They will pass harmlessly by."

"Here, in this safe spot, you must stay for a while, as you grow and become stronger. I will leave you alone here much of the time, Tateh, as my scent can easily be detected by the great predators. My presence would draw them to us. So, I will come to feed and care for you only when no danger is near. Do you understand, Tateh?" asked my mother.

"Yes, Mother" I said, "I understand."

"Sleep now, my son, and I will return soon," said my mother. She turned then, and started cautiously downward through the thick trees surrounding my safe spot.

I lay alone in my new home, hidden between the rocks and bushes, and peered carefully between them as I watched the graceful form of my mother walk silently from sight into the forest below. I trusted my mother completely and knew that all she had told me was true, but a lonely fear now accompanied me as I drifted into a nervous sleep in my new forest home.

I was awakened suddenly from deep sleep by a soft, crunching sound and the soft mewing call that I was sure was my mother's. She was very close now to the hidden bed in which I lay. The sun had traveled across the sky as I slept, and hung just above the trees opposite to where it had been when it rose this morning. This day, I realized, was almost over. I lay quietly, unmoving, listening carefully to the sound of the approaching footsteps. Closer, ever closer they came, then suddenly became silent. Just as my heart began to race, my mother appeared above the brushy veil of the safe place. With a great sigh of relief, I quickly stood. Mewing softly, and with my short tail wagging excitedly, I nuzzled beneath her and once again filled my stomach.

When I was at last done, we stood together watching the forest around us as darkness slowly gathered. Birds, one by one, flew into the trees to either a hidden nest filled with chirping young ones or to their chosen perch for the night. An occasional squirrel skittered down a log here and there with one last load of pinecones to add to its cache. The bird music of the forest, unlike the excited mix of the day, became soft and mellow, then slowed to an occasional questioning call. Finally, all was silent.

My mother laid down in the soft grass with me in front of her. I pushed myself backward until I was firmly snuggled against her soft warmth. Only the cracking sound of a weakened limb or the soft hoot of an owl perched somewhere in the darkening forest broke the silence. I drifted again into sleep.

This routine was repeated for many days as I became stronger and grew larger. My mother now took me on short walks in the surrounding forest. She taught me much about it, and the many animals with whom we shared our world. As my strength grew day by day, so did my confidence, curiosity, and my insatiable thirst to learn about the mysteries of my mountain home. Soon, I was able to follow my mother as she jumped the fallen trees that blocked our path, or when she climbed small ridges and crossed the streams of our forest home.

My impatience though, with spending my days alone was growing rapidly. My interest was no longer held by the flitting butterflies that danced around me on the forest breeze, or by studying the daily routines of the small animals that lived near my safe place. I watched them now with annoyance, waiting only for that time when my mother would return. Her return was always a gleeful reunion, a time when I would end the hunger in my belly. Then, in the softening light of evening, I would follow her through the forest where she would show me exciting new animals and strange new places. We would end our day lying together in the safe spot as darkness fell.

And so it was on this day, like the many days preceding it, I impatiently waited the return of my mother. A soft breeze flowed quietly through the forest, tempering the heat that had grown steadily throughout the day. The sun, whose place in the cloudless blue sky, now told me my mother would soon return. In all directions around me, the small animals of the forest worked diligently at their tasks in a wonderful harmony that even one so young as I could see.

Far off, somewhere in the forest I heard the call of *raven*. 'What a nice day it is to float quietly above the trees,' I thought. 'What a feeling of freedom that must be.'

Again, came the call of raven, but it was a bit closer now. Mixed with his raucous voice, I could also hear the reedy call of *magpie*. As their calls became louder, it seemed they had a different pitch today. A more anxious, excited tone tempered their echoing cries. Curiously, the forest around me, filled with song and chattering calls just moments before, had become suddenly quiet. All movement of the small animals, I realized, had ceased. None could be seen anywhere. A strange feeling of uneasiness descended upon me. I settled nervously into the grass where I lay quietly with my head down among the rocks and brush in my safe place. The disquieting cries of raven and magpie became steadily louder as they moved seemingly in my direction. Soon, the flying ones were calling excitedly from the forest near my hidden bed. Though I did not move or raise my head, I heard their flapping wings as they landed in the trees above me.

A shrieking wail echoed suddenly through the forest. It was a sound that shook me to my very core. It was a call I had never heard before, but one I instinctively knew was made by one who brings death. I lay quivering, head down, remembering carefully the ominous words of my mother, and tried to sink further into the forest floor. The terrifying scream again filled the forest. The frightful call was of longer duration this time, with a horrifying, mournful tone at its end. This predator knew, it seemed, it would soon feast. Above me, raven and magpie were calling and squawking excitedly. They were diving and darting aggressively at some unseen adversary on the forest floor below my knoll.

Again, came the terrifying scream. It was so close now that it seemed to shake the little trees amongst which I lay. Then, to my horror, I heard the soft crunch of footsteps climbing quietly upward from the forest behind me. Once more the silence erupted in a terrible, shrieking howl. *Wolf* was nearly upon me now. I lie in terror, afraid even to breathe, eyes squeezed tightly shut with my head on the grass. With all my strength, I lie motionless.

Suddenly, the world above me exploded in a crash of broken branches and flying dirt that for a moment caused me to open my eyes. In a blur of tan and brown, I saw my mother as she launched herself through the air above me. With hooves flailing wildly, she landed chest first on the skulking form of a large, black wolf. The impact of her body knocked the surprised wolf from the rock above me. Together they crashed from view in a chorus of enraged snarls and gasping cries.

Motionless still, with head down and eyes now squeezed tightly shut, I listened in terror to agonizing calls, and screaming snarls echoing from somewhere below. Amid the crashing sound of exploding branches and breaking brush was the resounding thud of my mother's lashing hooves. Slowly, the horrible battle moved off into the forest, and all became silent. Raven and magpie had sat quietly in the trees above my head and watched the terrible battle below them on the forest floor. Now, with only the soft whisper of wings, they glided silently away in the direction from which came the last sounds of the death struggle between my mother and wolf.

I lie unmoving, curled up tightly in the grass stricken with terror. Again, and again, the terrible event played in my mind. I saw the hulking black form, the yellow eyes, and the white snarling teeth of the wolf as my mother, flailing and kicking, swept it from the rock beside my bed.

The singing of birds and the busy movements of the forest animals around my safe place slowly returned to normal. I remained unmoving, though, as the day ended and evening settled over the land. I listened intently to the sounds throughout the forest as its many small residents retired for the night. I listened carefully still, long after the forest had become quiet. The sound I longed to hear, the soft, mewing call of my approaching mother, could not be heard.

I lie quietly alone in the darkness, shaking and motionless for what seemed an eternity. Suddenly, I heard the soft approaching footsteps of my mother! The happiness and relief I felt was nearly overwhelming, but I continued to lie quietly, frozen in the grass of my safe place, waiting intently in the numbing darkness. I was certain the sounds I heard I were footsteps. They became louder as they slowly climbed the small knoll on which I lay. The footsteps though, became uneven, and hesitated. Then, all became quiet.

'Mother, is that you?' I pleaded silently, as fear began once more to clutch at my chest.

Suddenly, the stillness was broken by a shuddering, deep grunt and a long breathy sigh. A bear, towering in the darkness near my grassy bed, stood on hind legs, slowly moving its head from side to side, drawing to its keen nose the alluring scent carried on the cool night air. The huge bear had been attracted by the wailing calls it had heard here earlier. Wolf had told all in the forest of his imminent kill. Bear, his nose held high now, sought to unravel the mystery of the recent death struggle between wolf and elk, the smell of which was everywhere. My heart pounded in my ears so loudly now, I was certain the bear would hear it and turn on me. A paralyzing fear gripped my body, but I continued to lie without moving, eyes tightly shut, as if I were dead.

In my head, I saw the soft eyes of my mother and heard her words again as she said, "Tateh, newborn calves have no scent. Our enemies, if you do not move, will not detect you. Trust me, Tateh."

As the dark form of the huge bear stood motionless near me, I said silently, 'I do, Mother, I do.'

Again, the bear filled its mighty chest with air and exhaled loudly. Then, with a loud thump, it dropped to all four feet and began to move forward, crunching softly as it walked slowly past me. The huge bruin hesitated and stopped, turning its giant head from side to side as he drew to his nose once again, the story in the air around him. He then continued slowly down the side of the knoll. My breathing came in soft, ragged gasps now. As I listened carefully to the fading steps of the great bear, I realized that its keen nose, though unable to detect me, had drawn it to the path my mother had taken during her crashing battle through the forest earlier. 'Would the great bruin find her,' I wondered?

As silence fell once more over the forest, my breathing quieted and my pounding heart slowed, and strangely, even my fears left me. In their place, though, was a deep fatigue and cold numbness. I lie filled with loneliness, listening desperately for the mewing call of my returning mother as the night dragged slowly on.

The dark sky began at last to lighten, and the first quizzical calls from waking birds rang through the forest. As the sky became brighter, the songs of the birds became one of loud celebration for the dawning of another day.

'Celebration,' I wondered sadly, as I watched the first of the small forest animals begin their daily chores. 'Don't they know what has happened? Don't they care?'

I became slowly aware of a gnawing ache emanating from deep within me as I began to crave my mother's milk. My mouth and throat were terribly dry. My breathing was becoming raspy. My

43

legs ached, and I longed to stand and stretch, but still, I lie motionless in the grass of my safe spot, listening and waiting for my mother's return.

I drifted into, and out of tormented sleep as the day wore slowly on. Once, raising my head with a start, I was sure I had been awakened by soft, mewing calls. My elation, though, faded as time proved finally that it had been but another dream, and I sank again into tormented sleep.

In my fitful dream world, I now walked again through green meadows and along mysterious rocky trails. In the distance, I suddenly saw the approaching figure of the magnificent bull elk that seemed always to be near.

As he stood before me, I could see a soft glow in his knowing eyes, and the words he spoke, I heard clearly this time. "Tateh," he said, "all is as it should be, and it is perfect."

My head snapped suddenly up, and I looked about my small world, fully awake now. Had I heard something? I slowly lowered my head but listened intently still. The sun was low in the trees now. 'This day will soon be over,' I thought sadly, 'and another dark, lonely night will be on me again.

There! What was that!?' I thought excitedly.

Listening intently, I heard it again! From somewhere in the shadowy forest came a soft mewing sound and then the steady crunch of approaching footsteps. My mind spun with uncontrollable emotion, but still I lie quietly.

Suddenly, above the veil of brush that surrounded my bed, appeared the chocolate brown head of my mother. Mewing softly, she looked apprehensively down at me. Relief flooded her face as I sprang from my bed bleating excitedly and walked stiffly to her side. As she lowered her head to nuzzle me, I noticed there was a jagged wound across her soft brown muzzle. Her shoulders, too, were clotted with blood from deep gashes there. She stood with her weight on only one back leg, the other, she held limply above the ground.

"I have missed, you little one," she whispered, as she drew me to her. "I am very proud of you, Tateh. You did well, my son. You did well."

She guided me gently beneath her, and I quenched the great hunger that had grown within me. We laid down then, with her behind me. Pressed firmly against her, I basked in the love and warmth that I had feared only a short time before, I would never again experience.

Together, we listened as we always did, to the animals of the forest, as one by one, they sought the security of their nightly homes. Each, with song, or by call, gave thanks for the day as they retired. I snuggled even closer to the warmth behind me. As I felt the steady, thumping beat of my mother's heart at my back, I thought silently, 'now, it is as it should be, and it is perfect.' I sank into a grateful slumber as I remembered the words of the great bull my dream.

Chapter Three

Anxiety and fear, fostered by the terrifying events of the past
few days, gripped me once more as I slept. The terrifying images
caused me to awaken with a start. With my heart pounding, fighting
to clear the remnants of sleep from my mind, I looked anxiously
around me at the dark forest that surrounded my safe place. Not a
sound came from the darkened forest, the towering trees around
me stood quietly in the murky light of early morning. As I became
fully awake, I felt the familiar warmth of my mother close behind
me. A wonderful sense of relief flooded over me as I realized again
that my mother was alive and had returned to me.

I stood slowly from my bed, careful not to wake my sleeping
mother, and watched silently as the first streaks of light pierced the
morning skies. None of the forest animals had moved or sounded
yet. I stood in the near darkness, basking in the feeling of
wholeness I once again felt. My mother continued to lie in her bed
behind me but having awakened now, lifted her head from the
grass. Quietly, we watched the stars disappear from the brightening
sky and listened as the forest around us came to life.

When the winged ones were once again at full voice and the
small animals of the forest were fully engaged in their daily chores,
my mother rose stiffly from her bed. After a few tentative, hobbling
steps, she turned to me with fear brimming in her eyes. "Tateh,"
she said, "when I returned here to the safe place last night, my

nose told me of *bear* and of his presence here the previous night. The fear that filled my heart made me nearly unable to force myself forward and look downward toward your bed. When I saw your twinkling eyes and heard your excited bleating voice, I was dizzy with relief. That you were alive and well told me of your great courage, Tateh, and of the trust you hold in the things I have taught you. You have listened well, my son, and you remembered my words. Because you did, I still have you. Remember this place, Tateh, but now we must leave it. Because of the trickery of magpie and raven, the great predators, bear and wolf, have come to know of it. Certainly, they return. It is no longer safe for us to be here."

Turning stiffly, my mother held one hind leg carefully off the ground as she led me slowly from the small knob that had been our safe place. Quietly, we moved into the forest below.

The early morning sun cast a soft light on the many rooted ones around us as we walked slowly along. The graceful lines of each plant or tree seemed even more vivid than usual. The wonderful light made the character of each stand out boldly even though they stood thickly together in a confusion of growth.

The rising sun, heating the upper reaches of the mountain peaks around us, pushed the cooler air down the mountain sides toward us. We walked steadily toward the sun with the fresh morning air flowing softly against our faces. We could easily scent all that was in our path long before it came to view.

"Always walk as we do now, Tateh, with the breeze in your face," said my mother as we moved steadily along. "In that way, your nose will tell you of what lies ahead. Avoid walking in the direct sunlight on the ridge tops," she continued, "the bright light shining from behind you there, will make your movements easily seen by others below."

My mother walked much slower than normal today. The gaping wound on her hind leg, and the mud-covered wounds on her chest and muzzle told of the near death struggle she had had with the black wolf.

"Mother," I said, "breaking a long silence, tell me about your terrible battle with wolf. What happened when you and wolf fought? Where did you go, and why were you gone so long?" I asked.

My mother stopped, and turned to face me. I saw her soft brown eyes fill with fear, then slowly soften as she looked deeply into mine.

"Tateh, my young son, I thought I had lost you when I heard the piercing howl of wolf near your safe place on the knoll. I was bedded nearby in a small draw where the breeze carried my scent safely away from you. From my bed I could easily hear all that happened in the forest around you. As I lie quietly waiting for the time to return to feed you, I suddenly heard the calls of raven and magpie echo from far off in the forest. I knew immediately that they spoke in a way that told of danger there. As I listened carefully to their ominous cries, I realized they moved in the direction of the safe place. You see, Tateh," continued my mother, "raven and magpie warn all living here of the presence of the dangerous ones in our mountains. But remember this, Tateh, they are also known as *tricksters*. They will sometimes guide the great predators to us, knowing that when bear or wolf has done his killing and eaten his fill, raven and magpie can then dine on the remains.

"As I listened to their anxious calls in the forest," she continued, "I realized that they were moving toward you, and I knew that this was their purpose. Springing from my bed, I crashed frantically toward our safe place. As I topped the knoll where you lay, I saw huge black wolf preparing to leap from a rock at its far side. I knew he would make short work of killing you. I sprang at him with all my strength," continued my mother, "knocking him to the base of our knoll. Then I stood, lashing with my front feet, striking at him as hard as I could. I bolted then, running through the forest, but stopped often to fight. I hoped to lure him so far from the safe place that should I lose the battle, the distance, and his injuries would prevent him from returning to you. For hours we fought as I drew him farther and farther from you. Finally, we were overcome by our unending toil. Exhausted, we stood silently facing each other, gasping for air. Our terrible battle had inflicted painful wounds on each of us. To my surprise, though, the wolf suddenly turned from me. His eyes burning still with anger, the black one skulked silently into the forest. Many times, I have heard tales of his lurid deeds. For me, it was very fortunate that this great wolf traveled without his pack, but even so, had the battle continued, he would have won.

"My wounds, Tateh," she continued, "were bleeding badly, and I knew I had to find mud quickly to lie in and stop the blood flow. I soon crossed a small creek and found a muddy bog. There,

I rolled and packed the wet earth on my wounds, then rested quietly in the mud while nature did its work. I knew I must lie there, Tateh, until the bleeding stopped, for I could not return to the safe place with the fresh blood scent in which I was now covered. I knew it would surely draw predators to us if I did.

"Sick with worry for your safety, I stayed for more than a day lying quietly in the mud as my wounds clotted and the flow of blood stopped. With a sickening fear for your well-being growing inside me, I was able finally, to rise without bleeding and returned as quickly as I could to you at the safe place."

Gently touching her nose with mine, I said, "I love you, mother, and I hope I can be as brave and courageous someday as you are. You have shown me the strength of your love. Without hesitation, you were willing to give all that was yours to give. I will never forget, mother, ever."

"You will do well in life, Tateh," said my mother, her eyes sparkling with love. "Your journey, I'm sure, will be one of wonder."

She turned, and with me following closely at her heels, started along the forest trail again. Oddly, the words my mother had just shared echoed in my mind from a long-ago dream, but I could not remember when.

We walked through a flat stretch of forest for a time where we had to cross many fallen trees that lay blocking the trail. Each tree caused my mother to wince and groan with pain as she lunged over it. We came finally to the base of a broad ridge. Here, we skirted the toe of the ridge and entered a wide draw to its side where we began walking upward on a deeply worn trail.

Our trail wound through stands of large trees that grew in the draw's bottom. The trail crossed from side to side, worn into the earth by ancient relatives as they found their way between the boulders and downfallen trees that had come to rest there. We climbed slowly up the canyon, nearing its top as the sun dipped low in the sky. The light was fading quickly when at last we crossed the ridge line at the head of the canyon and walked into an immense basin that lay beyond.

The basin was filled with small hills and plateaus covered with grass for as far as I could see. Large, bluish-green trees grew sporadically in gentle ravines that separated the tiny mountains. On some, the twisted, wind-beaten trees covered the small hills almost completely.

My mother soon stopped at the foot of a small bench-shaped ridge where we quenched our thirst at a small pond hidden near the edge of a grassy meadow. We then rested in the deep grass beneath sheltering trees where the meadow gave way to forest and watched quietly as darkness overtook the land. Pressed snugly against my mother and tired from the seemingly endless voyage of this day, I drifted quickly into a peaceful sleep.

I was awakened the next morning by the gentle prodding of my mother's nose. "It is time, little one," she said softly, "to continue our journey."

The sky had just started to lighten where the sun would soon rise, as we resumed our trek along the edge of the huge basin. The sky behind us slowly brightened and turned a deep red color as the sun slowly climbed from behind the mountains. We cast long, swaying shadows in the pinkish glow on the grass before us as we moved steadily along.

My mother still limped badly and was clearly in pain, but we walked ever onward through narrow ravines and over the tops of gentle, rolling hills. We stopped finally near the basin's edge when the sun was high overhead. Looking downward from an open saddle, we carefully studied an expansive canyon below.

The huge chasm fell from the basin's edge steeply at first, its decent becoming more gradual, finally, where it widened. From there, it continued to fall in a series of rolling hills and small basins. The canyon was covered mostly by a carpet of thick forest, but from many places in the trees, shimmering ponds beckoned tantalizingly from bright, green meadows. Even from our distant vantage point, the muffled rumble of a mountain stream could be heard echoing from its depths. Huge winged ones circled above rocky cliffs that rose from the canyon's steep sides. I forced my gaze finally from the incredible canyon and looked to my mother with questioning eyes.

"Yes," she said, then turned and started into the canyon with me following excitedly behind. A well-worn trail soon became evident as we slipped and slid through flows of loose rock, and on this trail we moved steadily downward.

As the canyon's descent became less steep, the path became less rocky. Soon, tall grass stood at the edges of the trail. Occasionally, my mother would lower her head and grab a mouthful of these rooted ones, then chew contentedly as we walked along. As I passed a spot where my mother had just taken a bite, I lowered my head and sniffed carefully at the grass there.

'It's great to lie on and play in, but I can't imagine ever wanting to eat this stuff when my mother's milk is available,' I concluded thoughtfully, as I followed my mother down the canyon.

We passed several ponds as we moved downward. Some were bordered by large rocks and had huge trees growing at their edges. Almost all of them were framed by tall, green reeds. The bright sunlight glaring on the pond's surfaces made it impossible to see into the water, but in those places where shadows lay across the surface, light green algae on the pond's bottom could be seen through the clear water.

As we walked deeper into the mysterious gorge, the size of the trees growing there became larger. The limbs on some of these giants were nearly as large as were entire trees in the forest of my birth. The reddish-colored bark that covered the broad trunks of these rooted ones was a maze of jagged grooves caused by years of expansive growth. Large tufts of green moss hung from their limbs in a splash of colorful relief against the tree's red bark and dark-colored limbs. On the ground beneath the towering rooted ones, the earth was shaded and moist. Here, small colonies of strange, round-topped little plants grew.

"Mmmm, fresh mushrooms!" said my mother, as she greedily snapped the tops of several into her mouth, as we passed by.

We had traveled a great distance down the canyon and the sun was high overhead when a strange aroma came suddenly to my nose. As we rounded a corner in the trail, we entered a large meadow that was completely surrounded by a towering forest. Brightly colored yellow and white flowers peeked bashfully from the abundant grass. The timbered edges of the meadow rose steeply to the top of jagged ridges that formed the sides of the great canyon.

As we continued across the meadow, my mother stopped suddenly and stared intently toward its lower end. There, ahead of us, was a large pond from whose surface, strange, white clouds of fog rose thinly into the air. The pond had no trees around its edge as had the smaller ponds in the canyon behind us. This one was surrounded only by deep grass. The forest again filled the canyon below the pond's far side and formed the lower end of the huge meadow.

"Come, Tateh," said my mother, her voice now brimming with excitement, as she started again toward this strange pond.

When we got to its edge, we gazed at the steaming pond and the wonders around it. The strange odor that I had smelled earlier, I realized, came from this pond. Staring through the mist that floated from its surface, I could see that the bottom was shallow on one end and was covered with shades of yellow and white algae, unlike the green algae in the ponds we had seen

above.

My mother looked at me, then turned toward the water. She slowly walked a short way into the steaming pond, stopped, and to my dismay, she flopped suddenly onto her side. With a great splash, she rolled onto her back with her legs kicking above her in the air, sending water flying in all directions. This she obviously enjoyed very much! She continued this strange rolling and kicking for some time. She rose from the pond finally and shook, sending a sparkling shower of water flying from her in the bright sunshine. She then turned to me.

"The water in this pond is special healing water, Tateh," she said. "It rises from deep within the earth where it is heated and becomes filled with minerals and goodness as it rises to fill this pond. This water helps the sick to be well again and the ones who have been injured to become strong once more. We will stay at this pond for a time as my wounds heal and you continue to grow larger and stronger. We must prepare ourselves, Tateh, to join the others."

"Others?" I asked. "What others, mother?"

"There are many like us here in our mountains, Tateh," said my mother. "Many mothers like me, during the season of *ducks returning*, went alone deep into the forest. They too, have brought young ones like you into our world. They now wait patiently in remote, safe places such as this one, caring for their young ones as they grow and become stronger. Soon they will journey to a place in our mountains where we will all join to form a great herd. It is

important, Tateh," continued my mother, "that we form this great herd, for there is safety in numbers. It is this safety that our kind needs as we live here in the mountains and teach and grow our young ones among predators such as bear and wolf."

"Wow!" I said, "There are others like us? A great herd? Other young ones like me? This will be wonderful!"

My mother turned and walked to the pond's lower end where the water became very shallow and gave way to slimy, yellow-colored mud. Here, she again flopped onto her side, sending yellow mud splattering all about her as she had the steaming water. She rose covered in the sticky yellow mud, looking very unlike the mother I had known only moments before.

With a very pleased look on her face she said, "Come on, Tateh, try it!"

Upon hearing this, I looked warily at the steaming water, and then at the mud-covered elk that was my mother, then back again at the water. Finally, with a determined sigh, I walked to the edge of the steaming pond and looked nervously in. Suddenly, a young, spotted calf elk appeared in the water below me. Startled, I jumped back from the edge of the pond.

"That is you, Tateh," said my mother. "It is your reflection in the water! It is what you look like," She said.

'Oh, my,' I thought to myself, 'it can't be! I am much larger than that strange little elk in the pond!'

But sure enough, as I looked tentatively into the water again, the same little calf looked cautiously upward at me. "That is really me?" I asked my mother incredulously.

"Yes, Tateh, that is the handsome little bull elk that I see when I look at you," said my mother.

Looking back into the pond now, I turned my head this way and that, flipped my ears back and forth, and even opened and closed my mouth, trying hopefully to disprove my mother's theory. Try as I might, though, the little elk in the water mirrored my actions exactly, confirming finally to be true what my mother had said. 'It is me in there. It is what I look like,' I thought dejectedly.

I wondered what the other calves in the great herd would think when they saw this little spotted calf that I now knew to be me.

'Well, no matter,' I decided finally, and stepped bravely into the steaming mineral water. Unlike my first creek crossing though, this time I did not panic or fall when my feet disappeared into the mud below the water's surface. I only stumbled a bit as the soft muddy bottom clutched at my feet. The water was wonderfully warm, and I soon stood with it lapping at my knees.

I began walking carefully through the pond in short circles. Soon, my tentative steps became splashing forays as I ran from the bank full speed into the pond, sending billows of steaming water splattering everywhere. I sometimes fell, tumbling headlong as I crashed into the water during my reckless charges, but I would jump up immediately from beneath the water to gleefully repeat the attack. My mother lay quietly in the healing mud at the edge of the grass, and with an amused look on her face, watched my frenzied water battles.

Having been lost in the joy of my newly discovered water games, the day passed very quickly for me. When only a red glow remained in the sky above the horizon where the sun had disappeared, my mother rose slowly from the mud.

"Come, Tateh, we will return to the pond tomorrow," she said as she stepped from the yellow muck and into the grassy meadow.

I followed her closely as we walked upward in the meadow toward its far side. The grass was so deep in places that I was able to see only my mother's legs in front of me as the grass parted and flowed past us as we walked.

We soon reached the large trees at the edge of the forest where the ridge began its sharp climb upward from the meadow. After satisfying my ever-growing appetite, we rested quietly in the grass beneath the trees at the meadow's edge. Together, we watched as our mountain world disappeared into gathering darkness. Lying tightly against my mother as I always did now, I sank into a wonderful sleep, thinking about the great herd and little brown spotted elk running everywhere.

It was not yet fully light when the familiar nudge from my mother's soft nose woke me once more. I rose from my bed and stretched. Upon feeling the gripping hunger that seemed always to be in my belly now, I slipped beneath my waiting mother and fed until I could hold no more. Stepping from beneath her finally, I noticed her looking at some distant point across the meadow.

Following her gaze, I saw a large, black animal walking toward the pond from the forest below it. The animal was tall with long legs and a sizable hump above its front shoulders. Bulky, flat antlers stood above the great animal's head, and even though it was still early in the season of the growing grass, its antlers had already grown far beyond the sides of his body. It had a large drooping nose, and a long black beard of hide dangled from beneath its chin, reaching nearly to the grass.

"Mother," I exclaimed, "what animal is that?"

"It is a bull moose, Tateh," said my mother. "I have seen him many times throughout my life here in the mountains. He is loved and respected by all who live here, for his life has been a long one. He stays here always, now. His remarkable life's journey is nearly done."

We watched as the old one waded into the warm water and lay down in it for a while. He rose then and walked to its edge, where he rolled in the sticky yellow mud as my mother had done. The old moose rose from the mud finally and disappeared into the trees below the pond.

"Come, Tateh," said my mother breaking the silence as she started through the deep grass toward the pond.

As we reached the area where the grass gave way to the yellow mud bog, my mother stopped suddenly, and stood quivering with her ears straining forward. She stared intently toward the timber at the far side of the pond where the big moose had disappeared.

From in the grass behind my mother, I peered cautiously through her legs. My heart began to pound and a terrible fear clutched at my throat as I saw the terrifying, black form of a huge wolf stalk slowly from the timber near the far side of the pond.

"Lie down, Tateh," whispered my mother tensely.

The huge wolf saw my mother immediately. Now both he and my mother stood quietly glaring at one another. Time stood still, and the silence seemed to roar in my ears. To my disbelief, my mother started forward toward the pond. The wolf did too. Each waded in a short distance, then lay down in the warm water facing each other, and quietly soaked. Shaking with fear and confusion, I watched from my hiding place in the grass for what seemed an eternity as this incredible event unfolded before me. Suddenly, they stood from the water, their eyes locked in an unblinking stare. In awe, I watched as each dipped their head in recognition of the other, then turned and walked from the pond.

My mother walked to where I lay trembling in the grass, and together we watched as the large black wolf limped slowly from sight, back into the timber.

"That is the black wolf I fought at the safe place, Tateh," my mother said at last, "the one that would have surely taken your life, had I not stopped him."

"But, you and he just…. I thought wolf was our mortal enemy, mother," I gasped, having again found my voice.

"Tateh," she said, "there are no enemies at this place of healing. The sick and injured come here only to heal, so they may live and continue their life's journey. When here, we easily see each other's hardships, and we understand that our struggles are much the same. Most importantly though, we realize that we must respect each other's purpose and remember that no one's journey is more important than another's. Because the path of wolf is often in conflict with the journey of our kind, does not mean that his journey is wrong and ours is right.

"Tateh, my young son, it is hard for you to understand, I know, but all who live in these mountains have a special purpose here. Sometimes that purpose, like the journey of wolf, may mean death to our kind, but we survive and flourish in spite of his treacherous work. Know your enemies well, Tateh, for your survival depends on it, but always respect their journey as you have seen wolf and me do today, here, at this place of healing water."

'Oh, my!' I thought to myself silently, quaking still from fear, 'It takes a great deal of courage and understanding to walk one's path here in our mountains.' I wondered then, 'Will I ever possess such courage as that which my brave mother had twice shown me in my young life?'

My troublesome thoughts were interrupted when my mother turning back toward the pond now, said, "Come, Tateh, let's soak."

Our day passed wonderfully as we soaked in the steaming water and my mother rolled again in the gooey yellow mud flat at its edge. The sun had already raced across the sky and was disappearing behind the ridge when my mother and I emerged from the steaming water and retraced our steps to our bedding place at the far side of the meadow.

With my hunger again satisfied, I lay snuggled against my mother and drifted into a peaceful sleep. My slumber this night was filled with secret mountain meadows where little spotted elk splashed gleefully through shimmering ponds of steaming water. Suddenly, I was again lying alone in the grass trembling with fear as I watched my brave mother and the black wolf staring at one another in the steaming water of the healing place.

Strangely, though, the mysterious bull elk of my dreams strode suddenly from the timber and stood silently in the water at my mother's side. The incredible vision of the great bull towering in the water beside my mother as she bravely faced the black one, I knew would play in my mind forever.

In the darkness of my dream world, I had seen with my heart that which my eyes had been unable to see in the light of day.

Chapter Four

My days passed rapidly now. Each one was filled with exciting trips to the pond that always meant warm, splashing water for me, and plenty of sticky, yellow mud for my mother. My mother's wounds had healed almost entirely, and her limp was nearly gone. My appetite had become voracious. It seemed I fed almost constantly beneath my mother as she grazed. I was growing quickly and was able finally to see above the meadow's deep grass as we walked to and from the pond.

We did not see the black wolf again. My thoughts now were filled with the time when I would finally see the other little spotted elk and would join the great herd at last, as my mother had promised.

This day, as did most, started with my mother's gentle nudge to waken me. Though fully awake, I continued to lie against my mother's warm softness. Together we watched quietly as the world around us came slowly to life. When the birds of the forest were again in full chorus and the little four-legged ones scurried once more at the edges of the meadow, we rose from our bed. I scooted quickly beneath my mother to satisfy my hunger.

With my belly full, I emerged from feeding to concentrate on the more important aspects of the day. I began with a few romping, bucking runs around my mother, then, snorting angrily, charged directly at her with my head lowered menacingly. Taken completely by surprise, of course, she jumped panic-stricken to the side, narrowly escaping my vicious attack. In retaliation of my shocking assault, she lowered her mighty head and pawed at the ground with rage. Engaging me suddenly with a mighty push, the fight began. Battling furiously, we pushed each other back and forth in the meadow. Mewing, snorting, and chirping, we angrily voiced our objections to each new onslaught made by the other. And so it was again, this bright and sunny morning, we bucked, and ran and pushed at each other, frolicking across the meadow. Breaking finally, into an all-out run across the grassy opening, the terrible fray continued as we splashed and fought to the far side of the healing pond. My mother was no match for me though. Our battle ended finally, as it always did, with my obvious victory.

My mother lay down and began to soak in the warm water while I continued to splash past her in mock charges. I ceased my playful conflict and came to stand in the water beside her when I saw a look of seriousness settle slowly over her face.

"Tateh," she said, "I am strong again, and my wounds are nearly healed. You have grown much during our time here and have learned much. It is now far into the season of *growing grass*, and it is time for us to join the others in the great herd."

With that, my mother rose from the warm water and walked to the yellow mud bog. There, she flopped on to her side and rolled and kicked with delight as she always did.

But now she stood and looked at me with a fix in her eye. "Your turn now, Tateh," she said.

Unlike my mother, I had not rolled in the yellow mud before. Nonetheless, I walked bravely forward. I slowly entered the mire and flopped onto my side in a great splash of mud. Soon, I was rolling and kicking joyfully in the sticky stuff. Finished at last, I stood from the muck and shook. I felt very bull-like after having completed my first wallow.

We walked from the pond into the meadow, then started along the trail that we had followed when we first came to this wonderful place. My mother stopped as we entered the timber, and together we turned and looked back at the steaming pond. The large, open meadow where we had so often played now stood vacant. Our bedding spot hidden in the deep grass beneath the trees at its far side, showed no signs of the many nights we had slept there.

"Remember this place always, Tateh, and the wonderful times we shared here, but look always forward, son, and go fearlessly onward," she said. Turning then, she continued up the canyon.

I was saddened to leave this special place but was excited to at last begin our search for the great herd. 'I'll come back here and stay forever, someday,' I promised myself silently as I turned and followed my mother up the trail.

We retraced the steps of our recent downward journey to the healing water. We walked again through the many meadows and past their ponds as we moved upward toward the basin above.

We walked, as always, with the breeze in our faces. The alluring new smells now floating there were incredible. During our long stay at the healing water, the season of *growing grass* had progressed, and now many rooted ones I had never seen before grew at the trail's edge. Each waited patiently it seemed, to be seen, sniffed, and even sampled.

We traveled upward through grassy meadows and walked cautiously through the dark thickets that separated them. As the sun drew overhead, we entered yet another dense woodlot. The trail was nearly overgrown by tall, leafy ferns that grew beneath towering alpine fir. Though no rain had fallen in weeks, the trail was still soft and moist on this shady, north-facing slope. Countless tracks could be seen in the mud, telling of the passing of the many animals that shared our mountain home.

Ahead of me, my mother suddenly lowered her nose to the damp mud before her. She took long, deep breaths, as she drew the scent of the earth slowly to her nose. Quietly, she studied the story it told. With a contemptuous snort, she raised her head from the trail, finally, and nervously scanned the forest around us. Satisfied at last that no imminent danger lurked nearby, she said, "Come here, Tateh."

There, at her feet, sunken plainly into the mud of the trail was a huge track. It was much larger than the tracks made by my mother, and had five toes at the front, with huge claw marks pressed deeply into the mud ahead of each toe.

"What is that track, mother?" I asked excitedly.

"Tateh, this is the track of bear, but a bear unlike the one you saw on the knoll of the safe place. This is the track of the great *silver bear*, the most ferocious of all predators who live in these mountains. We must be always vigilant and avoid him at all costs. He means almost certain death to those of our kind who cross his path when he is hungry."

My mother, with nose held high, moved her head slowly as she tested the breeze once more, then turned and started again up the trail. The tracks of the great bear were beneath us in the trail for a ways, then veered suddenly into a small canyon. The ravine was overgrown with underbrush and gnarly, close-growing trees. As we passed by the mouth of the draw, a nervous shiver traveled over me. In my mind I saw the great bear that probably lay hidden now in its upper reaches.

The trail continued to meander up the shady side of the canyon, but crossed finally, from the ominous stand of timber into the canyons' broad bottom. Here, the sun again bathed tiny flowers and grass that grew along the trail. All thoughts of the great silver bear were soon gone as I again became lost in the smells and beauty of the small rooted ones growing around us. My mother, too, seemed relaxed now, and sampled these tasty green plants often as we climbed steadily upward.

We walked at last into the grassy saddle that lay at the top of the big canyon. We turned to look again at the wondrous expanse from which we had just climbed. The trees and green openings far below us looked as beautiful as they had when I first saw them.

There was no hint however, of the wonderful healing water that lay hidden in the far end of the canyon. Exhilaration coursed through me, as I realized my mother and I would live always in this ancient place.

Turning from the big canyon, we continued through the saddle and walked into the basin beyond. Its grassy hills and small, tree-choked draws lay before us beckoning in the late afternoon sun.

Before proceeding into the great basin, we stopped near the edge of a scruffy, windblown patch of trees and surveyed all that lay before us. I watched with wonder as my mother listened intently in all directions and carefully sampled the breeze for any hint of danger. Satisfied at last that all was as it seemed, she led me from the stunted trees and started across the rolling basin.

The sun was not far from the horizon now, and from its low angle behind us, it cast a golden glow on the hills and trees ahead.

It had dropped from view when we came to a small pocket in the big basin where three open hills descended steeply to form the edges of a nearly round opening between them. On one side of the little meadow grew a clump of trees, and in its middle lay a pool of water with tall reeds growing at its edges. A small creek flowed from the pond and disappeared into a gentle draw that coursed between the hills and dropped into the basin beyond.

We walked down the hill and circled into the little meadow toward the setting sun. The fiery display that showed in the clouds reflected exactly from the pond's surface, but to my amazement became pulsing bands of red in the water as I disturbed its surface with my drinking.

Our thirst satisfied, my mother, with me feeding beneath her, grazed slowly through the little meadow toward trees that stood at its edge. Once there, we lay together quietly and watched the stars appear one by one in the darkening sky. I wondered where the great herd might be tonight and if we would find them soon. 'If ever there was an elk that could find them,' I thought, as I drifted into slumber, 'it would be my mother.'

My mother woke me the next morning long before the first birds sang. The stars shone brightly in the dark sky as I slipped below her to feed. An impatient stomp of her back foot soon told me that it was time to move on, and we started toward a faint glow that had begun to grow on the horizon. The radiance in the brightening sky became increasingly brighter until finally, the churning top edge of the sun appeared above the mountains. We walked toward a tree-covered bluff that stood far in the distance as the blazing orb climbed slowly into view.

The sun was nearly overhead when we stood among the trees on the once-distant bluff. We then moved up a broad ridge and crossed into a small basin. Before us was a canyon that fell gently away from the basin's edge in a series of stair-stepping meadows. The openings were circled by thick forest, and grassy knobs protruded from the trees in many places.

My mother stood quietly turning her head as before, listening carefully and sampling the breeze with her nose.

"Listen, Tateh," she said suddenly, her gaze now fixed on a point somewhere below.

Listening carefully, I could hear the wonderful sounds of elk. Many elk were calling to one another somewhere far below. My eyes wide with excitement, I looked anxiously at my mother.

"Yes, Tateh," said my mother, "we have found them."

As we walked quickly toward the elk sounds, the mewing and bleating of the cows and calves became louder. Soon, separate voices could be distinguished. We climbed a gentle rise that separated an unending series of meadows, and suddenly below us were many, many elk.

Cow elk with their heads down feeding stood for as far as I could see in the great opening before us. Jumping and bucking, miniature elk ran everywhere beneath them.

My mother looked for a long while, studying the big herd carefully. She then looked back at me. "Tateh," she said, "this is the great herd. Today, we will join them." With that, she started downward toward the herd, mewing loudly as she went, with me quivering excitedly behind her.

The feeding cows' heads shot quickly from the grass, and they stood frozen for a moment as they sought to identify the newcomers. All calf-play halted, and each quickly went to the side of its mother. The cows seemed to recognize the call of my mother, and each began mewing in reply as they started toward us, their calves following closely behind them.

When we reached the excited herd, they all gathered around us mewing and chirping excitedly. Spotted calves peeked shyly everywhere from beneath their mothers, their tails whipping back and forth wildly, as they studied this new cow elk and its muddy little calf.

"Wakhita, Wakhita!" the cows called happily to my mother again and again. "Welcome! Welcome to you and your fine new son. We have been waiting and wondering why you had not yet joined us," one large cow said.

I heard a series of quiet gasps as the excited throng of elk before us now saw the fresh wounds on my mother's nose and chest. They all knew then, of her recent near-death struggle with one of the great predators here.

"We knew you would come, Wakhita. An elk with your strength and wisdom will always return," the large cow said.

My mother stood looking happily back at the excited cows that surrounded us and at the little spotted elk each had hiding beneath them.

She looked proudly at me, then turned to the herd again and said, "This is a wonderful day, sisters. This is my son, Tateh, and we are honored to join you."

With me following shyly beneath her, surrounded still by excited cows and calves, we walked slowly down into the meadow. Stopping in its center, my mother stood silently in their midst. Meeting the eyes of each cow one by one, she proudly acknowledged each member of the herd and each of their calves that played now among them. Her gaze went finally beyond them to the meadow and beautiful clumps of trees that surrounded it. She looked at the blue sky above and deeply inhaled the many scents that floated on the breeze. She exhaled loudly with obvious satisfaction and lowered her head to feed.

Overwhelmed with energy and excitement, I could wait no longer. I trotted anxiously from beside my feeding mother toward the darting cluster of calves who now bound this way and that, throughout the meadow. As I drew closer, the calves ceased their frolicking play and gathered around me, looking and sniffing at me curiously. Carefully studying this energetic herd of spotted elk, I noticed I was a bit heavier and taller than they were. We milled stiff-legged and cautiously about one another for a bit, looking and sniffing, our small tails whipping excitedly. With unspoken acceptance, we broke suddenly into an elated run, bucking and jumping across the meadow. The little calf games about which I had dreamed for so long had at last begun!

The remainder of the afternoon was spent darting relentlessly through the herd of feeding mothers. We shook our heads menacingly, snorting and leaping into the air in great bounds while kicking all-out with our hind legs. We then sprinted away into the meadow, only to come running back at full speed at the unsuspecting cows to repeat our mock attacks.

When the sun hung just above the mountains, the mewing calls of the cows could be heard, and we all went quickly to our mothers' sides where we replenished the energy each would certainly need again tomorrow. As darkness gathered, I lay down with my mother behind me, at the edge of the big meadow. However, unlike my many previous nights, the soft murmur of elk talk could be heard in the darkness from the many other cows and calves lying around us. This had been a delightful day for me. I felt wonderfully tired from the exciting calf games I had shared with the other little ones of the herd.

As my mother and I listened to the sounds of the other cows and calves in the gathering night, I thought about our arrival here and about the many cows and calves that made up our herd.

"Mother," I said finally, "when the cows and calves gathered around us today, they called you 'Wakhita.' What is Wakhita, Mother? I have not heard you say this before."

"Tateh," said my mother, "it was a word used by the first two-legged ones who lived here among us long, long ago. To them, this word meant *sentinel*, one who watches out for others. This, the two-legged ones called those of our kind who led the great herds as we roamed the mountains. This name was passed down to me through the generations of our kind, and I am honored to have it be mine."

'Wakhita…. My mother is a sentinel,' I thought, as I drifted off to sleep.

The days came and went quickly. Each was spent feeding, running, jumping, feeding again, and sleeping as our herd roamed the open basins and ridges of our mountain home. There was indeed security and safety, it seemed, in the great numbers that comprised our herd.

One bright, warm afternoon the cows lay scattered through the meadow chewing contentedly on the rich grass there. Large groups of spotted calves ran as usual all about the herd in a serious game of calf play. In small, rowdy groups, or sometimes in long lines of racing calves, we charged away from the feeding cows. We crashed excitedly through the tall sage at the outer edges of the meadow, then, ran wildly back through the cows, continuing into the timber on the herd's far side. On one such run, as my group of calves bound recklessly through the sage, there erupted a sudden, snarling roar at the rear of our charging line. Recognizing instantly the horrifying sound of wolf, I stood for a moment frozen with terror. Finding my voice finally, I screamed *wolf,* as I turned frantically toward the herd to find my mother.

The cows, upon hearing the snarling attack and cries of death from imperiled calves, were on their feet in an instant. They thundered through the meadow, each calling frantically to their calf. The horrible, bleating cries from the brush soon quieted, then ceased, but the fierce snarling of our stealthy assailants rose in volume until finally, it became a terrifying chorus of wailing howls.

The terrible screaming of the wolves reverberated through the meadow as they celebrated their kill in the tall sage at the opening's edge. Cows and calves ran frantically in all directions around me. From everywhere in the rising dust of the meadow came the rumbling sound of hooves, the frightened bleating of lost calves, and the panicked mewing calls of fearful mothers.

Suddenly, above the sound of thundering hooves I heard my mother's familiar voice from somewhere in the dust. "Circle, sisters, circle!" she screamed above the din, as she loomed suddenly before me and nosed me roughly to the center of the meadow.

The cows, upon hearing my mother's call, formed a large circle in the meadow, all mothers facing outward with us calves cowering on the ground, trembling fearfully in the middle. A nervous silence fell over the herd then, as all cows stood perfectly still save for a nervous snort or the stomp of a foot. From in the sage came an occasional snarling outburst as the wolves continued their feast on the calves whose journey had ended there today. An eerie silence fell over the meadow then. The cows continued to stand circled shoulder to shoulder, facing bravely outward as all waited nervously for what was to come.

Time stood still. Then, softly at first, deep, rumbling growls erupted from unseen places in the brush around us. Increasing in pitch, they soon became terrifying, unearthly screams.

Suddenly, the attack began.

Through a jungle of tan legs, I peered in horror as the wolves rushed forward slashing, snarling, and screaming at all sides of the circle. The cows reared onto their hind legs and with their sharp front hooves, flailed frantically at the darting forms of the wolves. Dust again filled the air, and I could see only ghostly silhouettes as the cows reared, striking wildly at the dodging wolves beneath them.

For what seemed an eternity, I cringed in terror amidst a terrible din of painful cries and labored grunts. The thud of pounding hooves and menacing snarls filled the air as the clamor of our herd's valiant battle went endlessly on. Then, as suddenly as it had begun, the attack was over. The wolves sank silently into the surrounding timber and an eerie silence settled over the meadow. The brave cows stood fast in the circle, stomping and snorting and shaking their heads while calling angrily at the forest around us. The silence continued, though. The wolves had moved on. Their appetite for more killing had been dulled by the determined fight of the brave mothers and their earlier feast in the sagebrush on the calves they had killed there.

Suddenly, several cows broke from the circle and ran into the sage. Snorting and mewing with rage, they crashed toward a spot at the lower edge of the meadow from which came a soft, whining sound. Dust rose around them as they reared and slammed their hooves heavily to the ground there. Above the thunder of their crashing hooves and the rush of breaking sage, came the painful last cries of a wounded enemy.

The flailing cows stopped and stood quietly finally, as did the cows in the circle around me. The snorting, blowing, and angry stomping of feet slowly ceased, and all became silent. The terror-stricken calves that laid in the center of the circle around me began to rise. Bleating softly, they walked to their mothers and stood beneath them looking nervously about.

Standing beneath my mother now, I heard her say to the others in a loud voice, "Sisters, I am very proud of you. We fought hard today, and because of your bravery, our little ones and our herd were saved. We must go from here now, away from this place of wolves, for surely they will return."

Saying no more, she walked slowly through the cows who stood quietly gathered around her in the meadow. Her eyes were filled with pride as she met the gaze of each one she passed. Then, with me at her heels, she walked through the meadow and started toward the grassy crest far above. The cows formed a long line, three or four abreast, and with their calves trailing closely, moved quietly upward behind my mother.

When we at last reached the summit, the day's last rays of sunlight sliced between angry, towering clouds on the horizon, creating a fiery, red glow in the sky above us. All in the herd quietly turned, and look back at the sad meadow far below. The distant forms of two cow elk stood alone there still, their calves no longer at their sides. My mother somehow knew their journey would soon end. From deep within her chest came a long, quavering call that echoed downward to where the two cows stood quietly watching

77

us. Her eyes were filled with sadness as she turned and led the great herd down the far side of the grassy crest and into the gathering darkness.

Chapter Five

Flashes of brilliant, white light now shot through the sky above the horizon, outlining dark, boiling clouds that were rapidly advancing. Ominous, rumbling sounds echoed from the hills around us as the herd followed my mother through the darkness into the basin.

She stopped in a small meadow and turned to face the others who stood quietly in front of her in the darkness. She looked sadly into the faces of the many cows, some of whom she had known her entire life. Then she looked into the anxious eyes of their calves that stood nervously beneath them.

After a long silence she said, "Our two sisters whose calves were killed today have chosen to stay behind in the meadow. Together, they will fight the wolves when they return in the darkness tonight for more killing. With their lives, sisters, they will provide us time to lead our calves to safety, far away from that place of wolves.

"Rest now, and feed your little ones," she continued, "for it is our good fortune that the sky is filled with a storm that approaches from that place where the sun rests. When the rain begins at last to fall, we must travel as hard and for as long as we can. The rain will remove our tracks and wash away our scent that lies within them, and no wolves can then follow."

The cows, with calves following, turned and walked into the darkness to rest and prepare for the impending journey.

Jagged lines of light streaked from clouds that had drawn nearly overhead now, each one lighting the basin for an instant as brightly as if it were day. The once faraway rumbling had turned into great, booming roars that followed the flashing light almost immediately, and the wind stirred suddenly from the direction of the advancing storm.

I watched my mother as she stood above me studying the pulsing sky, her silhouette plainly drawn against the flashing light above her. Her thoughts, I was sure, lay with her two brave sisters far behind us in the darkness of the meadow from which we had come.

She lowered her head and said to me quietly, "It is time, Tateh. Follow me closely." With that, she started forward into the stormy night.

The nervous bleating of calves and the rumble of hooves filled the darkness as the cows and calves of our great herd quickly formed a broad, long line behind us. Beneath the flashing sky, as the wind swirled around us and rain began to fall, we moved together into the darkness.

The storm struck with a vengeance. The wind-driven rain stung our eyes, and the flashing light and booming thunder were nearly nonstop. As we walked across the basin, the hills and gullies, the thickets of trees, and the ponds that lay near them were all clearly visible in the exploding light that shot through the sky. The grass at our feet that only a short while ago stood tall and flowing in a pleasant breeze was pressed flat to the ground writhing in a fierce, driving wind. The ponds we passed, whose surfaces had earlier been smooth and glossy, boiled and splashed chaotically in the pounding rain. Still, our legion of churning brown bodies moved steadily through the terrible night, led by the plodding, dark form of my mother.

Down narrow draws, over rolling hills, and through dense stands of timber we toiled through the soggy night, pressing onward through a terrible storm that showed no signs of abatement. My mother looked back often in the flashing light at the long line of surging bodies behind her, and upon seeing that all was well, would lower her head once more and walk on. I wondered how my spotted friends were doing, and if they too, were filled with fear by the flashing light that hissed and sizzled through the sky and by the terrifying thunder that always followed.

We entered a steep draw where we slipped and slid in the mud to its bottom, then crossed a shallow stream where we climbed a small bank on its far side and entered a swampy meadow there. I looked behind me, and beneath the flashing light of the storm, I could see cows as they slid downward in the draw, with calves struggling in the slippery mud beneath them. Some tumbled helplessly down the muddy ravine and into the stream below it.

I walked endlessly on, my head held low against the raging storm. Behind me, I listened to the sound of clattering hooves against unseen rocks in the darkness and the sucking sound of footsteps in the mud. The first twinges of fatigue begin to burn in my young legs. I thought again of the other calves, especially my little friend Wicala, and wondered if exhaustion had begun to settle over her also.

My mother seemed to sense the ever-growing fatigue in the small dark forms who struggled beneath their mothers behind her, and suddenly she stopped.

Turning slowly to face the herd behind her, she said in a loud voice, "Little ones, when the muscles in your young legs burn and exhaustion gnaws at your will to go on, think of your brave mothers that lead you. Remember the courageous battle that they fought today as they gave all that was theirs to give, so that each of you might live. Think then, of the two brave mothers like them, who stand fearlessly together, fighting the wolves in that dark meadow far behind us."

The lightning flashed, and a deafening boom thundered around us. In the pulsing light, all in the herd had seen for an instant the love that shone in the soft, brown eyes of my mother as she stood before them. She turned then, and walked on.

We walked through countless meadows, weaving between ponds and swamps, then wound through the thick woodlands that separated the broad openings. In some of the meadows, the acrid smell of hot water came to my nose, the same smell I was certain that I had come to know at the healing waters, far away now in a distant canyon.

As we passed from the trees into yet another opening, there came to my ears a faint rumble somewhere in the distance. This rumble was not like the terrible thunder that followed the bright flashes of light in the sky. It was instead, a deep, unending sound. Curiously, the rumble grew louder as we crossed the opening, and as we came to the top of a gentle rise, my mother stopped and looked intently downward. Walking to her side, I followed her gaze.

There, beneath us, looming from the darkness at each blinding flash in the sky, was an immense canyon, whose rocky sides fell straight away to a depth that was staggering. Further up the canyon, a white torrent of water fully as wide as the canyon itself, fell thundering ominously into its depths, disappearing into a boiling white mist that rolled upward from the canyon's bottom. A churning white river appeared from the mist at the foot of the towering falls. The raging flow followed the canyon's bottom for some distance, disappearing finally behind gigantic walls of rock where the canyon turned from view. I turned to my mother wide-eyed, in awe.

"This is the canyon of the *yellow rocks,* Tateh," she said, as a huge line of cows and calves gathered around us on the crest. "The first two-legged ones called it that, Tateh. They thought it was a powerful place and came here often," she continued, turning again to view the canyon.

83

We stood for a bit longer on the rise above the magnificent gorge, watching in the flashing light and listening to the thundering roar of water that echoed from its depths. All in the herd, I was sure, felt the awesome power of the natural wonder before us. My mother turned finally and walked away from the canyon, leading us again across the stormy basin.

The storm at last began to diminish. The jagged streaks of light and deafening roars now came from the sky less frequently, and the rain seemed to ease as we moved steadily on. A dull glow began slowly to build on the horizon behind us, and I knew then that this horrible night would soon be over. As the grayness in the sky became brighter, the pouring rain ceased. The wind became calm, and the terrible, streaking light receded, hidden in the angry, dark storm as it moved beyond the mountains where the sun would soon rise.

My mother stopped at last near some tall trees at the edge of an opening. She looked upward into the slowly brightening sky where stars now shone between retreating clouds. She then lowered her head to the ground and breathed deeply the smell of the fresh, wet earth. She raised her head and looked into the eyes of the huge circle of cows and calves who peered wearily back at her.

"We have gone far enough, sisters," she said quietly. "We are safe now, we will rest"

She turned and stood quietly facing the direction from which we had just come, lost in thoughts only she could know. The cows and calves of our herd sank gratefully into the grass in the meadow around us. Unable to stand any longer beneath the stoic form of my mother, I fell at her feet and was immediately asleep.

I was awakened at last by a gripping hunger and raised my head groggily from the grass. My mother stood above me as she had before I slept, her head held high and her gaze fixed still on that place now far behind us. She lowered her head and nuzzled me as I wiggled beneath her and sought to chase the terrible hunger from my stomach. When I was done, my mother walked through the meadow with a throng of other cows toward a sparkling pond at the meadow's far end. Once there, they drank long, slurping gulps of the cool water, replenishing liquid lost during the terrible trek of the past night. They retired again in the grass beneath the trees at the edge of the ponds, where they were joined immediately by their still-weary calves. The remainder of the day was spent resting peacefully beneath a cloudless, blue sky.

Pressed safely against my mother, my mind was filled again with thoughts of our dreadful journey in the rainy darkness and about the fire that shot from the sky in the frightful storm. Slipping finally into sleep, I stood once more at my mother's side in the terrible crashing light as I dreamed of staring downward in awe at the roaring canyon of the yellow rocks.

I was awakened by the gentle movement of my mother as she rose from behind me and stood gazing at the meadow before us. Lying wearily beneath her, I squinted into the brightness of the blue sky where the sun's position told me the day was nearly half gone. I rose and slipped beneath my mother and fed, then walked with her into the grassy opening where she lowered her head and begin feeding on the lush grass.

One by one, the other cows and calves entered the meadow where the cows began to feed as my mother had. We calves, undaunted by the harrowing challenge of our stormy journey, began to bound about playfully in the meadow. In small gangs of spotted brown that grew steadily in number, we dodged recklessly between and around our feeding mothers. Completely forgotten were the frightful memories of wolves, and the crashing light of great storms as we sought only to burn the energy that had grown within us during our sleep.

We tired finally of our running game, and each calf walked through the big herd, bleating softly as it went, and upon hearing its mother's mewing reply, darted quickly to her and fed once more.

The sun shone from just above the horizon as I finished feeding. I looked to my mother, whose gaze was now fixed far off in the basin. After a long silence she said, "It is time, Tateh, to finish our journey through the high basin and into the more protected forest in the canyons which fall from its side. Come, son," she said, and turned and began walking across the meadow toward the descending sun.

The feeding cows, upon seeing my mother's deliberate stride as she crossed the meadow, immediately understood her purpose. They quickly formed a long line behind her, several elk wide, and with excited, bounding calves in tow, followed her again as we continued across the basin.

Our new journey was now pleasant, unlike our terrible trek of the past night. Behind me, cows called casually to one another and calves bleated excitedly as we moved onward toward the setting sun in a wonderful clamor of elk sounds.

We passed through many big meadows on our journey. Calves darted playfully from the wide column of brown bodies, jumping and bucking through the openings as our herd moved unfalteringly forward behind my mother. The numbers of our herd were so great that even when crossing the largest of meadows, the cows and calves near the rear of the line had not yet entered the meadow before my mother and I had passed into the forest on the meadow's far side.

Finally, in failing light, we stood at the edge of the great basin looking into a huge canyon that dropped from its side. The canyon fell gradually away and formed two small basins in its bottom that shone with lush greenness. The huge gorge then dropped away again to form yet others. Tall stands of trees formed dense woodlots between each of the basins, and immense trees covered the canyon's sides where they encircled still more islands of greenness there. Small ponds shimmered weakly from many of the meadows, and a soft rushing noise far below, told of a stream whose water made its way impatiently downward in the deep canyon.

My mother looked back at the herd, then to me, and started into the canyon. The trail was well used, and we traveled easily downward in the gathering darkness. Finally, as my mother entered one large meadow, she stopped and looked cautiously around, testing the air as she did so. She then walked slowly forward in the grassy meadow to its center, and lowered herself into the deep grass where I quickly joined her. The cows spread out in the meadow around us, and soon all were lying quietly with their calves in front of them, thinking still, I'm sure, of the events of yesterday.

We were greeted in the morning by a warm sun and clear blue skies. I jumped quickly from my bed in front of my mother and stood gazing excitedly around the big meadow. The grass throughout was tall and green. Wildflowers grew thickly everywhere, and in many places throughout the meadow, mounds of dirt stood above the grass where colonies of ants worked industriously in the warm sun. On one side of the meadow was a group of small ponds, and the stream we had heard from the canyon's top rumbled softly from beneath the trees there. I fed anxiously beneath my mother now, in a great hurry to fill my belly and enter the meadow. I knew my dappled friends would be there and that we would resume our all-important games.

I was soon running and charging menacingly through the meadow with the others. I loved my little speckled friends, especially one of the smaller ones, a little female named Wicala. Her name, she had told me, meant *faithful one*. She had a wonderful zest for life, but was a little smaller than, and not quite as strong as the rest. She had nearly lost her life during the horrible wolf attack and was now quite timid when we calves charged headlong through the brush at the edges of the meadow.

The grass here was rich and tasty, and the water was cold and pure. Several wonderful days were spent in this meadow, as we calves played, and our mothers fed on the abundant grass.

It was now late in the season of *growing grass* and countless rooted ones filled the meadow. The small animals, both on the ground and in the air above the surrounding forest were now accompanied by young ones. The voices calling from the forest from the day's first light to when darkness gathered, were many fold more than earlier. Countless young ones chattered excitedly throughout the day.

This morning began with the promise of another cloudless day as the sky above slowly brightened and the excited clamor of woodland voices began again in the forest around us. I lay listening to the growing hubbub of life as the meadow before me slowly appeared from the darkness, then rose and slipped beneath my mother to feed. When I was finished, we entered the meadow together where my mother barked loudly once to signal her intentions to the others. As cows and calves streamed from the surrounding trees into the meadow behind us, she turned, and with me following, started toward the trees at the meadow's lower end.

We moved downward on a wide trail, crossing the creek several times in the canyon's broad bottom. My mother led our herd carefully around small rockslides and skirted thick patches of blown-down trees through which we could not pass. Calves ran looping circles through the herd as we passed through the large green meadows. Happy chirping and bleating sounds echoed through the forest as we continued our descent.

The trail led us upward on the canyon's side where we wound between precarious rocky bluffs, and soon crossed into yet another huge gorge that lay beyond.

A stream sparkled invitingly from the bottom of this mysterious new canyon as it shimmered crookedly through the deep grass far below. Lower in the canyon, a thick forest choked its broad bottom, and from hidden places at the edges of tiny meadows, strange, white clouds rose above the trees.

"Why do the clouds hang in the trees there, on such a clear day as this, Mother?" I asked.

"It is steam, Tateh," said my mother. "It rises from the water of strange, foul-smelling ponds there. The water in these ponds bubbles always and is so hot that it cannot be touched. In some places," she continued, "the seething water shoots from the earth high into the air and steams so, that for a short while, even the mountains and trees behind them are hidden from view."

I followed behind my mother lost in thought, in wonder of this latest bit of knowledge I had learned about my mountain home.

We followed the trail downward on a narrow ridge walking between towering columns of rock and across narrow ledges of sheer stone as we descended ever closer to the winding stream.

Reaching the canyon's bottom at last, we walked from the forest into deep grass, where we moved with urgency toward the beautiful creek we had seen from above.

Cows and calves lined the grassy banks of the little stream and as all drank greedily from the cool water there. Soon, my mother turned from the water and continued onward once more. Leading us upward in this new canyon, she nipped greedily at the tall grass as she went.

A soft, hissing sound filled the canyon as the tall grass parted and flowed around countless surging legs as our legion of brown bodies moved steadily onward. We entered the timber at the head of the great opening and soon drew near one of the mysterious columns of steam that we had seen from far above.

The steam rose from a pond at the far edge of a small opening. As we neared the mysterious pool, I was amazed to see that its water boiled and splashed for no apparent reason. The churning billows of steam that rose from its surface caused me to wince and snort as I sought to expel the awful smell it carried to my nose.

'What animal could use a pond so terrible as that one?' I thought curiously, as we continued past and away from its hot, smelly steam.

As we emerged from a thicket of trees into yet another meadow, there stood before us many large, dark-colored animals. Indifferent to our presence, they fed unhurriedly in the opening before us. Each of the great four-legged ones had horns, but unlike the huge antlers of our kind, only one stubby horn protruded from each side of their blocky heads. Their bodies were large and thickset, especially at their front shoulders, and they were covered with dark, shaggy hair.

"What are they, Mother?" I asked excitedly.

"They are bison, Tateh," said my mother. "Once their numbers were huge, and they lived everywhere in our mountains," she continued, "but now only a few remain in special places like this one."

As we proceeded up the canyon, I looked back at the bison once more. There were many large ones, but unlike the cows in our herd, I realized, only a few of the bison had young ones at their sides.

The sun was dropping low in the sky behind us when we entered a tree-lined meadow in a small, hilly basin. At the edges of the basin, rocky walls rose almost vertically to form the rounded head of this big canyon. Far above us on the towering walls, white animals gleamed in the fading sunlight as they clung precariously to invisible rock ledges.

"What are those animals in the rocks above us, mother," I asked excitedly?

"Those are mountain goats, Tateh," she said. "They feed on strange rooted ones that grow on the rocks there. The goat's feet are such that they can walk nimbly on narrow ledges of rock and never fall from them."

I watched spellbound, as the amazing white animals continued easily across the sheer cliffs above us and disappeared finally into a craggy canyon hidden beyond.

With the incredible display in the cliffs now over, my attention focused on this new basin in which we now were. Wildflowers shown boldly throughout the meadow in the weakening sunlight, and several ponds surrounded by tall grass, lay near us at the meadow's lower end. On one side of the shimmering pools, white-barked trees with broad green leaves formed a large thicket. This colorful woodlot stood in bright contrast against the dark colors of the pine forest behind them. A small creek rattled through the meadow feeding the ponds from above and then disappeared into the forest below them.

My mother walked to the middle of the grassy opening, and looked carefully around her, testing the air as always. When satisfied that all was well, she lowered her head to the deep grass and began to feed. At seeing my mother's unspoken sign of approval, our herd spread out in the meadow and began to feed. The hungry cows with heads pressed to the grass, seemed unaware of their calves that fed greedily beneath them.

That night, as I lay against my mother in the fading light of our new meadow home, I thought again about the steaming ponds, the shaggy behemoths called bison, and the white goats that still clung, I was sure, to rocks far above us in the darkness. Each of

93

my days now were filled with remarkable discoveries such as these. 'What an incredible place this mountainous land is,' I thought silently, as I drifted into sleep.

The many different timberlands and meadows that filled our sprawling mountain home, I realized, were in many ways similar. The voices I now heard in the early morning darkness were ones I had heard many times calling from the forest surrounding each of the meadows in which I had previously slept. I lay quietly against my mother in the growing light and listened thoughtfully to the calls of the small animals echoing from the trees as I studied the grassy meadow and surrounding forest that was our new home.

Large trees surrounded the meadow at all edges, but one that stood at the meadow's lower end loomed well above the others around it. It had a massive trunk covered with dark red bark. Moss-covered limbs grew crookedly on all sides of the old tree, starting at a point high above the ground, giving way finally to a gnarly gray top that stood lonely vigil above the surrounding forest.

What had caught my eye, though, was a dark, narrow groove cut deeply into its trunk. The old scar coursed crookedly downward the full length of the tree from the twisted grayness at its top to the earth at its broad base. Resin had wept from the wound over time and now framed the dark gash with a dull, yellow color along its entire length.

"What is that strange, crooked line on that huge tree at the bottom of the meadow, Mother?" I asked.

"It is a scar caused by lightning, Tateh," said my mother. "That one is what we call a *lightning tree.* Being so much taller than the others around it, it is struck often in the raging storms such as the one through which we traveled not long ago. The lightning we saw on that night though," she continued, "flashed only in the clouds above us. The scar in that old tree was caused by a different kind of lightning, Tateh, a kind in which blinding bolts of light streak from the sky and hit the tallest of trees such as that one. When these trees are struck," she continued, "the lightning courses instantly down their trunks, and into the earth at their bases. Sometimes the tree, after being struck, will burst into flames. At other times, a deep groove like the one on that old tree is gouged into their trunk from the mighty energy of the pulsing light as it travels downward to the earth. During the great storms here, Tateh," she continued, "we never seek shelter under such large trees as those, for if it were to be struck as you lay beneath it, you would surely be killed."

I stared in wonder at the old tree, trying to imagine bolts of light streaking from the sky then down the old one's base.

"You will understand soon enough," said my mother solemnly, apparently reading my thoughts.

We arose then from our bed and walked into the meadow, where my mother lowered her head to the grass and began to feed. I stood lost in thought, studying the old giant that loomed at our meadow's lower end.

95

All thoughts about great storms and lightning trees soon evaporated though, as my speckled friends entered the meadow with their mothers, and the remainder of the morning was spent in gleeful calf games.

After a brief rest and a good feeding, we calves continued the joyful play that we had begun in the morning. The day had warmed considerably, and our mothers now watched leisurely from the shade as we charged recklessly across the meadow, fully engaged in our games.

In the lower end of our meadow playground, the grass grew in large, round clumps. Our feet, as we scrambled past, sank easily into the soil there due to the hidden digging and tunneling of little meadow voles working beneath the opening's surface. During one of our headlong, dashing assaults through that portion of the meadow, our hooves sank deeply as we ran, and a grassy nest filled with young meadow voles was dislodged and kicked to the surface. The tiny voles were totally disoriented at being so suddenly exposed to the sunlight. They scrambled across the ground in all directions beneath us, screeching woeful death cries.

Upon hearing their baneful cries, our small band of elk was immediately overcome by a strange excitement. The calves around me joined suddenly in a bizarre frenzy of running and jumping, as they thoughtlessly tried to kick and crush the screaming voles beneath their hooves.

I too, was nearly overcome by this curious new energy and stood frozen for a moment, watching in confusion. "Stop, stop!" I yelled upon gaining my senses finally. Rearing onto my hind legs, I flailed wildly in the air with my front hooves, trying desperately to gain the other calves' attention.

Upon hearing my cries, all stopped but one. A bull calf named Khiza glared at me defiantly, then continued to stomp and kick among the screeching voles. Khiza was fascinated by the sound of the dying ones beneath him. I ran at him with all my might and hit him squarely with my chest, rolling him end over end across the ground. The cows ran from the trees and gathered quickly around us, having heard the woeful cries of the meadow voles and my excited yelling at the other calves. They had seen my crashing assault on Khiza.

Khiza rose slowly to his feet, his angry mother glaring at me from behind him now.

"Why did you do that, Tateh?" she demanded angrily of me.

"He was killing the meadow voles for no reason and would not stop," I answered.

"Meadow voles, Tateh? You nearly killed Khiza to save little meadow voles?" she asked incredulously.

"Yes," I said bravely, holding her angry stare. "The lives of those meadow voles are important. Though tiny, they have a purpose here in these mountains, and no one's life or purpose is more important than another's, regardless of their size."

My mother stood before me now, her eyes wide with amazement at the significance of my words. She asked me finally, "Tateh who told you this?"

Hesitating at first, I blurted finally, "Woslolkia!" remembering suddenly, the name of the great bull in my dreams. "Woslolkia told me, mother."

A resounding gasp came from the cows gathered around us, and they stared at me through eyes filled with disbelief. After a long, puzzling silence, the baffled cows one by one, turned, with calves in tow, and walked back to the shady edges of the meadow leaving my mother and me standing alone in its center.

My mother studied me in silence for a long time, her soft, loving eyes filled with question. "Woslolkia," she whispered quietly at long last. "When did Woslolkia tell you this, Tateh?"

"He has walked with me many times in my dreams, mother," I said. "On countless nights the great bull has stepped from the shadows in my sleep, and we have journeyed together through the mountains. When I awake, the words he shared are always gone.... until today. Who is Woslolkia, mother?" I asked.

My mother drew in a long, ragged breath of air, then looked away down the meadow and finally back to me.

"Woslolkia," she said, her voice little more than a whisper, "was a great, magnificent bull elk. His heart was equally as large," she said, her voice becoming stronger now. "He was the monarch of our great herd. He led us through these mountains for many years, protecting all in our herd from the many dangers here. He was respected and loved by all.

"He was killed, Tateh, in the past season of the falling leaves as he tried to lead a bewildered herd of cows and calves to safety in a small valley below here. They had been foolishly driven there by another bull during the two-legged ones' *time of killing.* He was….. he is…. your father, Tateh," said my mother as she held my pleading stare. The emotion that filled her eyes said all that needed saying. She turned from me then and walked slowly away.

Bewildered, I stood alone in the meadow thinking about the gigantic bull that I now knew to be my father. I thought about the many times that he had come to me in my dreams and the many times I had struggled in the light of day to remember the words he had spoken. Now I understood the look of love that I had seen each time in his eyes and knew why that feeling of love lingered long after waking.

I stood quietly now, trying to understand all that I had just learned. I looked at the cows and calves standing at the edge of the trees.

'My father's great herd,' I thought proudly, suddenly feeling much older than the calf whose body I now occupied.

I looked at the beautiful meadow around me and at the mountains beyond it, whose ridges formed the ancient canyon in which I stood. All were once the domain of Woslolkia, I was sure. I looked finally toward my mother who stood with the others in the shade, staring quietly back at me.

Suddenly, I understood the great bull's words when long ago he had said, "I will walk not only beside you, Tateh, but within you as well."

The knowledge that I had acquired already in my short life was suddenly overwhelming. As I saw Woslolkia again in my mind, I was overcome with an intoxicating burst of energy and sprang forward lunging and bucking, kicking dirt and snorting… alone, across the meadow.

Chapter Six

Each new day in our mountain home seemed a copy of the many days before it. Each morning dawned clear and warm. I would rise excitedly, feed as quickly as possible, and then engage again in the exploration of my growing world, romping joyously through the meadow with my many spotted friends. How could I have known that these make-believe games at which my friends and I played so hard, were really youthful practice for challenges we would encounter in adult lives that were soon to come?

As the days progressed through the season of the growing grass, the sun's heat grew. We no longer played beneath the sun in the middle of the day but rather sought the cool shade found beneath the large trees at the meadow's edge. Here, we would nap beside our mothers through the heat of the day, rise again and feed, then meet in the meadow rested and ready to resume our miniature games of life.

As I would soon learn, hot days here in the mountains such as the ones we now experienced often ended with skies that were filled with menacing, black clouds and terrible flashing light. A spectacle caused by what my mother ominously referred to as "the thunder beings from the west."

So it was this day that as the afternoon turned to evening, dark clouds began to build in the sky above the mountains around us. The sun was hidden above the looming blackness long before it had finished its daily journey beyond the mountains in the west.

My frolicking calf business had ended for the day, and as I fed under my mother in the rapidly softening light, I heard the first distant rumblings in the sky. A sinister black line of ragged clouds approached steadily from the west. Darkness came quickly to our meadow. What had been distant rumbling became terrible crashes of thunder that reverberated in the sky above us. Brilliant flashes of light like those on that terrible night when my mother led our herd through the darkness now filled the skies overhead. Unlike that storm, though, jagged streaks of light now hissed suddenly from the sky and struck the earth, followed by deafening crashes of thunder.

'This,' I thought nervously, 'is the kind of lightning about which my mother warned me. The kind that scars the old trees.'

I stood nervously beneath my mother at the edge of the meadow as she quietly studied the threatening sky. She turned to me finally and said, "Come, Tateh."

She led me into a thick clump of small trees away from the towering forest at the meadow's edge. Pressed firmly against the warmth of her behind me, I lay shuddering with fright in the flashing darkness as I anxiously watched the growing storm.

From far off in the forest, we suddenly heard the ominous rumble of approaching wind and the crashing of trees that marked its rapid advancement. The frightful clamor grew closer until finally the wind burst upon us with a thundering roar. It whipped at the grass in the meadow and tore at the small trees in which we lay.

In the forest around us, the dreadful sound of snapping roots and the wrenching groan of trees echoed through the night as their trunks splintered and they crashed to the forest floor. Limbs, both large and small, flew through the darkness as they were torn from trees around us. Pine needles rained steadily down and blew in stinging clouds across the forest floor where my mother and I lay huddled tightly in the grass.

Between blasts of light and shuddering peals of thunder, the horrifying sound of the crashing forest filled the night as the sky borne assault continued.

Mingled now with the sounds of the storm's fury were the frightened squeals of calves and the reassuring mews of their mothers as they led their panic-stricken calves away from the edge of the meadow. They lay near us in the protection of the short dense trees and lowered their heads and necks over the young ones to protect them from the worsening storm.

The brilliant flashes of light were terrifying as they struck nearby in the forest, holding fast in the top of a tree for an instant, lighting the meadow around us as if it were day. Each was followed by a deafening boom. Rain began to fall and soon fell with such intensity that we could not see through it, even during pulsing flashes of light.

Soon, mixed with the rain, hard, white pellets began to fall and soon became an icy downpour that pummeled us from the sky.

"Hail," whispered my mother from behind me, her head close to mine as she covered me in the darkness.

The hail dropped from the sky with increasing intensity. The white pellets became steadily larger in size until finally, a sharp sting was felt at each spot where one hit my body. When the lightning flashed in the sky, I could see the cows and calves that cowered beneath the trees around us. Their flickering silhouettes were outlined clearly now by the white glow of hail that was building on the ground around us.

Suddenly, at the bottom of the meadow, a blinding flash of light filled the night. For an instant, a brilliant, writhing line of white held fast to the top of a huge tree there, followed immediately by a shuddering crash of thunder. 'The lightning tree,' I thought silently, as I shuddered beneath my mother.

After what seemed an eternity, the hail and rain diminished and the lightning moved slowly onward across the sky. The wind became calm and the forest quieted finally. I raised my head and looked about in the darkness. A soft whiteness shone from everywhere on the ground beneath the trees around us, and the sound of dripping water drummed softly throughout the forest. Soft mewing came from the quiet darkness around us as mothers soothed their shaken calves. All in our great herd lay in quiet wonderment, thinking of the incredible spectacle that we had endured.

"And now, Tateh," said my mother softly, "you have seen the light that shoots from the sky."

"Yes, Mother, now I know," I said, as I thought nervously about the terrible, streaking light. I wondered if the old tree at the lower end of the meadow had yet another scar.

The next morning dawned clear and warm as many previous days had. After feeding, we calves slowly gathered in the meadow where we looked in awe at the surrounding forest. Many trees had succumbed to the terrible force of last night's storm and now rested uprooted in the grass at the edges of the meadow. Others had splintered and snapped halfway up, their tops bent precariously over, resting on the forest floor. As I had thought, the great lightning tree at the foot of our meadow had a deep new gouge shredded down its trunk that already had begun to ooze pine pitch.

As the sun drew higher in the sky, the meadow quickly dried out and the romping games of life commenced for us once again. The terrorizing storm of the previous night was soon forgotten as our little herd frolicked in the sunny meadow, and soon it was time again to feast and sleep.

I opened my eyes in the late afternoon to the same beautiful blue sky and hot sun that had shone before my sleep. I rose, stretched, and quickly ate, then trotted with great anticipation into the meadow. My mother watched me from the shade as she chewed contentedly, lying beneath the trees at the meadow's edge.

I was alone in the meadow at first, as most of my dappled friends still slept beside their mothers beneath the trees. One by one, they awoke and walked into the meadow as I had, where we soon joined in a spirited game of pushing and shoving, a game of which we never tired.

This day was again calm and warm like all days in the recent past had been, but it seemed now that we romped harder than ever with energy lingering within us still from the excitement of last night's storm.

Soon we were a long line of miniature elk charging through the meadow. In large circles, we ran bucking and darting, bleating angrily as we defended our imaginary little ones from great beasts.

So caught up were we in our mock battles and pushing contests that we didn't notice the dark clouds of yet another approaching storm. Our surging line of calves now rushed downward in the meadow toward its bottom edge where we weaved through the forest beneath the brooding form of the old lightning tree. Our darting, headlong forays over fallen trees, between boulders and back again into the meadow, had become so intense that the beckoning calls screamed now by our mothers could not be heard above the clamor of our assault.

As our dashing line of young elk once again entered the timber, a brilliant flash filled the sky and a shuddering roar shook the forest as a large tree near us was struck. Bark and shredded pulp from the lightning-struck tree showered us from above, and calves ran panic-stricken in all directions through the forest.

The cows were on their feet in an instant, running toward the lower end of the meadow, calling frantically to their calves. Upon hearing my mother calling me from the meadow, I turned immediately and ran toward her. A group of calves followed me.

The dense underbrush to our side suddenly exploded in a great crash of splintering limbs as an enormous silver bear sprang from its hiding place beneath a tangle of fallen trees. With a terrifying roar, the giant thundered straight toward us.

We bolted in all directions from the great bear, which at first confused him. I shot around a boulder and jumped a large fallen tree. With the group of calves following closely still, I stopped beneath the great lightning tree at the bottom of the meadow listening frantically to locate my mother.

Suddenly, from behind me in the trees near the big log I had jumped, I heard the terror-stricken bleating of my friend, Wicala. From ahead of me in the meadow, I heard the desperate call of my mother. I froze for an instant, torn between the two plaintive cries.

Calves bolted past me on both sides, charging toward anxious calls from the meadow. I turned back, though, and lunged toward the bleating shrieks of my friend.

I sprang onto the large, fallen log where Wicala stood on the far side, her eyes glazed and screaming in horror, unable to jump the huge downfall. I could hear the terrible smashing and breaking of brush nearby as the great silver bear, having heard her cries of death, crashed through the dense forest toward us.

"Jump, Wicala! Jump! You can do it!" I screamed, as the enormous bear, roaring hoarsely, burst through the thicket of trees before us in a rush of crashing limbs.

For an instant, the great bear towered above me. Our eyes met, and the killing rage I saw froze me with fear. Suddenly, all was silent, I no longer heard the great bear's heaving breath or even his terrible roar, as his huge front paw slashed through the air toward me.

As if in slow motion, I saw Wicala scamper beneath the giant bruin and into the forest beyond. I heard my flesh tear, and I felt the shock of a crushing blow to my shoulder. The world spun as I twisted painfully through the air to land limply in the grass beneath the old lightning tree.

The enormous bear was immediately on me. Standing on his hind legs, he glared down at me in rage, washing me in rasping blasts of foul-smelling breath. His eyes were red with fury, and his shiny, dark lips were drawn fully back in a terrifying snarl that exposed rows of gleaming white teeth. Drool ran from both sides of his gaping mouth. I watched helplessly, unable to move, as the huge bear drew back his great arm.

I closed my eyes tightly shut as his huge paw swung downward. There was a blinding flash of light and a terrible crash, and then, all was silent.

I awoke and slowly raised my head. The forest around me was quiet and peaceful, but curiously, I did not feel the warm, soft presence of my sleeping mother behind me. I was alone now. As I studied this strange new forest in which I lay, fragmented pieces of a bizarre dream began slowly to fill my mind.

I remembered hearing the rumble of hooves somewhere near me in a strange darkness, as cows pounded headlong through the meadow toward the trees at its lower end. I remembered hearing the panic-stricken cries of calves that had somehow become lost as their anxious mothers called frantically to them. The great clamor of hooves and breathy cries of exertion had been all around me, it seemed, as in a frenzy, the cows had formed a defensive circle somewhere nearby. But above all that, I remembered the plaintive, echoing voice of my mother as she called again and again to me from a place I could not see.

As I lay quietly in this new place, struggling to clear the fog of sleep from my mind, I thought for a moment that I heard the mewing call of my mother ring softly from somewhere nearby. Her call was filled with sadness. Strangely though, upon raising my head to look, she was nowhere to be seen.

Suddenly, I remembered the terrifying confrontation with the great silver one in my horrible dream. The specter of the huge bear loomed so vividly in my mind that it seemed my dream must have been real. I sprang to my feet, nervously scanning the forest around me, but I was alone now. Remembering the crashing paw of the great bear, I looked anxiously at my body to verify the horrible memory as having been only a dream.

Curiously though, on my right side, there was now a dark, jagged gash where none had been. The wound ran from the base of my neck to the bottom of my shoulder. But oddly, I felt no pain.

A puzzling mist gathered slowly around me as I stood quietly contemplating my curious dream. I wondered of the whereabouts of my mother and the herd.

'Where is she,' I wondered, 'and why has she not come to me…. and the great herd, where have they suddenly gone?'

My eyes fell upon a faint trail that led from the grassy area in which I had just awakened, and I was somehow drawn toward it. The strange haze that had begun to grow around me became thicker as I started slowly forward on the trail. The path led me into a beautiful forest that grew across gently rolling hills. The forest floor was covered with bright, green grass from which peeked countless beautiful flowers.

The trail became more defined as I moved along. I felt no fear as I walked onward between fog-cloaked hills and through woodlots of towering trees. A growing sense of calmness settled over me as I continued along the trail in an ever-thickening mist.

The trail led me to the bottom of a small draw where I began climbing slowly upward. As I climbed higher in the canyon, a soft glow seemed to build ahead.

'The sun,' I thought, 'must be shining brightly at the top.'

I felt the presence of my father, Woslolkia, as I climbed upward, and somehow remembering his words, I whispered aloud, "Father, I will not fear in the fog that which I cannot see, for to all that now stands around me, I am related."

The fog soon became so thick that the trail beneath me could barely be seen, but the growing brightness that emanated above drew me steadily onward.

From somewhere in the mist, I suddenly heard the plaintiff call of my mother. I stopped and turned my head listening carefully. But now the only sound I could hear was the gentle whisper of this wonderful mist as it flowed slowly over me, pulling me ever upward toward the gleaming light above. I was suddenly overcome by an overwhelming urge to turn back and find her, but somehow knew such a search would be futile in this growing fog.

My attention was again drawn to the light that shown through the fog in the canyon ahead. 'I must be nearing the top,' I thought, as I started upward once again. The mesmerizing glow seemed even brighter now.

As I picked my way slowly upward, the brooding form of a downfallen tree slowly materialized in the fog. It blocked the trail ahead of me. The mighty roots of the fallen tree rose upward from the earth and reached far beyond the sides of the trail.

As I neared the tree, its towering roots rose from the ground and turned slowly in the fog. Standing suddenly before me, his tall, reaching antlers outlined by the bright light above him, was my father, Woslolkia.

Our eyes met as I walked to him. The many words he had shared with me now rang in my mind with clarity, and we stood facing one another in silence. No words needed spoken. The feeling of love and oneness that surrounded us was incredible.

"Woslolkia…father," I whispered at last, as I looked into his eyes, then, questioningly beyond him at the nearly blinding light that shown from just beyond where he stood.

"No, Tateh, my son," he said solemnly…. "It is not your time."

My eyes fluttered, and slowly opened. The amazing light and warm, caressing fog were gone. I lay alone in the grass at the edge of the meadow beneath the big lightning tree. My body was wracked with pain, and only with the greatest effort could I barely raise my head.

Seeing my movement, my mother jumped excitedly from the grass where she had been lying behind me and began mewing softly while she nuzzled me gently with her nose.

"Oh, my son," she said, "I thought surely you were gone. You have slept for many days."

She knelt at my head, and with her nose, gently guided me to her breast. I gratefully drew the warm fluid into my parched mouth and felt it course to my stomach, but the world around me began to spin, and as darkness overcame me, the fog once again descended….

Chapter Seven

I was suddenly enveloped once more, by a warm, swirling fog. Again, I walked through the mysterious forest through which I had recently journeyed. It seemed I was floating in the mist as I moved past the spot from which I had awakened earlier. Soundlessly, I continued slowly along the obscure trail that still bore the tracks of my recent passing. I was drawn ever onward toward the wonderful brightness that gleamed still, in the fog above.

Stepping suddenly from the trees in front of me was my father, Woslolkia. He seemed to have been waiting. He stood in the trail facing me as before, outlined by the bright light beyond him.

Studying me quietly, he said at last, "In that you have returned here, my son, I know that you are deeply troubled. You stand at a very bewildering fork in your life's journey. You are unsure of which path to take. Come, Tateh," he said. "Walk with me."

The great bull turned then, and started up the canyon in the warm mist. As I plodded quietly upward behind the looming bull, a comforting sense of oneness with him grew steadily within me. The ever-thickening mist that boiled around us seemed to hold and caress me warmly as it drew me ever upward.

The canyon gradually steepened, then split into two. Here, we turned and followed the smaller of the two canyons upward toward the alluring brightness beyond. At the top of the canyon, we walked between two rocky peaks whose tops we could not see in the fog, then onto a flat cliff that lay beyond. As we stared into the bright whiteness that surrounded us, it began slowly to part. A sprawling valley materialized far below us as the fog evaporated. I stood in bright sunlight now, blinking in marvel at what I saw.

This wonderous valley stretched in both directions as far as I could see. On the far side of the valley, towering mountains rose from its floor. The mysterious crags were covered with a purple-green color telling of the faraway timberlands that grew there. Jagged ridges formed mysterious canyons in the distant forests as the rocky spines rose from the valley.

The ridges merged finally, on ever-steepening terrain high on the mountain's sides. The thinning growth of rooted ones gave way, finally, to towering, jagged cliffs that formed a rocky barrier to all that was below. The mountains climbed ever-upward above the cliffs, covered with glistening snow, then, turned finally into craggy peaks that stood boldly against the deep blue sky behind them.

'What stunning beauty!' I thought. 'That is what these mountains upon which we stand must look like.'

Looming between the distant peaks, more mountains could be seen, and behind them stood even more. Each distant mountain range was a deeper color of purple than the one that stood before it.

"It is as you told me long ago, Woslolkia," I said. "There is no end. Our world goes on forever!"

As my eyes drifted downward from the beauty of the distant peaks, my eyes settled on a long, crooked, blue line that lay shimmering brightly in the rich greenness on the valley floor.

"Woslolkia, what is that blue line?" I asked excitedly.

"That is a river," said Woslolkia. "It is a surging body of water. The great river is formed by the union of countless streams, Tateh. Streams, like the ones that tumble downward from the canyons where we live.

"Where does the river go?" I asked.

"It flows across our Earth through many valleys where its life-giving waters are shared by countless others," said Woslolkia. "In some valleys, it is joined by yet other great rivers. Together they become a river so mighty that even large four-legged ones such as we, would not attempt to cross it. Far, far from here, this grand river enters an enormous body of water where at last, it comes to rest. This sleeping water, Tateh, is called the *ocean*.

"In this mighty body of water mingles the rivers from all the lands on our Mother Earth. In the ocean, Tateh, the river sleeps for a time, but is soon awakened by the powerful winds that blow there. Gathered by the gale's relentless lashing, the water returns to our mountain home hidden in the billowing clouds of mighty storms. It falls again to the earth to fill our mountain streams, and in this way,

Tateh," said Woslolkia, "the great circle of our water is completed again and again.

"The two-legged ones with whom we first shared our lands, called this water, *the water of life*. They said it was the *first medicine* given all things living here, by that which they knew to be the *Great Mystery*. With this abundant medicine, Tateh," he continued, "they knew all living things would flourish forever."

"Incredulously I thought, 'there are countless smaller circles at work within our great circle of life in this wondrous land.'

I stood quietly for a time, pondering the things Woslolkia had said, then asked curiously, "two-legged ones, Woslolkia?

Yes, Tateh," he said, solemnly. "The two-legged ones are curious animals somewhat smaller than are we. Unlike the hair and hide that covers our bodies, theirs is covered with what is known by them as, *clothes.* They walk upright on only their back legs, and are frail and weak in comparison to our kind. Long ago in the beginning, dark-skinned two-legged ones lived throughout our mountain home. Their numbers were small, and they lived in harmony with us and all living things around them. Those ancient ones, though, are gone. The two-legged ones that remain are white-skinned one's. They live in the valley below.

Looking downward, toward the home of the curious two-legged ones, I studied the valley carefully but none were visible. My eyes settled finally, on a long, dark line that seemed to be scratched into the land. The curious scar followed the river and ran from sight at both ends of the valley.

"What is that strange mark that follows the river, Woslolkia?" I asked.

"That is a trail, Tateh," said Woslolkia, "a route worn into the land by the passage of the two-legged ones."

"I can tell even from this great distance, that that trail is much larger and more deeply worn than any I have ever walked," I said. "And it is so straight! Why does it not turn this way and that, and follow the shape of the land as do our trails, Woslolkia?" I asked.

"It must be that way," answered Woslolkia. "The two-legged ones often travel their paths in wagons that are pulled quickly along by horses. At times, they travel at such a pace that if their trails were not straight, the two-legged ones and their wagons would tip, and fall from them."

"Wagons…? Horses…?" I asked, bewildered.

"It is very hard to explain, Tateh," said Woslolkia. "Horses are powerful four-legged beasts, larger even than our kind. Wagons, are wooden vessels in which the two-legged ones, ride. Horses pull the wagons on the trails of the two-legged, both day and night. In darkness the vessels have eyes of fire. The trail before them is clearly lighted, and the two-legged ones are able to travel as if it were day. Stay far from these trails, Tateh, for many of our kind have not returned after having ventured too closely to the two-legged ones and their strange vessels."

A chill passed through me as I quietly studied the ominous, dark line that lay far below me on the valley floor. 'I will never venture near that path of the two-legged ones,' I vowed silently.

As I struggled to understand the puzzling things that Woslolkia had said, my gaze fell upon a maze of much smaller, nearly invisible lines that crisscrossed in all directions on the valley floor. From this great distance they looked like silken threads spun somehow by a mighty spider.

"What are those strange lines on the valley floor, Woslolkia," I asked. "Are they the web of some great spider living there?"

"No, they are not the creation of spider," said Woslolkia. "They are fences, Tateh, barriers created by the two-legged ones to control the land and all things living on it.

"Fences, Tateh, are made when holes are dug in the ground by the two-legged ones. In these holes, they place short trees that have no roots or limbs. They are planted in a long, straight line. Between the trunks of these little trees is tightly stretched what the two-legged ones, call, wire. It is like a very strong vine, and like a vine, it has many sharp thorns.

"In this way, the two-legged ones create a barrier that makes very difficult the passing of any animal or even others of their own kind. Even as large and powerful as is our kind, only our strongest ones can leap consistently over them. Many of our young and old ones have become hopelessly entangled in the fences of the two-legged ones and have died struggling to free themselves."

Truly baffled now, I asked, "Woslolkia, how could one.... why would one ever try, or feel the need to control such a vast land as is ours? Are these two-legged ones so foolish as to believe they can possess and dominate something so powerful and mighty as are these mountains? I do not understand," I said.

"Nor do they apparently understand that, Tateh," said Woslolkia. "Though they believe that they can hold and control this land, quite the opposite is true. This mysterious and ancient place in which we live, indeed, possesses them and all of us who live here. It is controlled only by the mystical forces of nature, forces that the ancient ones knew to be the Great Spirit.

"These new, two-legged ones, Tateh, are driven by desires known and felt only by their kind. No other being that walks or grows in these mountains feels or understands their lust for possession, and their desire to dominate," said Woslolkia.

In several places on the valley floor, on pieces of land between the strange little lines, crawled what looked like small, black bugs. Across the valley floor they slowly crept, always in a straight path. Behind each of these tiny bugs rose a thin plume of dust into the air.

"What creeping crawler is that, Woslolkia?" I asked.

"That is not a bug," answered Woslolkia, "it is another kind of wagon used by the two-legged ones. It is very different from the ones upon which they ride when traveling their trails. This one is pulled by horses to turn the soil much the same as does the little meadow vole that lives here in our mountains."

"How is that possible?" I ask. "It seems nothing like the voles in our mountain meadows."

"Behind horses," explained Woslolkia, "the two-legged ones drag a strange kind of tree. This short tree has very sharp limbs that when pulled behind the beasts, digs as does the vole. The soil is turned in a way so grand, Tateh, that if all the meadow voles that live in all the mountains around us dug together, they could not hope to do in a season what the two-legged ones and their horses do in a day."

"Woslolkia," I said, "I am troubled by the things you tell me about these strange two-legged ones. Why do they live so differently than do all the animals around them? Why do they walk this land with footsteps so heavy that the land beneath their feet is forever changed?" I asked.

Woslolkia stood quietly for a moment, deep in thought.

"Tateh," he said finally, "it is because they have turned their backs on our sacred trust by which all here live."

"Sacred trust?" I asked.

"Yes, Tateh," said Woslolkia. "Our sacred trust is a bond held between all that live here and that which we know as the *great mystery*. It is a belief greater even, than faith. It is *knowing*. This belief, held by each of us, enables us to understand the great oneness in which all here, exist. It is a knowing, Tateh, in which no animal or rooted one is greater or more important than another. It is an unspoken vow that no animal or living thing will take more from our Mother Earth than is needed to exist. It is known by all that live in this great oneness, that our purpose here is only to find the courage to simply *be*, and to know that to each will come all that is necessary for them to complete their grand journey. That, Tateh," said Woslolkia quietly, "is our sacred trust.

"Long ago, Tateh," continued Woslolkia, "these new, white-skinned ones came to our land. For a time, they lived in harmony with the ancient two-legged ones and all living things here. They believed, and lived in honor of our sacred trust. But within their kind was a strange sickness that their dark-skinned brothers did not carry. A sickness called, fear, Tateh."

"Fear, Woslolkia?" I asked. "How did fear cause them to break our sacred trust?"

"For reasons unknown, the white two-legged one's belief in the great mystery began to wane. They became fearful of all that was around them, they became fearful even, of our Mother the Earth. They began to doubt that they would receive from her, all that they needed to complete their life's journey. As fear grew stronger within them, Tateh," continued Woslolkia, "so did their doubt in our sacred trust. Soon, the knowingness with which they had once walked, was gone. They no longer felt the oneness in which they had long existed with all living things here. Sadly, gone too, was their courage to simply *be*.

They began to seize a larger and larger share of the earths' bounty. As their sickness grew, they started to not only control the land, but to push others from it. They sought to make certain they would have what had become an ever-growing share of our land's wondrous treasures.

"Possession of the land soon came to be seen by the white-skinned ones as being somehow greater and more important than those they had pushed from it. Our belief, that all in life is exactly as it should be, and that it is perfect, was soon denied by them. They began to use the land in a bad way, Tateh. They tried to change our world to be perfect, in the odd way that they had come to believe perfect, to be.

"Soon, the two-legged ones no longer acknowledged the right of others to even exist. They came to believe that all living things around them lived only for their pleasure. Their inability to see the hardships that they brought to those with whom they had once lived in harmony, destroyed the natural balance of our ancient land. These two-legged ones now control all the lands upon which we four-legged ones once roamed freely, Tateh. They take the water from our great rivers to fill their tiny man-made streams. Some rivers are left nearly dry. The swimming ones, rooted ones, and countless animals that live in the valleys through which these rivers flow, all suffer by these selfish acts of the two-legged one's.

"Their ditches guide the water taken from our rivers to the land between their fences, where they grow only the rooted ones that please them. They eliminate all other rooted ones. Often, ones they banish are plants upon which our kind and others have depended since in the beginning.

"And even worse than their thievery of our water, Tateh," continued Woslokia, "is the irreparable damage they have inflicted on our rivers. Many of our once pristine streams have been forever ruined by the thoughtless digging of these two-legged ones. Digging, born from their ravenous lust for the shiny, yellow pebbles thought to be hidden in the gravel beneath.

"In our timberlands, the two-legged ones, with uncaring abandon, have fallen countless numbers of our great rooted ones to the earth. Now, giant, square meadows stretch for miles across our mountains where healthy forests teeming with animals, once stood. When the great trees were gone, the small rooted ones that lived in the shade beneath them, soon dried up and died. The flying ones and other small animals who were dependent on the trees, perished also. Even the soil once held in place by the myriad roots of the forest was washed away in the rain. The baneful, heavy steps of these two-legged one's has caused nearly irreversible damage to our natural chain of life. All, because they somehow became lost in their existence and forgot how to simply, *be*." said Woslolkia quietly, almost to himself.

"How can we stop them, Woslolkia?" I asked.

"We cannot stop them, Tateh," said Woslolkia sadly. "Only they, can stop themselves. If they do not change the way they walk their journey in life, the natural laws of our land will stop them finally, and all living things in this great land, including the two-legged ones, will perish."

"I hate them, Woslolkia, for all the evil things they have done to our land and to all those who live on it," I said, looking downward into the valley, my eyes narrowed with anger.

"No, no, Tateh," said Woslolkia softly, "do not hate them. Though they are lost, they are still our brothers. They do these things only because fear has grown so strong within them that they have forgotten that which they once knew well. Pity them, Tate, but do not hate them. Hope instead, that they will remember again that which they knew in the beginning and will join us to make the *sacred hoop,* our *great circle of life,* complete once more."

"I will try to do as you ask, "Woslolkia," I said at long last. "I will hope for the day when these two-legged ones walk again with us in oneness, but until that time, I will avoid them always."

"Perhaps the time is near, Tateh, when they will be shown the way home," said Woslolkia quietly, looking at me in a strangely knowing way.

"But….Woslolkia," I blurted, "surely those two-legged ones from there in the valley are not the ancient ones you have spoken of, the ones who walked in harmony among us in the beginning."

"No, Tateh, they are not the ones," answered Woslolkia quietly.

"What happened to those others, Woslolkia, the dark-skinned ones…., where did they go?" I asked.

Woslolkia drew in a great breath of air and exhaled slowly as he stood thinking for a moment. "Come with me, Tateh," he said finally, "I will show you."

As I turned to follow Woslolkia, I looked back toward the valley one last time, but the fog had settled around us again, and the valley could no longer be seen. We were shrouded once more in a mysterious world of billowing shadows.

We retraced our steps between the rocky peaks, then moved cautiously downward in the narrow ravine beyond. When we reached the place where the canyon had split, we turned and followed the larger canyon upward on a vague trail that disappeared into the mist ahead of us.

We walked carefully along a moss-choked stream that wound between looming boulders covered with lichen. We lowered our heads to creep cautiously beneath fallen trees that were suspended on each end by the rocky sides of the ever-narrowing canyon. Their dead, twisted branches reached ominously downward in the gloom. I marveled as Woslolkia turned his head side to side, guiding his giant antlers deftly through the gnarled maze as we went.

Brightness began to build again in the dark fog as we neared the top of the narrow canyon. As we climbed into a rocky saddle at the canyon's head, we entered a world of brilliant sunlight that shone from a magnificent blue sky.

On the far side of the ridge just below where we stood, the fog formed a churning, white floor that stretched across the sky before us as far as I could see. Though sinking slowly, the billowing deck of whiteness hid from view the ridges and canyons that I knew must lay below. Only the upper reaches of snow-laced peaks pierced the foggy blanket and stood shimmering defiantly in the distance beneath the luminous blue sky.

I stood quietly looking, hoping to commit to my memory forever the beauty which lay exposed above the clouds.

"Yes, Tateh," said Woslolkia, reading my thoughts, "few ever experience such a visual treasure as this one before you now."

As the writhing floor of whiteness sank, a rocky plateau grew slowly from the clouds in the distance. It was connected to the saddle in which we now stood, by a chiseled, boulder-strewn ridge. The sides of the plateau and the craggy ridge that led to it, were defined by broken cliffs and rock flows that fell steeply away, disappearing into the murky whiteness below them. Towering spires of rock stood among the plateau's rugged cliffs. Some had long ago fallen and lay in hopeless shambles while others stood in precarious columns, as if stacked by some unknown hand. Without a word, I followed Woslolkia down the far side of the saddle and onto the mysterious ridge. On an ancient trail worn into solid rock, we circled the towering spires we had seen from the main ridge. We wound beneath towering trees that appeared suddenly between gigantic seams of rock as Woslolkia led me onward. Our footsteps echoed eerily on the rocky trail as we moved cautiously between giant rocks against which long-ago fallen trees sagged precariously. Noiselessly, we proceeded through stands of short, gnarly trees. Ageless ones, that had been twisted and bent from years of enduring the violent weather that I was certain must occur on exposed ridges such as these.

We were often greeted by the shrill whistling calls of small four-legged ones as we crept slowly along shear rock ledges and jumped narrow fissures whose plunging depths were hidden in darkness. In places, the trail ahead seemed to vanish into a looming rock face. Upon reaching that spot, though, the trail would veer sharply through ominous shards of rock and continue through an unseen gulley or across yet another rock ledge.

We came to a spot where the ridge began to widen and walked, finally, onto the small plateau we had seen from the distant saddle. As I gazed in awe at the rugged rock flows and natural beauty that surrounded me, I realized that the ancient trail along the nearly impassable ridge was the only access to this magnificent place.

On the outer edges of the plateau along towering cliffs, stood huge rooted ones reaching far into the sky. The forest grew thicker toward the plateau's center where it opened suddenly to form a small, round meadow. The forest surrounding the meadow was dense and dark, colored in shades of grey and green, broken only by the bold, white trunk of an occasional aspen. In the meadow grew lush grass, and throughout, stood brightly colored flowers straining skyward.

In the center of the meadow stood a large, single tree shimmering before us in the sun. With gleaming white bark and vivid green leaves, the large rooted one stood alone, towering above the flowers and grass beneath it. The bark on its trunk bore the scars of its many years. From just above the grass, to a point above where even Woslolkia's great antlers reached, groups of vertical black lines stood in sharp contrast to the tree's white bark. The lines, in sets of four, had been etched deeply into its trunk.

"Here," said Woslolkia, "the great bears, stretching on their hind legs, had reached as high up the tree as they could. With their mighty claws, the bruins had pulled downward, leaving deep gashes in the bark that when healed, had formed these black scars. The tree's wounds were an ominous message for all who passed. It was a warning that told of the bear's ominous size and power."

Surrounding each limb on the tree's white trunk was an uneven circle of black bark. The dark circle clearly outlined the base of the white limb growing there. In its higher reaches, the large tree split, forming two smaller trunks. Angling away from one another, they reached ever upward above the meadow.

Many limbs grew from this point up, and each was thickly covered with oval-shaped leaves that rustled softly in the gentle breeze. The limbs spread in all directions, and this rush of green leaves and white branches stretched outward to form a sheltering canopy over the meadow beneath it.

"Woslolkia, this is the most beautiful tree I have ever seen," I said. "What is its kind?"

"It is an aspen," answered Woslolkia, "but really, Tateh, it is *all kinds.*"

"How can it be all kinds, Woslolkia?" I asked.

"The ancient two-legged ones," explained Woslolkia, "put this tree in the center of this meadow long, long ago. They believed that in the branches of this rooted one, the most magnificent of its kind, lived the spirits of all living things on our Mother Earth. They knew the spirits of their departed relatives and the spirits yet to come, lived among the branches of this great tree. They knew this beautiful rooted one was truly *the tree of life.* That is why, Tateh, that this tree is really, *all kinds.*

"Knowing this great tree represented all of life here in our mountains," continued Woslolkia, "the ancient ones believed that when all those living in our *great circle of life,* lived in harmony and oneness, this great tree would bloom and grow strong and tall."

As I looked more closely at the sacred tree, I saw nearly hidden in its dazzling greenness, leaves that were darkened with death and branches that were dried and twisted, the sap having left them long ago. "The doings of the new two-legged ones," I whispered aloud.

"The ancient ones knew this place to be very special, Tateh," continued Woslolkia, "and they came here often to celebrate their love for all that is the *Great Mystery*, as they stood and danced beneath this tree."

"Great Mystery," I asked? "What is the Great Mystery, Woslolkia?"

"It is the great unknown, Tateh. It is a force in our world that is far beyond our ability to understand. It is the mighty power that the ancient ones knew had caused all life to be, and indeed *is,* the spirit that lives in all things," answered Woslolkia. "They knew that not only had this mysterious power created our Earth and all the stars, they knew that indeed, it *is* our Earth and all the stars.

"Each year in the season of *growing grass*, in honor and celebration of the Great Mystery, these first two-legged ones came here. With their drums, they danced and gave thanks beneath this tree of life. To show the strength of their belief, for four days, without food or water, from the time when the sun rose, until it again rested, with all their hearts, they danced.

"On the last day of this sacred ceremony, Tateh," continued Woslolkia, "the two-legged ones would unite spiritually with the tree of life by physically bonding with the great tree. They did this by piercing the flesh of their chests with two small, wooden pegs. To each of these pegs was then tied one end of a strong leather thong. The other end of the thong was tied fast, high in the tree. To the beat of their drums they danced this way, joined with the tree of life by the flesh of their chests. They did this to celebrate and honor

131

the Great Mystery and the oneness of all things that they knew the great tree of life to be.

"As the sun dropped toward the horizon, signaling the end of the fourth day, they danced backwards away from the tree, drawing painfully against the leather thongs that bound them to it. As they danced forever backward, the pegs finally, would rip from their chests. The warriors would tumble to the earth, suddenly free from the great tree and all it represented. In that instant, they received the Great Spirit's most sacred gift of all. In their painfull breaking from the tree of life, came the gift of *choice* – the freedom to walk any path they chose. The freedom, even, to walk away from all that the sacred tree represented. But, with their breaking, the Great Mystery had also given them the gift of *wisdom*. A gift that enabled them to understand that even though they were no longer physically bound to the great tree, their spiritual bond with it and all things living there was much stronger than the leather thongs could ever be. They deeply understood the importance of walking in harmony with our Mother Earth and all others. Wooden pegs, and leather thongs were not needed. In this very difficult way, Tateh, they honored, celebrated, and proved to themselves and to all, the strength of their belief."

"Woslolkia, how could it be that the ancient ones who honored life and chose to walk in such a good way are no longer here?" I asked.

"The ancient two-legged ones, Tateh," said Woslolkia, "were simple, natural beings who lived in harmony with all around them and did not understand the need to possess and control. They were no match for the new, two-legged ones who came in such large numbers to our land. Like many of the four-legged ones and even the rooted ones, these ancient ones too, were pushed from the land by these new, white-skinned ones.

"Tateh," continued Woslolkia, "the old ones no longer exist as they once were, but as I have told you, when our life's journey ends, our bodies return to our Mother Earth, and our spirits live on forever. Look around you, Tateh," said Woslolkia, "using only the eyes of your heart. The ancient ones are here still, all around us. They live there in the tree of life. Their spirits dance before you on the breeze in the little butterflies you see all around you, and they live in the flowers and grass at our feet. Their words echo still from the trees and rocks, when the wind touches and gives voice to each. And, Tateh," continued Woslolkia, "as will we all, they too, will one day, return. Even now, it is said that the old ones sometimes dance beneath this tree during the full moon as they once did long ago."

I stood in deep thought, looking at all that was around me in the meadow. I carefully studied the beautiful tree of life that stood before us, then, lowered my eyes to the beautiful flowers and swaying grass beneath it. It seemed the small rooted ones were dancing with the butterflies in the meadow beneath the old tree. I looked toward the forest at the meadow's edge and listened carefully to the trees that whispered softly to us in the breeze. I raised my eyes to view the cliffs and spires of rock that stood guard behind them. It seemed I could feel the words Woslolkia had just spoken turn slowly to knowing deep within me. I Suddenly understood that much of what I would learn in life, I would see only with a quiet mind, through the eyes of my heart.

Turning back to the ridge upon which we had come, sadness settled over me as I thought of leaving this place of such beauty and spiritual power. 'Truly a secret place,' I thought.

Woslolkia, seeming to read my mind, said, "Do not feel sadness at leaving this place of wonder, Tateh, but rather happiness at having found it. Remember this trail, and look forward to your return here. This sacred place will someday serve you well, Tateh," he promised.

As we worked our way back along the ridge toward the hidden saddle, the churning fog descended upon us. The wonderful blue sky and sun that had shown only moments before were now gone.

Fear and panic grew suddenly within me and I hesitated… then, stopped.

"Woslolkia," I said, with a trembling voice, "I do not want to leave. I want to stay in this sacred place."

Woslolkia turned slowly to face me in the swirling fog. His eyes were filled with knowing.

"I am afraid," I said to him quietly, my eyes cast shamefully downward away from his. "I am afraid of life, father, I am afraid to go back. I fear the great predators that live there, the silver bear, and the wolf."

"My son," said Woslolkia, softly, "if it is your wish to stay in this beautiful place, you may stay and dwell forever among the trees and meadows here. But Tateh," he continued, "feel no shame for the fear you hold of the great predators in our mountains. Though you are very young, you have demonstrated to all those around you the great courage that already has grown within you. Once, as you lay motionless and unflinching at the feet of a prowling wolf and then a bear, at the safe place. You walk with me now, Tateh, because you had the courage to save Wicala. It is known by all in your herd that you turned from safety to face the wrath of the great silver bear.

"Soon, your size and strength will be a match for any that live in our mountains, Tateh. When next you face the great predators, you must remember that their greatest weapon is fear, the dread with which they freeze their victims when they attack. Do not cower from your fears in life, Tateh. Instead, look boldly at them, and they will vanish. When confronted again by the great predators, look them in the eye and stand your ground, Tateh. They will falter before your unblinking stare. Fear is not cast upon you by your enemies, but, rather, wells from deep within you. Their threatening presence merely causes it to spring to life.

"Tateh, though you are very young," continued Woslolkia, "you have been chosen to experience great fear. You have been forced to deal with the terror of impending death at the fangs of both wolf and the great silver bear. Each time, you found the courage to face them. From these great challenges, Tateh, has come a gift. You have learned to control the worst kind of fear known. The fear of death.

"Today, I have shown you how the white-skinned ones in the valley now walk the land, and I have told you of their breaking of the sacred trust. I have shown you, in this secret place, what the ancient two-legged ones once were and how they walked the land with honor in celebration of life. I have shown you these things, Tateh, so you will understand what the two-legged ones once were and what they have now come to be. Should you choose to return and walk the journey that will be yours, you will travel a path upon which you will face the most terrible predator of all. It will require all the courage that your life experience has caused to grow within you. Your path will lead you, finally, to the place of the two-legged one known as *man*. It is your calling, Tateh, to show our lost brothers the way home.

"You stand now, at a fork in your life's journey. You must choose if you will live, or you will die. Your kind needs you, Tateh, for the great bull you will be and the wisdom with which you will lead. But, if you choose to live, it must not only be for the sake of others. It must be your will, Tateh. You must do it for yourself. It must be your wish to experience all that is life, as you walk the magnificent journey that will be yours. Should you choose the path of life, the scar that you will bear on your shoulder will be a symbol of your bravery. It will carry deep meaning to all who see it."

My eyes fluttered weakly, then opened. The world around me began to focus, and the peaceful sounds of the forest became slowly clear.

Above me in the trees, small birds chirped happily as they flitted from limb to limb. Beyond them through the branches above, was a brilliant, blue sky. The familiar scent of the earth, the grass, and the great rooted ones around me, filled my nose. Bright splotches of sunlight shone blatantly between the jagged shadows of trees cast everywhere on the forest floor. A gentle breeze moved softly over me and played at the hairs at the tips of my ears.

I raised my head slowly from the grass to look around me and felt a great stiffness in my neck and shoulders. Behind me, I felt the wonderful presence of my mother as she stirred, then lowered her head to nuzzle me. I bleated weakly in response as her soft nose caressed my neck.

"Stay with me now, son. Please…. don't leave me again," she whispered.

Chapter Eight

As I struggled to pull myself from my strange sleep, I became aware of a measured throbbing that pulsed from deep within my throat, born from a terrible dryness there.

Lurching painfully upward from the grass, I struggled to rise to my feet, but oddly, I could not. Finally, with all the strength I could gather, I was able to straighten my rear legs beneath me and push my rear end from the ground. My mother then put her nose gently beneath my chest and lifted carefully until I stood wobbling painfully upright on all four legs.

Waves of sickness washed over me as I tried desperately to understand this terrible sea of pain in which I seemed lost.

"What happened to me while I slept, mother?" I gasped finally.

"We must cross the meadow now, Tateh, to the fresh water on the far side," said my mother evasively. "Come son, follow me, you can do it."

Pain throbbed in my shoulder, and my world spun dizzily as I took my first steps, but with my mother steadying me, I managed somehow to stagger across the meadow to the ponds there.

My legs trembled and threatened to buckle beneath me as I slowly lowered my head to the pond's surface. Gratefully, I sucked its sweet wetness into my mouth. The cool sensation that I felt within me was wonderful as the water hissed between my teeth quieting the burning dryness in my mouth. I shuddered with delight as the water rushed into my throat and found its way to my cramping stomach.

When the drought within me was quenched at last, I raised my head and looked carefully around me. Curiously, my mother and I stood alone at the meadow's edge. There were no cows lying beneath the trees around us, and my spotted friends no longer romped playfully across the big opening. From the forest surrounding the meadow came only the soft rush of the late afternoon breeze. The chirping and barking calls of cows and calves no longer echoed from the trees.

Bewildered, I asked, "Where is our herd, mother?"

"They have moved on, Tateh, to other meadows," said my mother. "It is our way, Tateh, to move often to new places where the grass is fresh and tall. The constant movement of our herd makes it more difficult too, for the great predators to find us."

'Moved on…. great predators?' I thought, as a bizarre memory sent a nauseating wave of fear ripping at my stomach.

Strangely, the horrifying specter of a great silver bear loomed unexpectedly in my mind. As I fought to shake the terrifying images that now streamed rampantly through my head, I realized that it had not been a dream. I knew then, why my mother had hesitated earlier to explain my crippling pain.

I reeled with weakness at my stunning realization. The memory of my horrible encounter with the silver one sprang abruptly to life. My legs became uncontrollably weak and the fear-driven sickness that clawed at my stomach caused me to choke and gag. In painful convulsions, I returned my precious store of water to the earth at my feet.

I looked anxiously around the meadow, fearfully searching the shadows beneath the trees surrounding it, then back to my mother. Following her eyes, I looked slowly downward to my shoulder where a mysterious, jagged gash was now healing over.

"What happened to me, mother?" I stammered, as the horrifying reality of the great bear sent waves of panic washing through me.

"The great silver one," I whispered aloud, remembering my terrible encounter plainly now. "Where did he go, mother? Why am I not dead? How did you save me?!" I cried.

"Son," said my mother in a trembling voice, "it most certainly was not your time to die on that day beneath the old lightning tree, nor, was it Wicala's time, either.

"Upon seeing the mighty blast of lightning strike the trees below the meadow that day, we mothers were on our feet and running to our young ones in an instant. As I ran frantically into the meadow calling your name, I heard the terrifying roar of a grizzly attacking somewhere in the forest below. Then, I saw you rush toward me from the trees at the meadow's lower end. To my

140

dismay, Tateh, you turned from my call. You left the group of calves that you had led from the woods and ran back toward the frantic cries of your friend, Wicala.

"I ran to the foot of the meadow calling desperately to you, when suddenly, Wicala dashed from the forest. I stood frozen with terror as I saw the huge bear strike you, knocking you helplessly from the log. Twisting awkwardly through the air, you landed finally at the foot of the old lightning tree.

"He was on you again immediately, Tateh. As he rose to his hind legs snarling and roaring, raising his mighty paw to finish his killing, a blinding blast of light filled the meadow. Lightning shot suddenly from the sky, and struck the huge tree under which you lay. The pulsing light held fast to the tree and shot crookedly from its massive trunk to the threatening, raised arm of the great silver one. With his mighty paw raised high above his head and a terrible snarl on his face, the enormous bear stood joined to the tree and sky by the blinding white light.

"Thunder roared and shook the forest as the great bruin was knocked to the ground, where he lay crumpled and trembling, surely dead. Wisps of smoke rose from his lifeless body.

"Slowly though, as I stared in disbelief, the great silver one struggled to his feet. Stumbling weakly, barely able to walk, he disappeared into the forest."

"Lightning... the lightning tree? That is why I am not dead, mother?!" I exclaimed. "Oh, mother, I groaned," as yet another wave of nausea filled my stomach, "I think… the farther I travel on my life's journey, the more I realize how little I understand."

"Yes, Tateh," said my mother looking around the vacant meadow quietly, "there are many mysteries here in our mountains.

"For several days I lay by you, Tateh," continued my mother, "as you clung barely to life beneath the big tree where you had fallen. You awoke once, mumbling words I could not understand, and I was able to kneel and feed you, but you were soon gone again.

"You have laid unmoving in the grass beneath the old tree for eight days, since your confrontation with the great bear, Tateh. You were nearly gone more than once. It was your strength and courage that brought you back to me, Tateh. Now you stand, and even walk again. You come from grand blood lines, son. I know your strength will soon return," said my mother.

My life, it seemed, had spun suddenly backward. My days now, as I slowly healed and grew stronger, were spent much as they had been when I was a newborn calf. I fed beneath my mother in the early morning, then rested in the shade at the edge of the small ponds through the day. I would rise and feed once more in the early evening, then limp painfully behind her as she fed in the meadow in gathering darkness.

As my days passed slowly by, walking endlessly through the meadow to strengthen my shoulder, I thought often of the other calves. I wondered in what wonderful new meadow they now

142

played their exciting calf games, games that we had once played together here. I wondered if I would ever again romp and cavort with them as I once had, or if I would limp tentatively, always in pain, as I did now.

'Will my mother and I ever again join the herd and roam with them in the beautiful canyons and basins of our mountain home,' I wondered? 'And the great silver bear... what of him? Did he now lie in a meadow somewhere nearby, racked with pain, healing and growing stronger, or did his life end later that day as he lay alone somewhere deep in the forest after having been so touched by the dreadful light?'

I could not help but hope the great bear was gone forever from this land, but each night I knew he would live again in my tormented dreams. Always, in the darkness of night he stood towering above me, scowling ferociously downward, his eyes brimming with rage. I would awaken as we were engulfed once more in blinding light. Gasping for air with my heart pounding in my throat, I would lie trembling, staring into the darkness. Awake then, far into the night, I would remember the words given me by the great bull in my dreams. As sleep would once again settle over me, I would whisper into the darkness, "have no fear, Tateh, look this one in the eye. It too, will disappear."

For many days, my mother and I stayed in the meadow near the small ponds. Eating, sleeping, and walking, I slowly regained my strength. It was now the season of *ripening berries,* and the grass in the meadow had grown tall. At the tops of the stems had appeared mature seeds soon to fall to the earth, beginning again their cycle of life. Each day on the afternoon breeze, the sky above the meadow was filled with the puffy white seeds of countless wildflowers. They shone in the sunlight as they floated magically through the air toward some unknown place where they too, would bring life in coming seasons.

Early one morning having finished feeding, I stood quietly beneath my mother as the sky began to lighten. Her head held high, her gaze was fixed on a place far beyond the meadow, a place known only by her.

After a long silence, she said finally, "Tateh, this wonderful meadow has served us well. You have experienced and survived some of our mountain world's harshest lessons here. You are stronger now, and able to travel. It is time that we go from here."

With that, she turned, and with me limping behind her, started slowly up the meadow.

There was no trail needed in the tall grass of the open meadows, so we meandered easily through them. When we came to the timber that separated the openings, my mother carefully chose a path through the trees that made my painful, three-legged trek endurable.

Our climb up the canyon through its dense forest and broad grassy fields was slow, but when the sun was high overhead, we stood once more at its top, near the edge of the great basin. Here, we stopped and looked back at the meadows and fingers of timber that comprised the bottom of what had been our canyon home. Memories of our life there, both good and bad, flooded my mind as I stared quietly into its depths. My mother too, I was sure, relived these memories. Without a word, she turned and started along the edge of the great basin.

With me hobbling along behind her, we slowly retraced our steps of that terrible stormy night long ago when we had crossed the basin with the great herd. Through many openings and pockets of timber we walked, stopping often to drink and rest ourselves near the small ponds hiding at the edges of the meadows there.

We came finally to a thick woodlot growing on a north-facing ridge, and I remembered suddenly that it was here, on our earlier journey in search of the great herd, that we had seen the silver bear's track in the trail. I shuddered with fear as the memory of my terrible encounter in the canyon now far behind, again filled my mind.

We walked slowly along the ridge, quietly passing the narrow draw into which the great bear's tracks had disappeared, then continued into the broad forest beyond. We came at last to the head of the familiar canyon where the healing water lay hidden far below. My spirits rose at the thought of the wonderful, warm water there. Knowing we would rest in the healing water at the end of our day, our pace quickened as we started into the canyon.

Our journey downward through the meadows and woodlands of the beautiful canyon was uneventful, and when the sun neared the far horizon, we lay once more in the healing water.

As I rested, quietly soaking in the warm water, I looked around me at the huge, timber-lined meadow that I had come to know so well earlier in the season of *growing grass*. I marveled at the natural wonders that surrounded me, wonders, that seemed I had first seen long ago.

When the healing water had at last soothed the pain that had grown in my shoulder during our journey, we rose from the pond. We walked slowly through the quiet darkness of the meadow to the bedding spot we had used earlier in the year beneath the trees at its far edge.

As the moon rose slowly above the ridge on the far side of the canyon, I lay snuggled tightly against my mother. Silently, I gave thanks to the mysterious power that had created this wonderful, healing place. I thought again about the many strange events of my short life. I shuddered as I remembered the terrible confrontation with the silver humpbacked one that had made necessary our journey here to the healing water. As I drifted into slumber, I wondered again where the great herd was now and about my many speckled friends with whom I had shared so much joy. I thought too, about Wicala, my little calf friend that I missed most of all.

Our days here passed slowly. I rose stiffly from my bed each day, fed beneath my mother, then together we would walk to the warm water and the sticky, yellow mud. There, I would soak for a while, then, roll in the healing mud. We would then return to our bedding place for rest.

Becoming bored at merely following and watching my mother as she fed in the meadow, I began to nibble occasionally at the seedy tops of the tall grass there. I soon acquired a voracious appetite for these lush, green-rooted ones that I had ignored for so long. I grew rapidly in size and strength now, and my hunger was no longer satisfied at my mother's breast.

My shoulder continued to heal, and the pain finally began to lessen. Sometimes now, we would even engage in a wonderful game of pushing and shoving while mewing angrily at one another as we once had. Left out though, was the part where we jumped and bucked and ran full out across the meadow, but it was joyous fun nonetheless.

As the days drew slowly past, it became finally, what my Mother told me was the time of *"yellowing leaves."* The days were still warm and balmy, but the sunlight now shone on the meadow with a softer hue. The light was cast at an angle from an ever-weakening sun that caused shadows of a greater length to stand behind all that it touched. The nights became cooler, and frost now occasionally covered the grass in the meadow till the sun rose to melt it away.

Now, each day after soaking in the warm water and a good warm-up romp in the meadow, my mother began to lead me up the steep sides of the canyon. We climbed upward through the thick forest, weaving between tall trees and even jumping some of the dead, fallen ones there. The climbing was at times painful, but my strength grew ever more quickly now.

147

As the days became shorter, frost often lay heavily in the meadow when we rose from our beds to graze. As the season of *yellowing leaves* progressed, there grew within me a strange feeling of uneasiness. I sometimes felt a need to be alone, it seemed, to prepare for something that I did not understand and could not find the words to explain.

So it was this evening, high above the meadow as we stood on a trail worn deeply into the side of the canyon, that this strange, new feeling welled once again within me. The sun had just dipped below the mountains, and my mother and I stood gazing at the beauty of the meadow below us.

Suddenly, from deep in the canyon below the pond, came a loud, whistling scream that ended with a series of deep, rumbling grunts. I was nearly overwhelmed by a curious excitement brought on by the piercing call. As I stood wide-eyed and trembling, looking toward the origin of the strange sound, a remarkable energy stirred within me. I felt an almost uncontrollable urge to seek out its maker.

"What was that noise, mother?" I asked excitedly.

"That was the call of a great bull elk, Tateh," said my mother, as she stared into the canyon toward the place of this unseen bull. "In this season of *yellowing leaves*," she continued, "the nights become cool and crisp and the days become shorter. The diminishing sunlight triggers within the great bulls of our kind, a growing urgency. They are driven to search out the cow elk and mate with them. Then, in the next season of *growing grass,* we mothers bring new young ones into the world. In this way, Tateh,

148

the survival of our kind is insured. The great bulls make calls like the one we just heard, as loud and as boldly as they can.   With grunts as deep and guttural as possible, they attempt to attract the cow elk to them and to warn all other bulls of their grand size and strength. The larger and stronger the bull, the louder and more formidable will be his call. It is nature's way, Tateh, that the cows are attracted to the mightiest bulls. The calves produced by this natural union guarantees the strength of our kind." She stood staring intently still, toward the direction from which the remarkable sound had come.

Finally, she turned to me and said, "Tateh, the bulls will gather their herds soon. They will often fight violently among themselves for the right to lead and mate with the cows of their herd. They will run all other bulls far from them. When the battle to lead is between two bulls that are nearly equal in strength, the fights are often long and brutal. The mightiest, Tateh, will always become the leader.

"The bulls are easily enraged, and are very intense during the time of mating," she continued. "They sometimes prod their herds forcefully along for great distances, trying often in vain, to outrun pursuing bulls. Sadly, the weaker of our young calves are often unable to keep up.

"Your strength has grown quickly, Tateh, during these first seasons of our land. Though you have healed much since your injury from the great bear, you still walk at times in pain with a slight limp. Should you become separated from me during this confusing time, remember all I have taught you. Return to this place where the grass is deep and rich, and the water is plentiful and healing. Wait here, and I will come for you, Tateh," she said.

She turned, and with me following, started down our trail toward the meadow where I knew we would soak and wallow before we bedded for the night.

As I lay by my mother that night, I stared nervously into the darkness around us. The mysterious, screaming call of the unseen bull we had heard earlier, echoed again and again in my mind. An uneasy feeling of impending change grew steadily within me.

Try as I might, sleep refused to come. Late in the night when finally, I sank into slumber, my dreams were filled with monstrous bulls. The huge ones screamed and grunted and chased young calves angrily from their herds.

Morning dawned, and as light slowly filled the meadow before us, I stood from my bed. Looking anxiously around me, I tried to shake from my mind the memory of my terrifying dreams. After careful inspection of the great opening, I was relieved to see at last that it stood vacant. The angry bulls that had filled my sleep were not present.

My mother stood from her bed and together we walked to the pond where we lowered ourselves gratefully into its warmth. As I lay beside my mother in the healing water, the stiffness in my shoulder melted gradually away, as did the fear that had grown within me since hearing the screaming call the previous evening.

Suddenly, my mother's head whipped toward the trees at the meadow's upper end, where she stared intently. Following her gaze, I stayed quietly beside her in the water, watching and wondering nervously what had drawn her attention.

Faint sounds, indiscernible at first, began to echo softly from the sides of the canyon far above the meadow. My mother stood and walked from the water as the indistinct sounds grew steadily louder. The sounds I realized finally, were the anxious chirping and mewing calls of an approaching elk herd.

Excitedly, I leaped from the water and stood at my mother's side as the first cows, with calves at their sides, entered the meadow above us.

"Mother, it's the great herd," I cried, as I started excitedly toward the cows and calves that walked steadily into the meadow above.

"Tateh, stay at my side," said my mother sternly.

Puzzled by the unfamiliar tension in her voice, I quickly joined her once more and watched curiously as the huge herd continued to pour into the meadow.

As the meadow above us filled with increasing numbers of brown and tan bodies, I realized that this was not the herd with whom I had grown up. The mewing and chirping calls coming from this herd were filled with an odd sadness and urgency. Suddenly, the brown sea of churning bodies parted, and from their midst stepped a gigantic bull.

The bull was lighter in color than any elk I had ever seen. His dark, thick horns were immense and reached far beyond his sides. Their gleaming white tips stood even higher above his head than did the antlers of the great bull in my dreams. I heard my mother quietly gasp as the huge bull struggled painfully forward between the parted elk.

The mighty one held one front leg off the ground as he stumbled and staggered in pain between the members of his now silent herd. As he continued slowly toward us at the pond, the cows and calves of his herd formed a wide line and followed quietly behind him.

When the great bull neared us, I saw a mighty scar on his shoulder. He had many smaller ones on his chest and sides. Scars, I was certain, that had been inflicted during brutal battle with other bulls over his many years as the leader of this grand herd. On his legs were smaller scars like those on the legs of my mother, scars caused by the sharp fangs of wolf.

The great leader's eyes were glassy, and from a wound in his side, oozed blood that coursed down his chest and dropped to the earth at his every painful step.

My mother's soft, brown eyes filled with a sadness that I had never seen in them before. She whispered to me softly, "come, Tateh," as she walked quietly from the pond toward the meadow's edge.

The great bull struggled to the pond finally, and with a painful groan splashed noisily into the healing water. His cows and calves began to mill nervously about in the meadow near the pond where he lay soaking. One cow, though, old and weathered, stood quietly at the edge of the pond near the huge bull.

My mother and I quietly watched the great bull and his nervous herd from our bedding spot at the edge of the meadow.

After a long silence, I turned to her and asked, "What is that bull's name, Mother? How was he so badly injured?"

"As I have told you, Tateh, mighty bulls such as this one, sometimes battle brutally for the right to lead the herd. Their will to mate and the great heart with which they fight sometimes brings death. This bull has been wounded in a battle such as that. He is one of the greatest leaders that has ever walked our mountains, Tateh," she continued quietly. "He has led his herd for many seasons with great courage. Through his incredible strength and kindness, he has brought much good change and knowing to our kind. That his cows and calves remain with him as he lies dying at the pond, and that no other bull has come yet to take them, is a testament to the love and respect felt for this great one by all who live in our mountains."

The day passed quickly as my mother and I fed at the edge of the meadow near our bedding spot. I watched with curiosity as the huge bull continued to soak quietly in the pond while his herd fed nervously in the meadow around him. I wanted to run into the meadow and engage the many spotted ones I saw feeding there.

The sadness though, that had settled over our meadow home had dampened even my urge to play.

As night settled slowly over the meadow, I rested comfortably once more, nestled against my mother. It seemed good to hear the soothing sound of soft mewing and chirping talk shared by the cows and calves of the great herd that lay around us in the darkness.

The moon rose above the ridge behind us, and as the meadow before us became bathed in a soft, bluish light, I heard the huge bull's splashing rise from the pond. I listened nervously to the plodding approach of his heavy footsteps, and watched in awe as his enormous silhouette struggled toward us in the moonlight. His gigantic antlers turned slowly as he stopped for a moment and looked toward where we lay. The huge leader then continued a short way beyond our bedding spot, where he lowered himself painfully into the grass at the meadow's edge.

Quietly thinking about the mysterious bull, I realized that curiously, my mother had not answered me earlier in the day when I had asked her the great bull's name.

I now whispered softly from the grass in front of her, "Mother, do you know the name of this bull, this amazing leader that has come here to die?"

"Yes, Tateh, I do," came her quiet reply. "When you are no longer a calf, and the steps with which you walk have become strong and firm, you will understand and know well the journey of this bull. His name, Tateh," she continued in a whisper… but the quiet solitude of our darkened canyon was shattered suddenly by a frightful, bellowing shriek. The deep, angry grunts of a great bull echoed from the canyon below us.

All thoughts of the mysterious wounded leader vanished as I leaped from the grass and stared nervously in the direction of this new, unseen threat.

From behind me in the grass I heard my mother's calming voice say, "It is all right, Tateh. It is a natural thing, and it will be over soon. Remember carefully, son, all that I have taught you, and all will be as it should be."

'As it should be?' I wondered nervously, as I settled once more into the grass against my mother.

Sleep refused to come to me, and I lay trembling anxiously in the moonlight as I listened to roaring bugles echo through the canyon. The terrorizing calls came now, with greater frequency.

Late in the night, clouds floated silently through the sky bringing blackness to the canyon as they covered the moon completely. At times lightning flashed through the clouds with the resulting thunder answered each time by another shrieking bugle. I lay awake in rain that fell softly from a thundering sky as the graying light of morning began at last to fill the canyon around us.

To my great relief, the shrieking bugles ceased finally as the skies began to lighten. The forest surrounding the meadow stood quietly now in the drizzling rain.

I rose anxiously from my bed, watching in the near darkness as the wounded leader's herd became slowly visible in the meadow around us. Their gigantic leader lay below us still, near the meadow's edge.

Suddenly, a screaming whistle pierced the gloomy calm from somewhere below the pond.

My mother stood nervously from her bed. With me trembling fearfully beside her, we listened to the screaming calls of angry bulls that seemed to echo from all sides of the canyon. There were several bulls, I was sure, and as they moved quickly our way from in the timber below, their piercing challenges grew angrier and more intense.

It seemed that the limbs and leaves of the small rooted ones around me shook at the force of each of the whistling screams. I looked nervously to the spot where the great herd bull lay. He lay with his head down, unaware, apparently, of the approaching bulls.

In a crashing explosion of breaking limbs and brush, two grunting bulls, with their great antlers locked, pushed suddenly into the meadow below the pond. They parted and faced each other lowering and tilting their antlers menacingly as they screamed their bellowing calls. They raked the earth with their towering horns, throwing clumps of sod and mud into the air. They sprang suddenly forward, colliding with a terrible, hollow, crashing sound. With their antlers locked once more, they violently pushed and twisted, grunting loudly as they fought back and forth in the meadow near the pond. They disengaged momentarily, only to crash together again, rattling and grating their antlers together, as chirping and moaning noises I had never heard before rumbled from their massive chests.

From a place in the forest near where these two bulls had come, a large group of cows, with calves frantically following, crashed suddenly into the meadow. They were prodded onward by an enormous bull. The bull was larger even than the two behemoths who were locked in violent battle near the pond.

With eyes wide and brimming with anger, the gigantic bull raised his head into the air, drawing to his nose the scent of the nervous cows and calves in the meadow before him. With antlers tipped back over his rear, mouth agape, and lips curled back, the enormous bull let out a hair-raising scream that I was certain shook everything around us.

He lowered his great horns and prodded his herd of cows into the meadow where he ran frantic, circling loops as he quickly gathered the many anxious cows and calves that had been led there by the gravely wounded herd bull.

After aggressively prodding the frightened cows into a tight herd, he threw his head into the air and looked wildly about the meadow. Seeing us standing in the trees at its edge, the enormous bull, with his nose to the ground, pranced toward us in a strange, stiff-legged trot. Upon reaching us, he lowered his horns and raked my mother angrily toward his waiting herd. Trembling, I followed fearfully behind them.

The two bulls fighting near the pond were still engrossed in their violent battle. They seemed unaware of this other bull and the many cows that he now prodded forcefully past them.

Their furious assault on one another continued unchecked as our angry leader pushed the enormous herd, of which my mother and I were now a part, toward the timber at the meadow's edge. A blinding flash of light filled the sky as our herd thundered past the gigantic old leader that lay silently there. As the deafening blast of thunder shook the canyon, the great one slowly raised his head.

Our eyes met as I ran desperately by him, and in that riveting instant I knew the great bull had seen to the very center of my soul. In his haunting stare, I saw the incredible journey of his great life. Still burning in his eyes was a fearlessness and knowing that I somehow knew would one day be mine.

Our charging herd became a long line of lunging bodies as the huge bull pushed us aggressively upward through the dense timber on the canyon's steep side. Any cow that wandered or lagged was quickly met by the heavy antlers of the angry bull and forced roughly back into the line. The pain in my shoulder was growing rapidly, but my need to stay fast at the feet of my mother drove me onward.

We came finally to a small meadow high on the canyon's side as the day became fully light. Our huge leader circled the cows, grouping them tightly in its center. The bull cut constantly through the anxious cows, his great head held low, while making a strange clucking sound deep in his throat. Transfixed, I watched the bizarre spectacle from the side of the meadow where I stood trembling among a large group of calves. I hoped not to be noticed by the angry bull.

Suddenly from the timber behind us came a loud, whistling wail, a bugle much louder than those made by the bulls we had left behind in the meadow at the healing water. The shrieking call was answered immediately by our leader with a thundering bellow. He lowered his great antlers once again and fiercely prodded the cows into motion, moving them rapidly along the ridge's top, away from the unseen bull.

Our huge leader called often as our herd rumbled upward on the ridge. His call was almost always answered by the roaring bugle of the mysterious bull that now pursued our fleeing herd. Our wild-eyed leader, upon hearing each earsplitting reply from the unknown challenger, would press our herd powerfully forward in a direction always away from the answering bull.

As we entered one small meadow during our flight along the ridge, we encountered a small herd led by a bull that screamed menacingly as our herd and enormous leader came into view. Upon seeing each other, the two bulls bellowed and grunted furiously, raking their horns into the ground and tearing bark from the trees around them as they thrashed them fiercely with their antlers.

Our leader bolted suddenly through the meadow toward the other bull and the two met with a resounding crash of antlers. Our leader nearly knocked the other bull from his feet. They disengaged for a moment staring intensely at one another. The lesser bull realizing the incredible strength of our raging leader, turned nervously from him and sank into the timber relinquishing his cows.

From the ridge behind us came yet another thundering call. Our leader's head shot into the air as he whirled to stare in the direction of this challenger that now followed our herd so doggedly.

Furious at the mysterious bull's unrelenting pursuit, our leader again lowered his antlers and raked angrily at our herd. Prodded onward at nearly a full run, our herd crashed desperately through the timber toward the great basin above.

Entering the gently rolling hills and openness of the great basin at last, our leader slowed and allowed our weary herd to stop. Towering at the edge of our exhausted herd, the huge one laid his head back and from his throat came a bellowing whistle that echoed far into the basin ahead. No answer came from anywhere around us. Satisfied finally that he had outrun his pursuer, he again gathered his cows into a tight bunch. He began walking stiffly through the nervous herd as he had before, a strange clucking sound again rumbling from deep in his throat.

The light slowly softened as the day drew to a close. Soon, some of the cows lay down to rest, while others, as did my mother, stood sadly watching what had become our outcast band of calves.

Our fuming leader continued to stalk stiff-legged through the cows. Holding his head low and tipping his great rack side to side, odd chirping noises emanated from his throat as he tested the scent of each. We calves, no longer welcome near the herd, stood fearfully at the side of the meadow, nervously wondering what was to come. There were not as many in the exhausted group of calves huddled around me as there had been when the day started. I wondered how long the pain in my shoulder would allow me to pursue my mother should our fuming leader again press our herd into flight.

The moon climbed slowly from behind the mountains and bathed all beneath it in a bright, bluish light. Resting quietly in the grass far from the herd, I could plainly see my mother bedded in the meadow, looking back at me in the moonlight. Resting in the grass around her were many other cows. Still, the huge bull paced through the herd, head low, tilting his head back and forth as he went. The moon reflected from the white tips of his great antlers, and his huge body was clearly outlined in its light. I shook with fear as I thought about the anger and intensity that now drove this huge one.

A piercing whistle from the trees at the edge of the basin suddenly broke the silence of our moonlit meadow. The great bull immediately prodded the cows to their feet and pressed them urgently across the basin. We calves sprang from the grass and followed the rumbling herd as closely as we could.

My shoulder was numb with pain now, but on and on I went, lunging forward with all my might in a shrinking group of calves. I was barely able to keep the herd in sight as we plunged onward through the basin.

As we reached the far side of the great opening, our leader stopped and gathered the cows again. The unseen challenger screamed from somewhere behind us in the basin. The bull immediately prodded the cows ahead, running even harder than before. Down a large, timbered canyon the angry leader recklessly drove the laboring cows.

Amid a struggling bunch of calves, I crashed downward through the night as I pursued my mother and the herd into the canyon. The great bull forced the cows ever downward on a rocky trail that led them through several meadows, then into thick forest again.

The ranting leader screamed almost constantly as he pushed the cows feverishly onward. Each of his furious bugles was answered immediately from behind. Our seething leader ripped at trees with his huge antlers as we went, ripping some from the ground. Moaning and grunting, he hurled them to the side with a toss of his head.

The bull, though crazed by his growing fury, realized finally that flight was futile. His unseen challenger would be fought. He quickly gathered his cows at the edge of a small meadow that sloped steadily away, then, stood alone in its center. Bellowing hoarsely in the moonlight, he raked and tore at the trees in front of him as he awaited the appearance of the unshakable challenger.

Our mysterious pursuer was nearing us in the forest above. I could hear him tearing up brush and ripping at trees as he prepared for the impending battle. His shrieking bugle had become a deep, rumbling moan, followed by a series of low grunts. Crashing and breaking timber told of his steady advance.

I could plainly see the shaken cows of our herd standing in the moonlight on the far side of the meadow. I stood alone quaking with fear, in a group of small trees on the opposite side. Calves stood trembling in the timber behind me as we waited fearfully.

Suddenly, from the trees above, stepped the massive challenger. Towering ominously in the moonlight, the bull glared across the meadow toward the leader of our herd, the rumbling moan reverberating still from deep within his throat.

The light shone on a huge set of white-tipped antlers that reached far to his sides and high above his body. His antlers reached well beyond his rump as he laid his head back and screamed thunderously at our leader. Our leader returned his bellowing challenge, and with a single raking motion, ripped several small trees from the ground. Some, hung tangled precariously from his massive antlers.

The challenger stood unmoving, glaring downward into the meadow as he studied the enraged bull below him. With a shrieking bellow, the mysterious challenger started forward. I stood mesmerized, hiding in my small clump of trees, as this terrorizing drama unfolded in the moonlight before me.

When the distance between the two bulls was small, the challenger stopped. The two huge elk stood motionless, glowering with hatred at one another in the moonlight.

With terrible, guttural grunts erupting from deep within them, the behemoths sprang suddenly forward. The two monsters collided with a thunderous crash that echoed from the trees around us. Grunts and moans and grating of antlers filled the night as the incredible bulls fought for supremacy in the moonlit meadow.

Crashing brutally together, with antlers grinding and rattling, one would push the other halfway across the meadow. They would part for a moment, grunting and wheezing, then would smash ferociously together again. The one who had been pushed backward, now pushed the other to the timber on the opposite side of the meadow.

Dirt and branches flew into the air as the floor of the meadow was churned by the straining hooves of the great bulls. They pushed against one another with such ferocity and strength that they sank into the moist dirt of the meadow halfway to their knees. The two seemed evenly matched as they snaked forward and back, destroying all that stood in the path of their terrible battle.

I tore my eyes from them for an instant and looked toward my mother. Her eyes were filled with dread as she stared back at me in the moonlight. My head spun instinctively toward the sound of crashing and breaking branches at my side. To my horror, I saw the huge, tan rump of a monstrous bull crashing toward me as it was forced powerfully backward by the lunging body and horns of the other.

In an instant, the bull was nearly on me, but lost its rear footing in the small trees in which I hid. As it did so, it could no longer push against its ferocious adversary. With its massive horns locked in the antlers of the other bull, it was pushed awkwardly onto its back nearly on top of me. I heard the resounding crack of breaking bone, and a sighing release of air from the downed bull as the other giant pinned him to the ground before me. Horrified, I scrambled to the side to prevent being trampled by the raging monsters.

The challenger had knowingly tricked our huge leader. He had tripped him by driving him backward through the short, thick pines in which I hid. Now, with his mighty antlers, he held our leader pinned to the ground there. The enormous bull, sensing victory, lunged again and again at the downed leader. Grunting and wheezing, the challenger slid the great bull through the trees with each powerful thrust, his antlers sinking ever deeper into the dying one's chest.

Realizing finally that the fight was over, the challenger raised his head, disengaging his antlers from the huge bull that lay motionless before him. With his enormous antlers shining wetly in the moonlight, the bull roared hoarsely as he glared toward the fearful herd that was now his.

My mother had panicked and had come running to me when she saw the bulls crash into the trees where I hid. The huge victor now saw me cowering at my mother's side, and with eyes sparkling with rage, lunged toward me. Adrenaline pounded through my body, and I tried desperately to spin away. His antlers caught me in the hip, sending me end over end careening helplessly downhill in the darkness.

I struggled dizzily to my feet, and with all my might I lurched downward through a tangle of dense trees. I could hear the bull crashing closely behind me. Downfallen trees and invisible branches reached upward in the night, ripping at my belly and legs. Tripping finally, I tumbled helplessly downward, skidding to a rest, lodged firmly beneath the twisted roots of a fallen tree.

Panic-stricken, I lay trapped, waiting frightfully for what I knew would now come. The huge bull though, had given up the chase. He could no longer hear the crashing path of my escape. With the ever-thickening forest making the passage of his broad antlers nearly impossible, he had decided the pursuit of this puny calf was no longer worthwhile. With a contemptuous snort, the bull turned away. The angry moan of battle rumbling again in his throat, he retraced his steps upward toward his newly won herd.

Afraid even to breathe, nearly choking with fear, I lay shaking as I listened to the crashing footsteps of the retreating bull. My breath came in ragged gasps, and my heart pounded in my chest.

"Run, mother," I whispered softly, fear clutching at my heart as I pictured in my mind the terrible punishment that would surely be hers.

A powerful bugle rang suddenly through the darkness from somewhere above. I could hear the soft rumble of hooves, the mewing of cows, and anxious chirps of calves as the bull gathered his new herd, and surely my mother, in the moonlit meadow above.

Soon, the sounds of the herd faded. The thunderous bugle of the new leader, though, told me of their path as the big bull pushed the herd upward toward the basin.

The canyon became silent finally. Only the eerie screech of an owl hidden somewhere in the darkness pierced the night.

As I stared into the darkness, my mind was filled with the terrible screaming calls of the fighting bulls. I shuddered as I remembered the haunting, guttural sound made by the big herd bull as he crumpled backward toward me in the trees. The soft, moaning sigh of breath that had escaped his throat, I now realized, had been his release of life as he died, pinned beneath the mighty antlers of his relentless challenger.

My mind reeled at the thoughts of my shattered life brought on so suddenly by this bizarre season of mating.

My mother was gone, and I lay trapped, alone in the darkness.

The great bull that had driven us from our home at the healing water only a day ago, lay dead I knew, in the meadow above.

Chapter Nine

After what seemed an eternity lying quietly in the silent darkness, I began to fight my way from beneath the tangle of roots under which I had slid during my panicked escape. Struggling free finally, but wracked still, with fear, I crept quietly into a thicket of tall bushes and lay listening carefully to the sounds of the night.

Bright shafts of light from the moon shone through the dense forest around me. The luminous blue light cast eerie shadows on the tangle of downed trees that lay scattered before me on the forest floor. As the night wore slowly on, the moon dropped beneath the mountains, and I was plunged into total darkness. I felt more alone than I had at any time in my short life.

'Is my mother alright?' I wondered, as my mind was filled again with thoughts of my narrow escape from the angry new leader of the herd. In my mind, I could still plainly hear the terrible rumble of his screaming bugle. His scent was a smell, I was certain, that had been burned into my memory forever.

Pain shot through my shoulder as I stood slowly from my brushy hiding place. New injuries had been inflicted during my fearful headlong flight to escape the wrath of the huge bull. My shoulder throbbed with pain, its fresh scar having been torn open, and blood dripped on the ground at my feet. I stood quietly hiding for the remainder of the night, anxiously studying the dark sky for the first hint of light to appear.

At last the sky began to lighten, and the forest around me began slowly to stir. Birds soon chirped happily, and squirrels scurried about on the forest floor. From the trees around me, I heard the muffled rumble of beating wings as grouse burst from their nightly perches, flying upward through the forest toward the meadows above.

From far above, in the direction from which I had been chased, I could hear the call of raven. Already, the black scavengers had found the carcass of the dead bull. Raven's call today was one of excitement, though, not the frantic, anxious call I had heard during my confrontation with wolf long ago.

With great caution I walked from my hiding place and began climbing upward through the dense forest. I slowly followed the skidding, erratic tracks made during my harrowing escape from the angry bull the previous night. When the forest above me began at last to thin, I could see many ravens and magpies perched among the trees at the meadow's edge. Having learned long ago not to trust them, I circled away from the chattering birds and crossed the meadow far below the spot where they sat calling.

I climbed quietly upward through the forest on its far side to a spot opposite where the unruly flock sat in trees, hopping from branch to branch as they croaked and chirped excitedly. Beneath them on the meadow's floor, I could see the horns of the dead bull looming from the grass where the great leader had died the night before.

Suddenly, from near the towering antlers rose the black form of a large bear. I instinctively froze and stood motionless, afraid to move even my eyes. The bear though, was totally absorbed in the good fortune of his recent find and was unaware of my presence only a short distance away on the far side of the meadow.

The big bear scanned the meadow around him and tested the air with his keen nose. Satisfied that all was well, the bruin settled again into the grass to gorge himself on the bull.

I crept cautiously into the trees away from the feeding bear, then turned and began walking quietly upward again. I listened carefully to the chortling calls of the ravens behind me, thereby making certain of the bear's exact location. Far above the noisy flock finally, I breathed a sigh of relief and no longer felt in danger from the feasting bear.

As I thought about the dead herd bull below, the anger I had felt toward him at the treatment of my mother and me, softened. I saw him in my mind, strong and alive only a day ago. Now he was feasted upon by others.

I remembered the words of my mother. "The dead one is only gone as you knew him to be, Tateh, for it will live again, soon, in the form of those who feed on it. The dead one will live even in the leaves of the rooted ones who grow near the spot of its passing. They too, gather strength from the lifeless body as it passes back to our Mother Earth."

The picture in my mind of my mother telling me this earlier in the season of *growing grass*, caused the aching loneliness I felt for her to return. But I remembered the words she had spoken as we stood on our secret trail high on the side of the canyon above the healing water.

"Tateh," she had said, "should you become separated from me, go to the place of the healing water. Wait there, son. I will return."

Her words now fresh in my mind, I climbed with renewed strength toward the top of the canyon.

I walked upward on freshly churned dirt in the trail where the night before our herd had crashed downward from the basin above. Their tracks were plainly visible where they had climbed again with their new leader to reenter the basin, pushed onward to a place only he knew.

Dropping my nose to their fresh trail, I could smell the scent of the many cows and calves that had recently passed this way. The scent most overwhelming of all, was the terrifying scent of the angry bull that now drove the great herd and my mother to places I could not imagine.

As I climbed toward the top of the canyon, the throbbing ache in my shoulder worsened, and small drops of blood continued to fall to the ground beneath me as I walked. I hoped no predator would cross my trail and pursue the one leaving these tracks.

At last I came to the top of the canyon. Tracks in the freshly torn earth told of the place where only last night my mother and the herd had crossed into the basin. I had told myself again and again that the herd would be here still, and I would rejoin it and be with my mother again. The basin before me lay empty. The churned earth from the many hooves of the herd was the only sign of elk I could see.

The grassy knolls and green trees in the basin whispered softly to me in the breeze beneath the afternoon sun. A sparkling pond nearby beckoned me as I became aware of the thirst that had grown in me since leaving the pond of the healing waters more than a day ago.

The water of the little pond was wonderfully good, and I marveled at the feeling within me as it passed down my throat and into my stomach. I walked through the pond to a muddy area where it gave way to the grassy meadow beyond. Here, I lay down and gently pressed my injured shoulder into the cool, dark mud. I hoped it would stop the bleeding and begin the healing of the reinjured scar there. I stood from the black medicine long after the sun had dipped below the mountains in the west and the moon had risen behind me in the east.

No longer bleeding, I walked to a thick clump of trees where I rested in tall grass and quietly studied the basin that lay shimmering before me in the soft light of the moon. I lie awake far into the night listening carefully for the wrathful call of the bull that had taken my mother, but I heard nothing.

I lowered my head as slumber settled gently over me. Soon, I was walking an obscure trail in the bottom of a dark canyon listening, and searching carefully for my mother. I entered a large opening where the fog that seemed always present in my dream world, floated near the tops of the rooted ones that surrounded it. In the center of the meadow, standing beside a large pond, was the magnificent bull that walked often in my dreams. As I approached him, I could not return his steady gaze, and when I stood before him finally, I stood in silence with my eyes lowered to the ground at his feet.

"Tateh," he said at last, studying me carefully, "your heart is very troubled."

"Yes, Woslolkia," I answered, "I am a coward. I could not do as you told me. I was not able to look my fear in the eye and stand my ground. I ran from the great herd bull, Woslolkia," I said, "and he took my mother."

"Son," said Woslolkia, "you are a young calf. Your time has not yet come to fight the great bulls. Your mother knows that, Tateh. All will soon be for you as it should be, son. Look into the pond, Tateh," he said quietly.

Slowly, I looked into the pond at my feet, where looking back at me from the water was the most enormous bull I had ever seen!

"Woslolkia!" I exclaimed, jerking my head from the water, but the great bull was nowhere to be seen. I was alone again in the grass beneath the small trees, staring into the darkness of the basin.

With my heart still pounding from my exciting dream, I studied the star-filled sky for the first light of another day and wondered curiously about the enormous bull that had stared back at me from the water.

I started across the basin once more as the sky first began to lighten, hoping to find the canyon on its far side that would be the one in which lay the pond of the healing water. The soothing black mud of the bog had sealed my wound. No longer bleeding, I walked steadily toward the rising sun across the big basin.

Twice before, I had made this journey across the basin, and dropped into the canyon of the healing water, but it had always been behind the trustful steps of my mother. During these trips, I had studied the rooted ones and other curious things at my feet, things much more important, it had seemed then, than directions and landmarks.

I moved nervously along, remembering as best I could the path to the canyon, hoping I would recognize the natural features at the basin's edge that marked the head of the huge canyon.

As the sun climbed in the sky to a point directly overhead, I came at last to the far side of the great opening. I followed a gentle fold in the earth that led me to the head of a sweeping canyon where I stood on a small rock ledge looking downward into an immense, tree-choked gorge. It was the canyon, I was certain, in which lay the pond of the healing water.

With the mixed feelings of relief at having found the canyon, and the loneliness of now entering it alone, I started nervously downward on the rocky trail toward its bottom. The grass was still deep, but no longer green as it had been earlier in the season of *growing grass*. It was very dry now and stood in various shades of yellow and golden brown. Its taste was still wonderful though, and I sampled it often as I walked downward.

The day passed quickly as I moved through large meadows, past sparkling, blue ponds, and strode through the thick woodlots that separated the openings.

As the sun sank lower in the sky and its yellow light became softer, I suddenly smelled the acrid aroma of the healing waters that lay hidden below.

I entered the top of the large opening where the wounded herd bull and his huge herd had entered just days before. At the meadow's lower end, I could see the familiar cloud of steam that rose from the surface of the wonderful pond. The yellow mud bog at its side shone softly in the retreating light. Both looked just as they had when first I had seen them. I looked to the side of the meadow at the trees under which my mother and I always slept. The grass beneath the trees stood vacant in the weakening sun, and a wave of loneliness flooded over me as I realized once more how alone I truly was.

I walked to the trees where just two days before, my mother and I had bedded. I slowly lowered my nose to the earth and drew deeply at the scent that rose from the flattened grass there. A sense of calmness settled over me as I smelled my mother's familiar scent. Bolstered by the sense of her presence, I quietly scanned the familiar surroundings around me.

Suddenly, I remembered again, the wounded bull that had come here with his enormous herd. My eyes shot anxiously to the spot where the huge one had lay dying at the edge of the meadow. His antlers no longer towered from the grass there, and as I nervously studied the meadow and forest around the healing pond, I realized all were vacant now. Strangely, the great bull was nowhere to be seen.

With uncertainty, I walked to where the bull had lain and thrust my nose to the grass where it lay pressed flatly to the earth. Curiously, only my own scent rose from his bed. I smelled no trace of the wounded one in the flattened grass.

'How could that be?' I wondered, as I realized that he, and the old cow that had stood faithfully at his side, had somehow moved on. Perplexed, I pondered the strange events and the disappearance of the mysterious bull as I continued slowly into the meadow toward the steaming water at its lower end.

As I neared the pond, the sun sank beneath the canyon's far side, and my mother's words rang softly in my mind once more. "Come here, to this place, Tateh, where the grass is tall and the water is good, and I will come for you."

"I am here, mother," I said softly into the darkness, as I lowered myself into the warm water of the pond. As the curing heat of the soothing water coursed through me, I felt healing begin not only in my shoulder, but deep within me, also.

My days were filled with loneliness as I soaked in the healing water. I wondered about my mother and longed for the day that she would return. I thought often about the great bull who had come here so gravely wounded, and wondered still about his name. I clearly remembered the sadness that I had seen in my mother's eyes when she saw the mysterious leader. And I thought of the angry bull who had taken the great one's herd, only to be killed himself later that day in a dark, remote canyon.

My shoulder healed quickly, and now at the end of each soak, I began to climb the canyon's steep sides on the trails worn there by my mother and me only a short time ago.

I lay each night at our bedding spot by the trees, and as I drifted to sleep, again, I would hear her words, "Tateh, should you become separated from the herd, go to the place of the healing water. Wait there, son. I will return."

I rose each morning to soak, then climbed quickly up the steep trails above the meadow, determined to strengthen myself so that I would never again be separated from the herd. I repeated this routine again and again as I passed the lonely days waiting for the promised return of my mother.

One dark night as I lay sleeping beneath the big trees at my bedding spot, my dreams were filled suddenly with the screaming whistles of huge bull elk that echoed from the canyon below the healing pond. I rested safely against my mother as I had long ago, but now, I did not tremble with fear, but waited instead in silence.

The screaming bulls and the sound of their crashing battle came closer and closer. As the bulls exploded into the meadow below the pond, I stood from beside my mother and stared intently toward them. They saw me immediately and bellowed thundering challenges in my direction. But now, I stood without moving, watching them silently as my anger grew. Rage pounded within me as I started toward them with a low, rumbling moan boiling from my throat.

To my amazement as I drew near, their eyes filled with fear and they turned and bolted from me, crashing into the timber from where they had earlier come. Walking past the pond as I returned to my bedding spot, the reflection of enormous antlers moving along the pond's surface caught my eye. Looking curiously into the water, I was shocked to see looking back, the gigantic bull that Woslolkia had shown me before.

My head snapped up as I awakened, my breath coming in short gasps. My pounding heart slowly returned to normal as I realized finally, that I was safe in my bed beneath the trees at the meadow's side. It had been only a dream, but one in which I had not shrank from the scream of the great bulls. I had stood my ground this time and protected my mother. As I scanned the darkness of the meadow, I realized the stars were gone now, and I was sure I could hear the faint rumbling of thunder.

Unable to sleep, I lay awake, nervously watching the sky as threatening flashes of light and the ominous roar of thunder crept slowly closer. Suddenly, below me in the canyon, I heard the moaning sound of wind. Steadily, the sound grew louder until I could plainly hear the frightful clamor of its advance as it whipped and tore at the trees like some unseen beast. With a great roar, the raging gale burst suddenly into the meadow. It whipped the grass mercilessly against the earth and tore at the trees along the meadow's edge.

The sound of breaking tree tops and the terrible groan of falling trees filled the darkness. Everywhere around me, rooted ones of all sizes succumbed to the wind's terrible ferocity and crashed to the forest floor. The lightning flashed from all sides of the sky, and the earsplitting peals of thunder that followed were almost continuous. Trembling with fear, I lowered my head to the grass, waiting for the pelting rain I knew would follow, but the clouds that boiled through the sky were filled only with lightning, and no rain fell.

On the canyon's side across from me, I suddenly noticed an ominous, orange glow in the timber. Yellow flames soon leaped from the tree tops there, fanned by the shrieking wind that ripped still at the forest.

Jumping to my feet in panic, I turned and saw fire surging from the trees in writhing torrents on the canyon's side behind me.

The lightning sizzled through the sky without end, and the sound of thunder was deafening.

To my horror, I could see an orange glow growing ever brighter above the trees in the canyon below the healing water. And now, to my nose came the terrible, stinging smell that I instinctively knew was smoke.

Boiling clouds of the blinding stench quickly filled the meadow before me. Gripped from deeply within by terrible, fear-driven panic, I crashed from my bedding spot into the meadow.

Quickly lost in a world of blinding smoke, I stopped. Suddenly, a message from long ago echoed through my mind. I stood fearfully without moving in the raining ash and choking smoke as I again heard the unspoken words.

"Never flee uphill from fire, Tateh. It will almost always overtake you," I heard the great bull from my dreams say once more.

"But the fire is all around me, Woslolkia. Uphill is the only way," I pleaded into the darkness, as glowing clouds of smoke rolled horrifically across the meadow before me.

A blinding flash of lightning shot through the sky, and as thunder reverberated through the fiery canyon, Woslolkia stood suddenly before me. His enormous silhouette stood ghost-like before the twisting glow of fire and churning clouds of smoke around us.

"Woslolkia!" I cried, as our eyes met.

A strange calmness settled over me, and when the huge one turned silently and disappeared into the billowing darkness, I knew to follow.

Without a noise, the great bull moved steadily forward through the blinding haze. His plodding silhouette disappeared often between clouds of smoke and ash as I followed him fearfully through the sea of heat and swirling smoke.

Finding the pond, the great bull walked deeply into the water without hesitation, and stood with only his head and antlers above the pond's surface. I quickly followed Woslolkia into the pond and stood anxiously beside him. With my head barely protruding from the water, I watched in terror as the terrible yellow flames leaped from the trees around me, dancing into the sky in spiraling torrents.

The hot smoke and ash driven into my face by the fierce wind made it nearly impossible to open my eyes or even breathe. The stinging heat I felt on my exposed nose and face was greater by far than any I had ever known.

"Woslolkia," I said fearfully, turning slowly to him, "will we"...but the great bull was gone. I stood alone now in the pond, the deafening roar of the raging fire was my only companion. I watched in horror as twisting flames curled from the trees beyond the place where he had just stood.

Glowing embers rained into the deep grass of the meadow from the thundering flames in the forest around me. Soon, the flames roared through the tall grass at all sides of the pond. It danced wickedly across the meadow as if with a life its own, consuming all in its path.

The thundering fire surrounded me completely now. Holding my head barely above the water's surface, I drew the smoke-filled air into my lungs, then submerged completely between breaths to cool myself from the stifling heat. The billowing smoke and ash became so thick finally, that I could no longer see even the edge of the pond.

The water became hotter and hotter as the raging wind drove heat from the fire over its surface. Glowing embers fell steadily from the smoke, hissing angrily as they hit the pond's surface in the darkness around me.

I was more afraid than I had ever been at any time in my life. I was certain this would be my last night. An eerie, orange glow filled the sky, and the deafening roar from the blazing forest grew continually louder.

Once, as a hot blast of wind parted the smoke, I thought for an instant that I saw a strange form in the water across from me, but the hunkering apparition was immediately engulfed again in the blinding smoke. Endlessly it seemed, I stood in the ever-heating water, breathing, then submerging, all the while holding my eyes tightly shut against the burning smoke and ash.

The orange glow around me seemed to soften, finally, overcome by soft gray light that began to build in the sky signaling the beginning of a new day. The wind that had whipped the fire into a raging blaze began to diminish, and the roar from the surrounding fire slowly quieted. I was able to stand at last, with my head out of the water.

The water of the pond was now very hot. I wanted badly to get out, but the searing heat carried by the billowing clouds of smoke and ash around me told of the scorching earth present in the meadow and surrounding forest. The day wore agonizingly on as I stood in the hot, ash-covered water of the pond, choking in the thick smoke and cinders floating on the breeze.

The luminous sky above the meadow began to darken as the sun, hidden high above the smoke, dropped steadily toward the horizon. As darkness slowly advanced, the air around me became still, and the driving clouds of gray and brown smoke began at last to rise straight upward. Through the billowing towers of rising smoke, a grotesque landscape slowly appeared. The green forest that just one day before had stood growing at the edges of the meadow was now an eerie maze of twisted blackness. The devastation stretched for as far as I could see into the smoky canyon.

The smoke was no longer driven in blinding clouds across the pond's surface, and at times I could see the curious form that I had seen earlier in the water across from me. Partially obscured still, in the smoke, it seemed as though it floated on the water at the far side of the pond. As darkness gathered, the smoke decreased.

Panic tore at my heart, and adrenaline pounded through my head as I suddenly recognized the strange form highlighted by the weak glow in the darkening sky. I was suddenly again beneath the old lightning tree, staring into the enraged eyes of the grizzly. On the water's surface across from me in the pond was the huge, oval-shaped head of a great silver bear. It stood quietly submerged, watching me from the protective water in which we had both taken refuge. My mind raced, and my body became numb with fear as the darkness of night slowly engulfed the meadow, hiding the great bear from my view once more.

The moon rose slowly above the canyon's far side, filling the smoky sky with a dull, brown glow. The blackened trees in the surrounding forest stood twisted and ghostly in the eerie light. Now, I could clearly see the ominous silhouette that quietly faced me at the pond's far side.

The great bruin's presence was terrorizing as the night dragged slowly on. At each crash of a falling tree, or snap of failing roots in the burnt forest, I was gripped by a terrible, gasping panic. The moon dropped at last beneath the mountains to the west, and the sky began to brighten above the mountains where the sun would soon rise. As the night turned slowly to day, my horrifying partnership with the great bear wore on.

Gone, were the waking cries and songs of morning that only days ago had echoed from the forest around the pond. The only sounds heard now were the terrible sounds of burned trees as they sagged and broke, crashing in a cloud of black dust to the forest floor.

The immense heat rising from the burned forest around the pond had greatly diminished, and as the sun rose and shown weakly through the smoky sky, the great silver bear stood suddenly from the water.

My emotions had long been drained. I stood exhausted, staring helplessly from the water as the huge bear towered before me. The hair on its ears was singed, and its nose was blistered and red from the heat of the great fire. It stood without moving, looking silently at me for what seemed an eternity. But now, instead of anger, I saw acceptance in the great silver one's dark, brooding eyes. A bond had somehow grown between us during our odd alliance in the protection of the pond.

Finally, with a deep huff, the great bruin turned from me and sloshed noisily from the pond. As it made its way toward the blackened forest, I noticed that the huge bear limped badly. On its front leg was a wide, black scar that ran from its shoulder to its huge paw, where two, long, thick claws were missing. As the grizzly walked into the burned trees, it stopped and turned slowly back toward where I stood watching from the pond. At last, the huge bear turned and continued into the blackened forest. I shuddered as I realized that I had again looked into the eyes of the great silver one that long ago had nearly taken my life. But this time, I had not blinked.

Alone now, I stood quietly in the water thinking about the horror of the thunderstorm and about the frightful fire that had ravaged my canyon. I thought about the haunting appearance of Woslolkia, and how he had led me to the safety of the pond. I pondered the unlikely alliance I had shared with the great silver one, as together we had somehow survived the great firestorm in this protecting water. It all seemed like a dream now.

'It was no dream,' I thought, as I walked from the water and stepped onto the bank at the pond's edge. The blackened, smoldering trees of a once-green forest stood in terrible devastation around me.

Both sides of the big canyon and the meadow that surrounded the pond were charred and burned. Smoke still rose from many of the trees throughout the blackened canyon. In awe, I studied the ghostly scene around me. It was hard for me to imagine this place as being as green and lush as it was only days ago.

Only blackened trees stood at that place on the canyon's side where my mother had spoken the words that now filled my mind. 'Go, to the place of the healing water, Tateh,' she had said. 'Wait there. I will come.'

Sadly, I realized, I could not stay here. I would have to go from this place to find grass and clean water. 'How would my mother ever find me now?' I wondered sadly.

Above me, in the trees at the top of the meadow, I suddenly saw a movement. A large, black form stepped from the trees and entered the meadow. It stopped and looked warily across the opening toward the pond where I stood, then started again, in my direction.

'A moose,' I thought nervously, as it walked steadily my way.

The mysterious animal strode purposefully across the meadow and as it drew closer, it stopped and stared intently toward me.

I stood frozen, unable to move as I helplessly returned the black one's stare, my mind refusing to believe what my eyes saw standing in the blackened meadow before me.

My mother, her sleek, tan body, now black with soot and ash, stood quietly studying me. Her eyes were filled with disbelief.

I exploded with joy, as all my fears and pent-up emotions burst to the surface. I ran wildly to her filled with indescribable happiness, bleating excitedly, bucking and jumping with my short tail whipping wildly back and forth.

My mother stood quietly over me staring downward, shaking her head slowly as she studied in disbelief this singed and blackened little calf that was her son. She saw the blisters that had formed on my nose and the reddened skin that showed through the singed hair on my ears. My swollen eyes drained a dark trail of soot down my cheeks, and my eyelids were blistered from the embers that had rained from the fiery sky.

She stood with her head held low over me, holding me closely to her chest. I heard her quietly choke and gulp for air, as her eyes too, began to drain.

'Must be the ash,' I thought silently as I stood beneath her, basking in her love, trembling with unbelievable happiness.

Chapter Ten

My mother and I stood near the pond in the blackened meadow for a long time, basking quietly in the feeling of our impossible reunion. Finally, my mother stepped back from me and looked me in the eye.

"Tateh," she said, "you are a very brave little bull. There is no doubt that you will become a great leader of our kind. With your leadership will come much wisdom and knowing as you walk your path on your life's journey. There are no words to explain the fear that I felt in my heart for you when the huge bull chased you from my side after having killed our leader in the canyon. As the bull forced me back toward the herd, I reminded myself of the great strength and courage of your father, and I knew those virtues lived now in you. I knew also that you had heard my words well and would remember all I had taught you.

"As I traveled for many days with the herd, I told myself again and again that you had found the canyon of the healing water and would be waiting there when I returned. You cannot imagine, Tateh, the emotions that welled within me, when free from the herd at last, and on my way to where I knew you would be waiting, I saw smoke boiling into the sky at the far side of the basin. When at last I stood above the canyon of the healing water and saw the devastation that lay in its depths, I was nearly paralyzed with fear.

"That you stand before me, alive and well, means more to me than anything I have ever known in my life. The courage it took for you to stay in the pond as the fire burned around you is hard to imagine. I am very proud to call you my son, Tateh."

She stood looking at me for a while, and the love I saw in her eyes told me more than words could ever say.

"Tateh," she said, finally, "we must go from this place now. We must find a place where green trees afford us shelter, and the grass stands tall and will satisfy our hunger. Before we leave though, we will soak one more time in the healing water."

She turned and walked into the pond with me behind her, and stood in the deep water near where just a short time before I had survived the fire's fury.

Standing beside her in the water, I looked around the pond at the ghostly forest that stood blackened and silent, and remembered the thunderous roar and angry flames that had danced through the trees. The water was still very hot, but still, a chill passed over me as I looked to the far side of the pond where the great silver one had recently stood. But gone was the fear I had felt then, because now, all was as it should be. I stood once more at my mother's side.

In a short time, we walked from the pond and into the yellow mud at its side. We sank to the mud and rolled and kicked as we always had, covering ourselves one last time with the wonderful, sticky stuff. Satisfied, my mother stood from the mud. For a long while she studied the strange, blackened landscape that surrounded us in the canyon.

"Tateh," she said finally, "it is hard to believe, I know, but the grass here will be deeper than ever in the next season of the growing grass. In a short time, the burned forest around us will live again too. Come here often, Tateh… and remember."

She turned then, and together we started across the blackened meadow toward the basin above.

As we reached the timber at the head of the meadow, we stopped and looked back. All that was below us, from the meadow to the tops of the ridges that formed our canyon, was black. From some of the larger trees, thin trails of smoke twisted crookedly into the sky. As I viewed the steam that rose from the healing water in the bottom of the meadow, I relived the events I had recently experienced there. My mother looked at me as if she, too, somehow saw the troubling scenes that now played in my mind. With a knowing look, she turned, and with me following happily behind, continued toward the top.

Walking behind my mother as we climbed briskly from the canyon, I realized that my forced sanctuary in the fire-heated waters of the pond had somehow speeded the healing in my shoulder. I walked now with very little pain and no limp at all.

The ponds that we passed in the burnt meadows as we climbed higher in the canyon were all dark in color from the ash and embers of the fire. In one, small fish floated lifelessly on its surface.

Ravens circled in the sky above the canyon, looking for victims who were unable to escape the fire's raging onslaught. In places, large numbers of the huge, black birds sat chortling in the trees. Their ominous presence marked the discovery of yet another unfortunate one.

To my surprise, as we climbed closer to the top of the canyon, we found small islands of green, where the fire had mysteriously parted and left the forest untouched. We stopped at these little patches of life and gratefully sampled the grass as we moved toward the top.

The sun was just above the horizon in the west as we stepped into the basin above the canyon of the healing water. The fire had burned to the top of the canyon but had not entered the basin. Here, the grass stood tall and thick and shone a bright, golden brown in the setting sun. The green trees that now surrounded us stood in sharp contrast to the burnt trees through which we had walked in the canyon.

We stopped in a meadow where a large pond shimmered in the sunset beside a group of trees. We waded eagerly into the inviting water to roll and clean ourselves.

After removing the black ash in which we had become covered, we satisfied our growing hunger in the grass at the pond's edge. When darkness crept over the basin at last, we lay beneath the trees and listened to the soft murmur of the breeze as it passed gently through the basin. I rested thankfully against the warmth of my mother, and all was good again in my world.

In the distance echoed the unexpected whistling call of a bull. I stiffened nervously and started to rise.

My mother stopped me, saying softly, "It's ok, Tateh. The season of the bulls is over now, even though younger ones such as the bull you just heard continue to roam the mountains making their calls. These bulls do not gather herds though, Tateh, they merely roam about, voicing their frustration with the large herd bulls who chased them during the season of mating."

We heard no more of the bugling calls, and as the uneasy feeling drained from me, I sank into a deep and secure sleep, the first in a long time.

We enjoyed many days roaming aimlessly around the great basin, feeding, rolling in the waters of the many ponds there, and lying in the sun during the warm part of each day. To my great joy, some of the cows and calves with whom we had traveled earlier in the great herd, joined us. We calves played again at our games as hard and joyfully as we ever had.

One morning, as we drank and waded in one of the large ponds in our new basin home, my speckled friends and I splashed noisily through the water around our mothers as they stood with their heads down, drinking. Suddenly the cows threw their heads into the air, and stared intently toward the far side of the pond. We calves froze immediately and also looked in that direction.

From the trees on the far side of the pond emerged an enormous bull elk. It walked slowly to the water, and ignoring us completely, lowered its massive head to drink. On his huge rack, several of the ivory-tipped tines were broken. On some, just the tips were gone, but on one side near the top of his rack, one of the great bull's tines was missing completely. The bull bore fresh scars on his broad chest and shoulders. On one side, a long, dark scar ran nearly the length of his ribs, proof, I assumed, of the violent battles in which he had engaged during the season of mating.

When the bull finished drinking, he slowly raised his head and through narrowed eyes, looked steadily at the cows. The shifting breeze suddenly brought his awful scent to my nose. I shuddered with fear as I remembered this ruthless one who had killed our leader and chased me through the darkness. I quickly splashed to my mother's side as anger welled within me, and I stood defiantly between her and the big bull. I was determined that this time, I would stand my ground and protect her. The enormous one turned uncaring though, and walked slowly into the trees from which he had come.

Our days continued sunny and warm as my dappled friends and I darted with reckless abandon between our feeding mothers in the golden meadows of the great basin. The nights however, were becoming increasingly cold. As the sun rose above the mountains each morning, the grassy meadows nearly always sparkled beneath a layer of frost.

One morning as our small herd arrived at a pond for our morning drink, I noticed that the water had a strange, dull look. As I lowered my head to drink, my nose struck abruptly against what was now the solid surface of the pond. In bewilderment, I looked to my mother.

With smiling eyes, she said, "It is ice, Tateh. When the nights here become very cold as they do now, the top of the ponds freeze," she said.

I watched as she dropped her front foot heavily through the pond's hard surface exposing the water beneath and then lowered her head and gulped greedily.

Tentatively, I struck the pond's surface with my front foot as my mother had, and just as it had for her, a jagged hole appeared beneath my foot in the hard surface of the pond. As I cautiously sampled the exposed water that now jiggled nervously in the opening, I quickly decided that the ice had not damaged the water at all. In fact, it was colder and tasted even better than usual. Quite pleased with my new discovery, I quickly drank my fill and was off to play games of life with the other young ones.

The blue skies above our mountain home slowly turned to gray as the day progressed, and as evening approached, the sun became hidden entirely behind gathering clouds. Darkness came early beneath the stormy skies, and a cold breeze washed over us as I drifted into slumber lying snugly against my mother.

Later that night, I was awakened by a tingling sensation on my nose. As I became fully awake, I was astonished to find that in my slumber, I had been covered beneath a strange blanket of whiteness. More, in the form of tiny flakes fell silently still, from the darkened skies. Panic-stricken, I sprang immediately to my feet and shook.

"It is snow, Tateh," said my mother sleepily, awakened by my wild hopping and kicking as I freed myself from this strange stuff that had entrapped me in my sleep. "When it becomes so cold," she continued, "that the tops of our ponds here become frozen, the raindrops freeze also as they fall from the sky. They float gently downward and cover everything on the ground beneath a blanket of whiteness."

'Hmmm..., snow,' I thought suspiciously, as I pressed my nose tentatively into the cold, white, fluff at my feet.

Seeing my mother's lack of concern with the white flakes that continued to silently build on her, I lay cautiously against her once more and was soon asleep.

In the morning, there was a deep layer of the strange whiteness on the grass of the meadow. We calves soon discovered the great joy of running, kicking, and sliding in it. It even seemed fun to fall into this soft stuff called, snow.

It had slowly become the season of *falling leaves.* The cold snow, it seemed, had somehow caused the colors of the leaves to change on both large and small rooted ones. Only the large trees with the tiny needle-shaped leaves were green now. All others were various shades of red, brown, and yellow. On those mornings when the rising sun shone brightly from behind these frost-covered rooted ones, our small herd often stood quietly admiring their beauty as their sparkling leaves danced wildly in the brightness.

On one such morning, as we stood feeding in the rising sun, I heard a series of strange calls echo from somewhere near us in the basin.

"What animal calls in that strange way, Mother?" I asked.

With a nervous sigh, she said, "It is the talk of the two-legged ones, Tateh."

She rapidly led our herd to the far side of the meadow where she turned and looked anxiously back, watching the trees at its far side.

"We can move quickly from here into one of the small canyons that drop from the great basin's side, Tateh," she whispered anxiously, without turning her head.

'What could these strange animals be that strike such fear into one as wise as my mother?' I wondered silently.

The strange, garbled call made by these mysterious two-legged ones became steadily louder, until at the top of a gentle hill in the distance, they appeared. Down the center of the open hillside, two brightly colored animals, walked on only their hind legs through the meadow while calling to one another in a soft, rumbling drone. As they moved closer, their scent came to us on the breeze. It was a scent like no animal I had yet smelled, a mixture it seemed, of many scents. And smoke… they smelled of smoke! It was not like the billowing smoke I had smelled in the great fire, though. It was a foul-smelling one. The smoke to my dismay, could be seen floating at times from their mouths as they chewed on short, white sticks.

They walked through the meadow in front of us, unaware of our presence as we watched them nervously from its edge. When they had disappeared from sight, my mother turned, and with me following closely behind, led our herd down a small canyon away from them.

In the safety of the canyon, far away from the two-legged ones in the basin above, my mother stopped and turned to us.

"Sisters," she said, "it is nearly the time of the *killing ones*. There is no longer safety for us in numbers. Our herd, even though it is small, makes it more difficult for us to hide from the ones who come to kill. We must separate, and we must each go our own way. The two-legged ones fear the darkness, so tonight, sisters, when night comes and it is again safe for us to travel, climb to the high timbered ridges where the two-legged ones seldom go. Hide there with your young ones until the deepening snow signals the end of *the time of killing*. We will gather then as always in the hills below these mountains where the snows are not so deep. There, we will find safety in numbers once more, and we will endure together the *season of renewal*."

Our mothers stood for a bit, looking knowingly at one another while my spotted friends and I stood quietly beneath them.

We wondered what this *time of killing* was and about these strange ones that walked on only their hind legs.

That night when darkness had fallen, the cows looked sadly toward one another. With their calves beside them, they turned, and without a word, walked silently into the blackness.

When all the cows and calves had departed, my mother led me silently upward in the darkness toward the basin above. We skirted through sparse trees at its edge for a time and dropped finally into another canyon that fell from the basin's side.

We walked down this canyon in darkness for what seemed a long time, then began to climb its steep, rocky side. Eventually, we came to the top of the ridge where we entered a small opening. Here, my mother lay down in the darkness at the meadow's edge, and lying against her, I was soon asleep.

I awakened the next morning as darkness slowly gave way to light, revealing the small opening in which my mother and I rested. Our meadow sat high atop a ridge that climbed steeply from a broad valley far below. The rocky ridge flattened temporarily at the lower end of the opening in which we lay, then climbed steeply again at the meadow's upper end. A large, timber-choked canyon nearly identical to the canyon from which we had climbed in the darkness, lay on the opposite side of our ridge. The trees surrounding our meadow nearly hid the opening from view. The grass here grew tall, and a soft murmur from the meadow's edge told of a spring that fell quietly away into the canyon beyond.

My mother had chosen this place wisely, the place where she now said, "We will spend the many days of this terrible *time of killing*."

When the first rays of sun hit our ridge, my mother and I rose from our grassy beds and began feeding in our small meadow.

As we ate, I turned to her and said, "This *time of killing,* Mother… tell me about this strange time."

"Tateh," she said, "I try to forget about this most horrible time that comes each year to our mountains, and each year when it ends finally, I deny to myself that it will ever come again. But each year during the season of *falling leaves*, the two-legged ones return. I knew the day would come when I would have to teach you about them, and their *time of killing*. Sadly, my son… that time is now.

"During the season of *falling leaves*," she continued, "when the leaves on the rooted ones turn the bright colors of red and yellow, and when the days turn cold and the first snows come, so too, do the two-legged ones. They climb into our mountains from far below in the valley. They come, Tateh, to kill our kind.

"Many of them are like wolf," she continued. "They hunt only for the strange excitement they feel when killing one of our kind. They want mostly to kill our herd bulls, for they lust to possess the antlers that the great bulls carry. To have their wondrous antlers, they feel, is to somehow possess the mysterious power of the great bull, his strength, his courage, and his knowledge of the mountains.

"Many will stop at nothing to have these antlers for their own," she said.

"How do such spindly creatures as are these two-legged ones, kill such large and powerful four-legged ones like our herd bulls?" I asked.

"The white-skinned, two-legged ones who come to kill, Tateh, are known by our kind as, *ones who carry thunder,*" said my mother, her eyes now brimming with fear.

"During the time of killing, they carry *lightning sticks.* Sticks, that when pointed at one of our kind, belch fire with a thunderous roar. Often, the one at which the lightning stick was pointed falls to the ground dead. Sometimes though, the unfortunate one is only wounded and dies days later, alone in the woods, at the fangs of wolf. Many in our herds bear scars caused by the lightning sticks of these killing ones.

"As the time of killing continues, Tateh, the snow quickly builds in our mountains where many of our kind hide safely from the white-skinned ones. As the snow becomes increasingly deeper, digging for the grass that lies beneath it becomes very difficult. The deepening snow forces weaker ones of our kind downward from the safety of the mountains in search of food. Many of them perish at the hands of the two-legged ones who live there. Were it not for the trickery and the tools of death possessed by the two-legged ones, it would be them, who starved," she added in barely a whisper.

"Eventually, Tateh," she continued, "as the snows become deeper in the *season of renewal*, the white-skinned ones lose their hunger for killing. As suddenly as it began, the time of killing is then over, and the two-legged ones come to the mountains no more.

"When it becomes evident, finally, that the killing ones are truly done, we return to our natural way of life. We then spend our days eating grass to fatten our bodies as much as possible. We rest to grow our strength in the short time we have before we must face the harsh storms of the *season of renewal*.

"So, my young son, for now, it is here in this secret place where we will stay during the time of killing. In this spot, long before we are seen, we will hear or scent any who come close. In only a few bounds, we can be out of sight in any direction we choose. Food and water is plentiful here, and we have the protection of the forest during the times when the snow comes."

After a long silence, I said finally, "Mother, I do not understand. You have taught me about the great predators of the mountains. You have helped me to understand even the strange dependency upon one another that we and the predators share. But this time of killing, and the white, two-legged ones who carry thunder, I do not understand."

"Do not try to understand it, Tateh," said my mother softly. "Simply learn to survive and to endure it. Then, when it is over, force it from your memory, and as all here do, deny to yourself that it will ever come again."

She turned from me then, and lowered her head to feed as if she had already forgotten, and it was somehow, again, the wonderful season of *growing grass*.

Snow came sometime during the darkness, and when our small meadow was again bathed in the early gray light of day, all around us was covered in a blanket of snow. The limbs of the trees surrounding our meadow drooped with its weight, and the grass in the meadow lay flat beneath the white blanket. My mother and I lie unmoving, covered completely by the snow. Quietly, we watched the sky brighten and the first yellow rays of sun slice between the peaks of the mountains to the east.

Suddenly the early morning calm was shattered by the sharp crack of thunder, and we jumped anxiously to our feet from beneath the snow. Again, and again, came booming reports from somewhere above us in the basin. I knew the frightful sounds must surely be the sound of the lightning sticks of *the ones who carry thunder.* We stood nervously waiting, concealed in the trees at the edge of our small meadow. My heart raced as we stood quietly watching and wondering if the two-legged ones would somehow find us in our secret spot.

Above in the timber, we heard a loud crashing and breaking of brush as one of our kind ran recklessly through the trees toward our meadow from above. A young bull burst suddenly from the timber at our meadow's upper end. With his head and neck straining forward, his small, uneven antlers lay back over his driving shoulders as he ran. His eyes were wild and unseeing, and with mouth agape and tongue hanging to one side, he gasped for air as he lunged powerfully toward the bottom of our meadow. He did not see us standing in the timber as he crashed frantically by, and soon his pounding footsteps and the smashing sound of his headlong flight faded, and all became silent. We stood alert and trembling as we carefully studied the forest above for the slightest movement there.

Then from somewhere below, suddenly came an ominous sound I had never heard before. From in the timber where the bull had disappeared only moments before, came short, raspy wails followed by labored, groaning huffs. The sorrowful cries soon ended, and silence fell again over the forest. We continued to stand quietly for a long time as we watched for any movement in the trees around us and listened carefully to the sounds of the forest.

My mother decided finally to solve the mystery before us and walked from the concealment of the timber with me following cautiously behind. The bull had left deep, sliding ruts gouged into the mud and had kicked dirt and small limbs through the snow in all directions in his frenzied run to the timber below. We soon understood his headlong flight through our meadow and the haunting cries we had heard from below. In his snowy tracks was the bright crimson splatter of blood. The bull had been touched by the lightning stick of the two-legged ones.

My mother lowered her head to the bull's tracks and breathed deeply the scent that rose from them. She raised her head and looked nervously around us. "Tateh, we must leave this place at once," she said. "The white-skinned ones will soon come, following this bull."

With that, she turned, and we hastily dropped into the thick timber that lay on the far side of our meadow home. We moved quickly down the side of the ridge and into the canyon beyond.

Upon reaching the bottom of the narrow ravine, we followed it downward for a time. We left the canyon's bottom finally, and walked a short way up its far side. Looking downward from the trees, we could still see the canyon's rocky bottom and the snowy tracks that we had made there only minutes before.

My mother turned, and reversing direction, walked upward along the canyon's steep side. We continued to watch the snowy tracks we had made during our hasty downward retreat in the canyon's bottom. In a short time, my mother lay down in the concealment of thick brush with me lying safely behind her. With only her head above the brush, she tested the wind and carefully watched for movement on our descending trail in the canyon below.

The sun was high in the sky now, and its warmth was causing the heavily laden limbs in the trees around us to dump their snowy burdens. The resulting "whoomf" sound of snow hitting the forest floor reverberated everywhere throughout the canyon. Bright shafts of sunlight slicing between the trees shone warmly upon us as we lay quietly watching the canyon below, and I was soon lulled into a feeling of sleepiness and well-being.

Suddenly, without moving, my mother whispered tersely, "Tateh, lower your head, and don't move."

Through the twisted brush of our hiding place, my mother and I watched silently as two white-skinned, two-legged ones, moved slowly down the canyon below us. Carrying their terrible killing sticks, they carefully followed the tracks we had made earlier in the snow. When they had walked down the canyon to a point where we could no longer see them, my mother rose and we quietly climbed upward through the trees away from them.

We moved cautiously uphill, always into the breeze, testing for any scent that did not belong in our mountains. In this way my mother and I climbed steadily until just before dark. When in the thick trees at the edge of the big basin, finally, we lay again in the snow. With our heads up listening and watching, we waited anxiously for darkness to settle.

Several more thundering booms like the ones that we had heard earlier in the day echoed from far away across the openness of the basin as night fell. Finally, in darkness, all became quiet.

We rose from our beds and walked quietly into the basin, where we moved steadily toward its far side. We stopped often in the safety of darkness and pawed at the snow-covered mounds that lie in the meadows along our way. Exposing the large clumps of grass that lay beneath, we ate quickly, and moved cautiously on.

There were many tracks in the snow of the great opening where small herds of our kind had passed sometime earlier in the day. In some tracks lay dark splotches of blood which told of a wounded one that traveled still with the herd.

As we neared the far edge of the basin, we heard from somewhere far off, the mews and bleats of cows and calves calling excitedly to one another in the darkness. These calls though, were not calls such as the ones made by our kind during the happy season of *growing grass*. They were, instead, the haunting calls of distress. Turning our heads from side to side and listening carefully, we knew that the journey of the wounded ones that traveled with the herd had ended there in the darkness. We looked at each other sadly, and with the tormented cries ringing from the darkness behind us, started toward the safety of the deep canyons below the basin's far edge.

Soon, the great opening before us tipped sharply away, forming a series of deep canyons. My mother led me around the heads of the first two canyons, then slipping and sliding on a frozen trail, we moved quickly downward into the next.

A stream sounded in the canyon's bottom, and the vague trail we followed was littered with fallen trees, stacked on one another to a height that made crossing them very difficult. We continued downward, struggling through the darkness across the downfallen maze, then picked our way carefully across boulder-strewn rock slides.

We turned from the canyon's bottom finally to climb the steep, rocky ridge that defined its north side and entered a grassy meadow at its top. The opening spanned to each side of the ridge and climbed gently upward along its top to a rocky cliff that stood at the meadow's upper end. A tall, uneven ring of grass at the meadow's edge told of the small pond it surrounded there. Towering trees at all sides of the grassy opening concealed it completely. The rocky ledges at the head of the meadow prevented the approach of two-legged ones from above. As it had been in our last meadow home, should the need arise, we could easily escape danger into a canyon on either side of the ridge.

We bedded at last in the trees beneath the cliff as the skies began to lighten, and rested gratefully there throughout the day after our demanding journey of the last day and night.

Here, in this hiding place beneath the rocky cliff, we spent many days. There were no more close encounters with the ones who carry thunder, and only occasionally did we hear the echoing boom of their lightning sticks. Once, far off on a distant ridge deep in the valley below us, we saw a two-legged one as it climbed slowly through an open meadow.

'What a wonderful trick nature played on these two-legged ones, making them so slow and easily seen,' I thought silently, as I watched it climb out of sight.

We now spent our days resting in the safety of the trees near the base of the big cliff. At night, in the security of darkness, we pawed through the snow in the meadow for the thick grass which lay beneath.

As the days of the killing season passed slowly by, the snows came with greater frequency. Each day, the snow was closer to my belly as I pawed through it to reveal the precious grass beneath.

One day after we had satisfied our hunger digging through the snow of our meadow home, my mother stood quietly in thought, gazing at the tree-covered slopes that lay at each side of our secret ridge.

After a long silence she said finally, "Come, Tateh," and started downward through the trees toward the canyon below our ridge top home. In the canyon's bottom, there were no tracks or signs in the snow of the two-legged ones having traveled there. We climbed to the top of the next ridge, and dropping into the bottom of the canyon beyond, found the snow lying undisturbed there, also.

This climbing of ridges and crossing of bottoms we repeated many times. Still, we found no sign of the white-skinned ones.

My mother, satisfied at last that the time of killing had indeed ended, turned to me and said solemnly, "It is over, Tateh. The two-legged ones will come no more. We can travel now without fear to places where the snow is not so deep and the digging for grass is much easier. Soon though, the storms will force us to the foot of the mountains in search of food. There, we will join the great herd and graze on the windswept foothills for the rest of the *season of renewal*."

We spent our days now on the sunny sides of tall ridges, digging in the snow for the grass beneath. Each day, with our hunger satisfied, we bedded comfortably and rested in the warmth of the ever-weakening sun.

Late one afternoon, as we lay high in the rocks above a large sprawling valley, we saw a strange bank of dark clouds approaching slowly from the direction where the sun rests. As we watched, the clouds began to boil mysteriously downward between the distant mountain peaks. Flowing ever downward like a massive gray river, the clouds crept silently across the great valley. When the billowing sea of gloom started upward toward us, my mother said anxiously, "Come, Tateh." She rose quickly from her bed and led me off the ridge toward the sheltering timber on its opposite side.

We had no more than entered the trees when the storm hit in a terrible fury of wind and swirling snow. The wind howled through the large trees around us, freeing their sagging limbs of snow stacked deeply on them from previous storms. It cascaded around us in giant torrents, that when mixed with the snow now falling from the clouds, made it impossible to see things that only moments before had stood clearly before us.

My mother found a thicket of dense brush hidden in a woodlot of large trees. Here, she lay behind a fallen tree with me tightly against her, and together we listened to the growing fury of the storm.

211

The wind thundered through the trees with a vengeance. Limbs straining beneath the increasing burden of snow could be heard snapping and breaking all around us. The large rooted ones groaned and creaked loudly as they swayed in the driving wind. During strong gusts, the tops of some snapped and crashed to the forest floor. The cold quickly intensified, but the growing blanket of snow under which we soon lay, shielded us from the stinging bite of the wind. We had eaten well in recent days, and with our stomachs full, the heat created naturally within us, kept us warm as the driving snow covered us ever more deeply.

For two days and nights, we lay beneath the snow as the storm raged through the forest around us. Then, in the darkness of the third night the terrible storm ceased as quickly as it had come. The sudden silence awakened us, and we poked our heads from beneath our snowy blankets. In wonderment we peered through the quiet darkness of the forest. Above us, stars twinkled between snow-laden trees that stood quietly around us like towering ghosts. The only sound was the occasional hiss of falling snow as the trees around us began to shed their icy burdens.

When at last, the skies began to slowly lighten, we rose stiffly from our beds and shook the deep blanket of snow from our bodies. To my amazement, the snow was now well past my belly in depth. I could move only by lunging forward in the deep, furrowing tracks left by my mother as we struggled slowly toward the ridge top above.

Near the crest of the ridge where trees no longer grew, a deep snow drift had formed on its downwind side during the storm. Plunging forward with all my might, the snow above my head now, I struggled exhaustedly as I fought this snowy barrier. Lunging again and again, I wallowed finally through the terrible drift and joined my mother on the ridge's top.

The terrible, driving winds of the storm had swept the ridge nearly clear of snow. Short, yellow grass lay exposed and now beckoned us in the weak, morning sun. We greedily filled our empty stomachs, satisfying a hunger that had grown from two days lying beneath the snow of the violent storm. We bedded then in the sun. As I gazed at the beauty of the snow-covered mountains around us, I thought silently about the mystifying power that seemed always at work here. A power so incredible that without warning, it had transformed the wondrous beauty before me into a raging enemy against which we had struggled for survival.

My mother breaking the silence finally, said, "Tateh, it is time now that we go from these high reaches in our mountains to the foothills near the bottom."

Rising then from her bed, she began meandering down the ridge with me following. Together we fed downward toward the valley far below. As we continued down the ridge, the snow became less deep, and walking became easier even where the wind had not blown it off.

On the flat, rolling hills far below, we could see small, brown specks. "Those specks," explained my mother, "are other elk

213

grazing. These were the cows and calves of our great herd," she said, "ones that had already dropped from the mountains after the end of the two-legged one's time of killing."

The sun was just above the mountains to the west when my mother and I descended to a spot where the great ridge flattened out.

"We will join the herd tomorrow, Tateh," she said, as she lay down facing the sun with large rocks at her back. I quickly joined her, and together we watched as the sun sank below the far mountains and darkness swallowed the great valley below us. As I drifted into sleep, I thought excitedly about the small, brown specks my mother had said were elk feeding on the hills below.

'Would the calves that surely ran playfully there remember me still, and would the games of life be played by us once again?' I wondered.

I squirmed against my mother in the darkness as suddenly in my dream, I stood once more in the meadow where the two great bulls had fought for the right to lead the herd. The enraged challenger stood once again above the lifeless body of our huge herd bull. Again, the furious one saw me standing below him at timber's edge, but strangely, I no longer stood at the side of my mother. He whirled and lunged at me as he had before, but now I did not move and instead stood glaring back at him. He stopped for an instant, confused by my lack of fear, then sprang forward with all his strength. As our bodies met in a thunderous collision, I awoke. My head shot from my snowy bed and my heart pounded wildly in my chest. As the fog of sleep slowly cleared from my mind, I lay quietly against my mother and watched the valley below us emerge from the early morning darkness. Trembling still, I pondered the meaning of my ominous dream.

'Where is the great bull now,' I wondered, 'and will we meet again?'

My mother, feeling my nervous movement, whispered softly from behind me, "It is ok, Tateh. In time, the dreams will pass, and knowing will come to you." She arose from our bed then, and after testing the air with her keen nose, said, "Come, Tateh, let's go see the others."

We dropped quickly from the big ridge and in a short time walked on the bare, rolling hills at the valley's edge.

'The grass on these little hills is not as tall as was the grass in our mountains, but with no snow to paw through, it will be easy to fill my stomach,' I thought as I followed excitedly behind my mother.

We topped a gentle crest, and below us finally were the cows and calves with which my mother and I had spent the season of *growing grass*.

As we walked happily into their midst, they gathered around us as they had when my mother and I first joined them long ago.

"Wakhita, Wakhita!" they cried.

Then, through eyes filled with wonder, they looked slowly down at me and saw the jagged scar on my shoulder.

215

"Tateh," one cow said, "that you are alive is most difficult to believe, but that you are the son of Woslolkia, there is no doubt. My young daughter, Wicala, owes her life to you because of your fearless actions in the face of the great silver one. I see that you will bear forever on your shoulder the sign of your great courage. We are honored, Tateh, to have you in our midst." I looked happily at my mother, whose eyes now brimmed with pride. Looking proudly back at the cows and calves that formed a great sea of brown and tan before us, we stood quietly for a moment meeting the gaze of each. My mother turned, and with the herd now following behind us, we walked to the center of the meadow where she lowered her head and began feeding.

Soon, all the cows were feeding again, and we calves romped happily about them. It was not with the carefree abandon as before, though. We had grown, and life's harsh realities were becoming known by all of us. The games of life had become serious, and the struggle for survival, we were coming to understand, could not be taken for granted.

Chapter Eleven

My first days on the rolling hills of our new winter home were filled with wonder and much learning about not only this new place, but also about the *season of renewal*. There were many of our kind here, more than I had ever seen before. There were also four-legged ones much like us, but smaller. These, my mother said, were *deer*. And there were other four-legged ones a bit smaller even than the deer. These were extremely fast. Their small, fleeting herds looked almost like shadows cast by moving clouds when they charged across the valley floor below our wintering place. These swift, four-legged ones, my mother told me, were *antelope*. There were many great winged ones soaring in the skies above our new home, and of course, raven and magpie were present in large numbers also.

Our days were filled mostly with grazing along the rolling hills eating the short, yellow grass that remained from earlier seasons. We then rested in the sun on those days when it was not hidden behind gray clouds that often filled the skies now. I was amazed at the numbers of our kind that had gathered here to endure together this harsh season.

One day as my mother and I rested on a grassy knoll, I carefully studied the hills before us. They were covered by four-legged ones who stood quietly grazing or like my mother and I, resting in the sun.

"Mother," I said finally, "with the many different four-legged ones I have seen here, I have seen no sign of bear or wolf. Where do they go during the *time of renewal*?" I asked.

"Tateh," said my mother grimly, "wolf is certainly here. He is a very cunning one though. He is seldom seen because their great packs travel in the darkness of night. They stalk our land looking always for opportunities in which they can easily kill those of us who have grown old and weak. Wolf is one who cannot be trusted, Tateh. If wolf somehow gains a favorable advantage, he will gladly kill even the strongest of us.

"The great bear, though, does not join us here in the wintering place Tateh," she said. "Bear spends the *season of renewal* sleeping far above us in the mountains."

"Sleeping?" I asked incredulously.

"Yes," she said, "he fattens himself by gorging on any food he can find during the warm seasons. Then as the *season of renewal* approaches, bear digs a warm burrow deep in the forest beneath an upturned tree stump where the snows will cover him deeply. There, he sleeps through this harsh time buried beneath the snow, waking finally when the snows covering his burrow begin to melt."

"Is there ever a season during which we are free of predators, Mother?" I asked.

"We are hunted in all seasons, Tateh, by two-legged, four-legged, and even the winged ones," said my mother. "We must never drop our guard. We must be vigilant always."

The joyful calf games played so tirelessly in the past were seldom done now as we had learned that energy squandered in play may soon be sorely missed. Nevertheless, we calves still enjoyed a good romp now and then.

One cloudless day after feeding, as our mothers lie warming in the sun on the hillside above us, we calves pursued each other, running with abandon across the open hills. We plunged into small ravines where we lunged playfully through the deep snow that lay in their bottoms.

Our reckless herd of rowdy calves stopped finally in the bottom of one ravine and stood panting as we rested for a moment in the deep snow there. Suddenly from above on the hillside, Khiza came running at us. When just above us, he launched himself into the air and landed with a great splash of snow just above where we stood. A loud cracking sound reverberated through the snow around our surprised herd, and to our horror, the snow in which we stood began suddenly to slide downhill.

Terrified, we bleated and screamed loudly as we bounced down the draw with ever-increasing speed, lost in a blinding mist of thundering snow. As the small ravine widened near its bottom, the torrent of snow began at last to slow, then ground to a halt with a shuddering groan. Calves were scattered across the draw straining and struggling to free themselves from mounds of snowy debris.

Wrestling free from my snowy entrapment, I lunged toward Wicala, who was twisting frantically to free herself from the snow. I was unaware, though, of Khiza, who charged toward me from above. As I reached Wicala, he smashed into me from behind. Hitting me squarely on my injured shoulder, I tumbled down the snowy hill in searing pain.

The cows who had been watching from their resting place on the hillside above the ravine had seen it all. Arriving quickly, they stood breathlessly before us. When satisfied that all the calves were safe and free from the snow, the cows turned and stared angrily at Khiza.

Khiza, and his mother who stood behind him now, glared defiantly back at the other cows. My mother walked from the group of cows and stood facing Khiza's mother. She quietly returned the angry stare of the defiant cow.

After a long silence, my mother said quietly to her, "Go from the herd now. You are no longer welcome among us."

The angry cow and calf turned, and with the herd watching in silence, disappeared over the rise beyond the ravine. I limped to my mother, and with the herd, walked from the ravine.

Over the coming days, the snow came often, and the wind became colder and more biting each day. The white-headed winged ones sat feeding often on the lifeless bodies of the weaker ones in our herd who could not withstand the harsh conditions of this time of renewal. Ravens and magpies sat in the snow around the huge birds as they fed, squawking impatiently at them as they waited their turn to feed.

Each morning when we stood and shook free from the blanket of snow that had fallen in the night, there seemed always to be some in our herd that lay motionless beneath the snow and did not rise.

One morning as we fed in a roaring south wind pawing patiently in the snow for the grass beneath, we felt the driving wind gradually slow, then become still. My mother looked up from her feeding and scanned the surrounding hills nervously as she felt the first gentle gusts of wind that had suddenly sprung from the north. Though puzzled by her uneasiness, I followed her without question as she fed steadily toward the down-wind side of the broad ridge we were now on.

Boiling grey clouds raced across the sky and soon blocked the sun completely, and the cold became even more biting. Snow began to fall from the skies and the wind steadily worsened. The storm that had begun only minutes before, soon shrouded the feeding herd around us in torrents of swirling snow.

As the storm's intensity grew, my mother led the herd onto the south side of the ridge, away from the driving wind. Here, we bedded in a stand of bushy trees that stood amidst a jumbled field of huge boulders. I lay nervously against my mother, trembling in the piercing chill of the raging north wind. I could see many other cows and calves lying beneath the trees around us as we slowly became buried beneath the drifting snow.

From behind me in the snow, my mother said, "The storms from the north are the worst, Tateh. Let the snow cover you deeply, son. Don't shake it off. It will shelter you from the terrible wind. Be brave, my son. We will be fine."

Darkness came, and the relentless gale worsened. My mother had chosen our bedding spot well though. The large rock directly behind us caused the snow to drift deeply, and we soon lay in a dark, silent bed beneath an icy blanket. Occasionally, I would raise my head from my snowy den to see if the storm had eased, but my eyes and nose were met each time by clouds of stinging snow driven by the furious wind.

For five days and nights, our herd huddled beneath the snow in a relentless blizzard of whiteness. The snow fell unceasingly from the skies, driven in billowing clouds across the ground by a screeching wind that made it impossible to see more than a few paces.

Finally, in the darkness of the fifth night, I felt a gentle nudge from behind me. Poking my head through the crust of the drift that had entombed us, I was met not by the freezing wind, but instead by a quiet calmness. The storm was gone, and the sky was filled with stars. Buried still in our snowy beds, my mother and I quietly surveyed our storm-torn surroundings. The dark sky slowly brightened, then turned to a luminous purple color as the sun began to rise on a brutally cold morning.

Knowing that the storm had passed, my mother and I rose stiffly from our beds. Around us, we saw many in the herd lying still with only their heads poking from the snow. Others, like us, had risen and were shaking the snow from them as they looked curiously about.

My mother walked slowly to the snow-covered forms of cows and calves that had not yet stood. Lowering her head to each, her keen nose told her the dismal story that lay beneath the snow. She would mew softly, then, walk to the next. Certain, at last, that only those who had succumbed to the raging storm lay still beneath the snow, she turned, and led our herd sadly from the protection of the timber.

Following quietly behind her, I thought about my young friends and their mothers as I walked past the silent mounds of snow. I wondered about the terrible brutality of this life we four-legged ones must often endure, and I silently promised to remember the ones who had not risen.

'How is this a *season of renewal*?' I thought sadly, as I walked past them toward the open ridge beyond.

The winds of the storm had blown the ridge bare, and the herd now stood with their heads down, feeding the gnawing hunger that had grown strong within them beneath the snow of the howling storm.

Sadness had now settled over our herd. As the cold, bitter days of renewal wore on, it was rare that we calves romped or engaged in friendly pushing matches. Our days instead were spent feeding in the cold wind, trying to eat enough grass to ensure that we had the strength needed to survive another night.

Each night we lay in our snowy beds nervously listening to the howling ones who fed on those in our herd who in the previous night, had succumbed to the brutal cold. As the days of this cruel season wore on, the sun slowly became stronger. Finally, some afternoons could be spent lying in comfort among warming rocks on the hillsides here.

One day as we rested in the sun, a two-legged one appeared suddenly on the hillside close below us. This was not a white-skinned one as the ones in the season of killing had been, though. It was covered in colors much the same as our kind, and the skin on its face was dark. Its hair hung in braids to its shoulders, and it carried no lightning stick. The strange, dark-skinned one stood quietly below us studying our nervous herd carefully. All in the herd rose from their beds waiting to flee, looking anxiously from the two-legged one to my mother. But curiously, my mother did not run, but instead, stood calmly watching this strange one below us.

With anxiety building within me, I turned nervously toward my mother. The two-legged one suddenly noticed the dark, jagged scar on my shoulder. It became excited then and did a very curious thing. Facing me, the dark-skinned one raised its arms toward the sky. Lowering them slowly, it pointed toward me. Then with clenched fist, it gently struck its chest four times. It then sat cross-legged in the snow and quietly watched me.

To my relief, my mother finally turned and led the nervous herd across the ridge and away from the strange two-legged one.

Safely away now, I looked questioningly at my mother. "Why did we not bolt immediately away when the two-legged one appeared, Mother, and why did this one look and act so differently from those we have seen before?" I asked.

"Tateh," she said, "the two-legged ones harm us only in the *season of falling leaves*, during the time of killing. This two-legged one had no lightning stick and walked calmly among us as it is said the ancient, dark-skinned ones once did."

'Hmm, these two-legged ones are strange… and why did he point at me?' I wondered.

That night as I lay sleeping peacefully beneath a starry sky, Woslolkia stood suddenly before me in my dream. We stood on the windswept hills looking down at our winter range. His mighty head turned slowly away from me as he looked down the mountain. Following his gaze, I saw my mother and I below us as we quietly watched the strange dark-skinned one that we had seen earlier in the day. Again, the two-legged one excitedly raised his arms toward me and slowly retracted them, touching his chest. Then as before, it sat quietly in the snow and watched us. "Why does this strange two-legged one do this?" I asked the great bull.

"He honors you, Tateh," he said. This two-legged one is a descendent of the ancient ones who long ago walked peacefully with us in our land. He has seen the jagged wound on your shoulder. To his people, your lightning shaped scar is the sign of the sacred ones they call the *Wakia*, the great *thunder-beings*. By pointing to you and then touching his chest, the dark-skinned one brings to his heart your sacred power. He will bring great joy to his people in the valley when he tells them of this sacred bull calf he has found in the mountains." The one that bears the great sign of the Wakia.

Perplexed, I turned back to Woslolkia with questioning eyes, but the great bull was gone. I lay in the darkness again against the warmth of my mother. For a long while I stared into the night around me remembering Woslolkia's words.

The days slowly warmed, and on the ridges facing the sun, tiny rooted ones began to appear at last in the soil at our feet. The two-legged ones came more often now, and to my amazement, each time they saw me, they acted much as the first dark-skinned one had.

As the days passed, the sun strengthened, and we moved steadily north along the low ridges of the great valley. We fed on the small, green, rooted ones that had grown tall enough finally to eat. As we lay resting late one afternoon, I noticed at the top of a narrow valley on our ridge's far side, a strange line that stretched across land there.

"What is that line above that small valley, Mother?" I asked. "That is a fence, Tateh," she said. Puzzled now, I asked, "A fence?" "Yes, tomorrow I will take you there. I will show you," she said.

226

As I slept that night, I dreamed of my Father, Woslolkia. Oddly, I could not see him, but from somewhere in the past I heard his words of warning,

"Only the strongest of our kind can cross them, Tateh," he said ominously. "The old and young often die hopelessly tangled in them. Stay far from their fences, Tateh."

I awoke the next morning with the huge bull's strange words still echoing in my mind. The sky had begun to lighten, and the stars were nearly gone. All in the herd lay with their heads up watching as the sky slowly brightened above the mountains behind us and shone upon the tops of the mountains to the west. Soon, bright sunshine bathed the valley floor, and as its warming light fell upon us, we stood from our beds and began feeding.

As the day warmed, many of the grazing cows and calves became full. One by one, they lowered themselves to the grass to rest in the warm sunshine. My mother, her hunger satisfied last, raised her head from the grass and said, "Come, Tateh, I will show you the fence."

We dropped down the north side of our ridge through stout, brushy timber and into a narrow valley that lay beyond. We walked steadily up the small valley and soon stood before the fearful object of my dreams… a fence.

It stood taller than me, and it had many vines, which my mother called wire, stretched tightly between short, limbless trees.

On the wire were many sharp thorns. I shuddered as I thought of being tangled in such a terrible thing as that.

My mother broke the silence finally, as she said, "Tateh, stay away from fences. They are very difficult to cross. Young ones such as you must crawl under them. Only the strongest of our kind can leap over them."

With that, she turned, and we retraced our steps down the pleasant little valley to the ridge. We climbed its side and soon lay in the sun with the others.

The snow was melting quickly during these sunny, warm days, and the snow line had receded to the mountain's top. The mood of the great herd was again happy, as all regained their strength feeding on the green rooted ones that now grew quickly in the sun. The nights too, were becoming warmer. Gone, now, were the haunting calls of feeding wolves that until only recently had echoed often through the darkness from the canyons around us.

One afternoon, after much nibbling on rooted ones, we lay resting in a breeze that blew softly from the west. Clouds began to build slowly over the mountains there, and what was once a gentle breeze soon became a howling wind.

With an uneasy feeling, my mother and I stood from our beds. With many of the cows and calves following, we walked over the ridge onto its leeward side and lay in the protection of thick timber away from the strengthening wind. The once pleasant afternoon soon became dark and threatening. As the rest of the herd joined us in the trees, fleeting clouds obscured the sun.

The first flakes of snow fell from the sky as darkness came, and we were soon covered in a deepening blanket of white. The snow continued throughout the night. The wind whipped it fiercely against us, causing large drifts to build around our motionless bodies as we listened from beneath the snow to the ever-gathering storm.

There was no relief from the storm as the sky lightened the next morning. All in the herd continued to lie beneath the deepening drifts. The soft light of the stormy day turned eventually to darkness as the day ended, and still, the storm raged on. The wind continued to strengthen, blasting us unmercifully with driving snow.

Sometime late in the night, I awoke suddenly with a troubled feeling. Raising my head from beneath the snow, I peered cautiously into the darkness. Blinking my eyes against the sting of the wind driven snow, I thought for a moment I heard footsteps crunching softly in the snow near me, but the raging wind made it impossible to be sure.

Suddenly, from the stormy darkness came the terrible, shrieking wail of wolves and all in our herd exploded at once from beneath the snow. The night was filled with the clatter of rumbling hooves as snow flew from the shadowy forms of lunging bodies. From everywhere around me came the terrified bleating of lost calves and the labored snorts and grunts of their panic-stricken mothers.

Above the roar of the wind and clamor of churning bodies, I heard my mother's strong, clear voice yell, "circle, sisters... circle!"

At her frantic urging, our herd quickly formed a protective circle in the darkness. With snow hissing against us in a deafening wind, we peered with squinted eyes into the snowy blackness around us. The terrible scent of wolves told of the circle that they had formed around us in the snowy night. Their scent was easily read by all, but their stealthy footsteps could not be heard above the roaring wind. The circle of brave cows, with calves in the middle, stood nervously readying themselves. Filled with dread, they waited for the attack they knew would soon come.

With vicious, earsplitting shrieks ringing from the darkness at all sides of our herd, the wolves suddenly struck. Terrible, guttural snarls were answered by sharp cries of pain from the cows as our desperate battle for survival began.

The wolves plunged again, and again, into the circle of cows. Spinning, and ripping with their sharp fangs, their streaking forms were impossible to see in the darkness of the stormy night. Their darting presence was known only when the pain of their slashing teeth was felt. The horrible assault went on and on. The cows labored exhaustively as they kicked and flailed with all their strength at our invisible enemy.

From across the circle behind me came a terrible gasping cry as one of the cows succumbed to the savage attack. Moaning and grunting, she was dragged to the snow by the wolves. The woeful cries of the dying cow soon ended as did the attack on our terrified herd. The cows stood trembling fearfully, facing outward still into the darkness. With eyes straining anxiously against the driving snow they waited quietly for the terrible life-struggle to begin anew. A soft, bleating cry came from within our midst as a young one there realized that the desperate cries of death had been those of its mother.

From the darkness came only the sound of the raging storm, interrupted occasionally by terrifying, snarling outbursts as the huge pack of wolves devoured the unfortunate cow.

Time stood still, it seemed, as the wind roared relentlessly around us, battering all in the herd with blistering clouds of snow. I lay filled with terror, cowering in the icy darkness, as I watched the shadowy forms of the cows standing bravely around me, awaiting what they knew would soon come.

A piercing howl rang suddenly from the night, as the leader called upon his pack to resume its treacherous assault. Again, the night was filled with tearing fangs, menacing snarls, and the gasps of the fighting cows as the exertion of the death struggle began to take its toll. Twice more, I heard the agonizing death cries of falling cows above the roaring wind and the horrible sound of the howling attack.

Again, I heard the brave voice of my mother above the terrible din of the battle. "Reach deeply, sisters! We will beat these ruthless demons!" she vowed. "Don't give up!"

The shadowy forms of the wolves slowly became visible as the dark skies began at last to lighten. The attack ceased as it became lighter. Wolves could be seen everywhere around the herd in the weak morning light. Some stood growling menacingly at the shaken cows, while others lay panting in the snow. Still others tore at the bodies of cows that had been killed earlier. The leader, a huge, black wolf, sat panting alone on a large snowdrift beyond his unruly pack. He stared coldly through yellow, glowering eyes at our exhausted herd.

Staring at him between the heaving sides of the weary cows, I realized in horror that we had met before. A dark scar that coursed from the top of his broad head to between his eyes was the scar I had seen on the wolf at the place of the healing water. An injury, I knew, that had been inflicted on him by the lashing hooves of my brave mother as she fought for my life long ago. I remembered how she and the black wolf, only days after the frightful fight, had stood silently facing each other in the water of the healing pond. I could plainly see them in my mind as they dipped their heads to one another in respect before parting. A chill passed over me as I remembered the words she had said after the wolf had walked from view that day.

"There are no enemies here, Tateh. We come to these waters only to heal and strengthen ourselves so that we can continue our life's journey."

I shuddered as I realized that this dreadful attack on our herd was yet another part of the black leader's journey.

A short, yipping howl from the huge wolf started the onslaught anew. The wolves were easily seen now as they twisted and turned, slashing at the cows that fought doggedly on, their strength nearly gone in this terrible struggle for life.

The wolves no longer stopped their killing to gorge themselves as cows, one by one, were pulled to the snow kicking and moaning, to die. The wolves were now completely caught up instead, in the frenzied killing of all in our herd.

My mother's voice rang still again, "strength, sisters, strength," she cried. "Our young ones depend on us!"

But exhaustion had overcome the brave cows, and they could fight no more. Completely drained from the terrible fight, the cows began to bolt from the circle with their calves running desperately in panic behind them. Wolves tore savagely at their legs as they fled.

Wolves darted unchecked through the broken circle now. Slashing and tearing at the cows from both the front and rear, they turned their terrible wrath on the helpless calves that lay cowering at the center. Their frenzied howling and the anguished death cries of our herd filled the air as the wolves sensed the nearing end of the mighty struggle.

Suddenly I heard the terrified voice of Wicala from somewhere outside the broken circle and watched in horror as a large, gray wolf pulled her kicking, heaving body to the snow. From deep within me welled suddenly an anger and rage that I had never before known.

Filled with a strength possessed only by those about to die, I sprang from the circle running headlong toward Wicala's assailant. With all that was within me I leapt through the air and landed squarely on the gray wolf with all four hooves. The wolf screamed in agony and rolled away from Wicala as its ribs snapped beneath the weight of my crashing hooves.

The attack on the herd stopped instantly, and all around me became suddenly quiet. The wolves had heard the anguished, yelping cries of the black leader's mate. Snarling and howling viciously, they sprang suddenly toward me. Without fear, I turned to face them in the driving snow.

The scene before me seemed suddenly to slow, and gone even, was the horrific wail of the charging wolves. I watched almost with curiosity as they crashed toward me. Cows and calves ran in all directions behind the sprinting wolves, freed temporarily from the deadly attack as the wolves killing lust was focused now, on me.

I rose to my hind legs and struck at them with all my might as the wave of onrushing killers hit me without slowing. Knocked immediately backward, I lie kicking helplessly at them in the snow.

Loud, yelping cries of pain rang suddenly from the wolves who tore at me as my mother, kicking and flailing, landed in the middle of the slashing, gray bodies.

"Run, Tateh!" she screamed, as she lashed and struck with all she had, sending wolves rolling and yelping in all directions around her.

Suddenly I was up, my feet barely touching the ground, it seemed, as I ran blindly through the driving snow.

Close behind me I could hear the vicious snarls of pursuing wolves, but behind that, amidst a din of howling and yelps of pain, I heard my mother scream again, "run, Tateh, run!"

Looming suddenly in front of me was the fence… the terrible object of my dreams. Gasping for air through mouth agape, I lunged forward with all my might. The muscles in my legs burned, and my lungs ached as I battled through the deep snow toward the ominous specter.

The shrieking wails of wolves and painful cries of my mother battling behind me, became a distant clamor as my own labored breathing roared in my ears and my heart pounded in my chest.

As the fence drew nearer, the words of Woslolkia rang suddenly in my mind. "The strongest of our kind can cross them. Young and old ones have died tangled in them."

I heard my mother's labored voice scream from behind me then, "go under the fence, Tateh... go under! Run...you can do it!"

As I came to the fence, I closed my eyes, and for reasons that I did not know, I leapt with all the strength I could beckon.

All was silent as I soared through the air. Suddenly, there was a terrible screeching of wire as I landed hopelessly tangled in the fence. Blind with panic, I lunged again and again, but the wire only cut deeper into my legs and held me fast.

Two wolves were on me now, ripping and tearing at my hind legs as I fought wildly to free myself from the twisted wire of the fence. I heard the heavy footsteps of my mother behind me then. Turning, I watched in terror as she lunged through the air toward the two wolves tearing at me in the fence. She groaned mightily as she hit the wolves and the fence with all the strength she had. The wolves rolled through the fence as the wire screeched and snapped, flying through the air in both directions away from me.

With my chest heaving wildly I lay on the ground exhausted, unable to move. Horrified, I watched helplessly as the wolves turned their rage on my mother.

Gasping for air as she fought, she screamed again, "run Tateh... go! The safe place... go!"

My strength came from a place unknown to me, and I was suddenly on my feet again plowing through the snow, lunging forward with all I had. Turning, I saw my mother behind me still at the fence, standing on her hind legs flailing wildly. Wolves tore at her flanks as she dropped again and again on the darting, churning bodies beneath her.

Suddenly beside me as I ran, was Woslolkia.

"Look always forward, and go fearlessly, Tateh," I heard him say, as together, we crossed the hill that lay beyond the fence.

The nightmare of snarling howls and the labored screams of my mother faded behind me. Alone now, I struggled forward through the snow. Above the sound of my rasping breath and pounding chest, I heard my mother's pleading voice ringing clearly in my head.

On and on across hill after hill, then upward in a small canyon, I ran. With my chest heaving painfully, I stopped for a moment. Trembling violently still, I stared frightfully around me as I gulped cool air into my burning lungs. Torn hide dangled loosely from a spot low on both of my rear legs where the slashing teeth of the wolves had cut deeply. In my tracks I left a steady trail of blood.

The fear I felt for my brave mother weakened my resolve to climb further upward in the canyon away from her, but her pleading voice echoed again in my mind, "run, Tateh, run... the safe place!"

Doggedly, I climbed upward in the driving snow to the canyon's head, then crossed the ridge that formed its south side and struggled painfully into a small basin beyond.

The snow was deep now, and the terror of the wolf attack and my long, climbing flite at last took its toll. My legs buckled helplessly beneath me, and I tumbled into a deep, wind-blown trough beneath a tree. My strength was gone, and I lay trapped in the snowy blowhole beneath the tree's reaching boughs unable to move. With eyes bulging and chest heaving, every muscle in my body was cramped with pain.

I lie imprisoned beneath the tree for the rest of the day and following night, not caring if I lived or died. I wanted only for my mother to find me. Racked with pain, I lay quietly in the snow seeing again and again, my brave mother as she reared on her hind legs striking at the leaping wolves. Her courageous fight, I knew, had enabled me to flee the wolves unnoticed.

I lay chilled and quivering the next morning when the skies at last lightened and the first rays of sun hit the forest floor around me. The winds had ceased, and the skies had cleared in the night. The deep snow of the terrible storm began to melt quickly beneath the heat of the rising sun. The day passed slowly as I lay painfully hiding beneath the tree in a steady rain of melting snow. The patter of water in the trees around me continued long after the day had ended and the sun had dropped beneath the mountains to the west. Though another day had passed, I lay unmoving still, listening anxiously for the mewing approach of my mother. After having overpowered the wolves at the fence, I knew she would find me as she always had.

I only hoped the wolves would not follow....

Chapter Twelve

Wet and miserable, my legs throbbing with pain, I hid for another day and night beneath the tree. The forest, as far as I could hear, was filled with the whooshing, plopping sound of falling snow as the storm's icy grip was quickly loosened by a warming breeze. The drum of dripping water was continuous as the melting snow rained through the branches of the trees around me.

The animals of the forest were again out after the long storm, and their anxious calls rang through the trees as they attempted to locate one another. As the chorus of voices became more numerous, I listened more intently for that one special sound that would signal my mother's approach.

I was filled with crippling guilt for having left her to fight the wolves alone. A near panic of loneliness set in at times as I thought of my mother and all that she had brought me to know. But mostly, I thought of the incredible love she held for me, a love so strong that twice she had chosen without hesitation to sacrifice her life so that I could live mine. I knew there would never be anything in my life as important to me as my mother. Most of all, I had learned to trust her and to do as she said, without question. My survival, she had told me many times, depended on my trust for her. Over and over, I reminded myself that it was for this reason that I had done as she said.... I had left her at the fence and had run to safety over the ridge. Again, and again, in my mind I saw my brave mother rearing to her hind legs, lashing with her front hooves as she fought so desperately for my life.

Remembering again her pleading words, "The safe place, Tateh, go there," I somehow drew the strength to drag myself painfully from my soggy bed beneath the tree. I looked cautiously around, then started slowly through the trees of the small basin.

'Perhaps,' I thought, 'my mother is already at the safe place and is waiting anxiously for me to arrive there.'

The thought of her waiting on the small knoll at the safe place brought a surge of happiness to me. With a warm feeling and renewed purpose, I walked from the small basin and onto the open side of the main mountain.

The past two days and nights had been very warm, and the fresh snow from the big storm was mostly gone on the open ridge. I worked slowly across the main mountain toward the south, stopping finally at a spot high above the open hills that only days before had been my home.

The small creeks that were in almost every canyon created a soft rumbling sound that echoed across the mountains around me. The once gentle creeks were now brown and frothy, swollen with melting snow from the *season of renewal* and this most recent storm.

The rolling hills below me were vacant and lonely now. No tan bodies could be seen feeding there as they had been just days before. The only signs of life were the many black winged ones that circled in the air, swooping and disappearing often into the trees of the little canyon. They now fed I knew, on the cows and calves of my herd that had died there. My loneliness welled again within me as I stood looking at the familiar hills, and I was nearly overcome by an urgency to rush downward and find my mother. Her desperate words came suddenly to me again, and I turned reluctantly and continued upward.

Soon I was on the ridge my mother and I had walked when we descended from the high country early in the *season of renewal.* As I started upward on the broad ridge, the sun hung low in the sky over the mountains to the west. I walked a short distance and found the spot where my mother and I had slept the night before we joined the herd on the rolling hills. I lay down in our old bedding spot and watched quietly below as darkness overtook the land.

As I slept, my mother's words rang unendingly through my mind. "Go Tateh, to the safe place…. Never trust them, Tateh, be always vigilant…. Go under, Tateh, go under….. You can do it!", I heard her say.

And again, I heard the words Woslolkia had said as he ran beside me during my escape from the wolves; "Look always forward, Tateh," he said, "and go fearlessly there."

Awakening suddenly, I raised my head and listened anxiously to determine what had drawn me from my troubled sleep. A lonely, piercing wail echoed from far below in the darkness. Shaking instantly with fear, I jumped from my bed with my heart pounding in my ears and limped with all my strength upward again through the darkness.

I climbed wearily around huge rock outcroppings and through small stands of timber. I was far above the rolling hills when the skies at last began to lighten and the sun rose above the mountain before me. As I continued slowly upward toward the basin above, I thought often of the wonderful feeling of freedom and the happy words my mother and I had shared on our recent journey down this ridge after the time of killing had ended.

It was very strange to walk this ridge alone now, but I told myself again and again, "she is at the safe place waiting for me." Filled with certainty, I would climb again with renewed strength and growing anxiousness, toward the great basin above.

I stood, finally, nearly exhausted at the upper reaches of the ridge overlooking the huge basin. My body ached and the wounds on my legs throbbed, but hope flooded over me as I viewed the familiar beauty of this wonderful place. The heavy snows from the *time of renewal* had only recently begun to recede here, and the soil of the great basin had not yet become warm enough to spur the growth of new grass. The grass from the previous year lay pushed to the ground in a yellowish-brown mat that stretched for as far as I could see across the basin before me. The large clumps of trees that stood scattered across the basin, however, shone with the bright, green color of renewing life.

Loneliness settled over me as I remembered again standing in the great opening as my mother explained to me, "This shade of green, Tateh, is worn only by the big rooted ones when their life-giving sap, triggered by the ever-brightening sun, rises from their roots to fill their branches and needles once again."

Large patches of gleaming snow lay melting at the downwind sides of the many small woodlots that stood before me in the basin. On the tops of the ridges, large cornices of snow formed by the mighty winds of the *season of renewal* stood looming like shining white cliffs in the late day sun. A few ravens dotted the skies across the great opening looking for their evening roosting place, and occasionally the call of squirrel echoed from the trees around me.

The white clouds that floated above me slowly became pink as the sun sank below the mountains behind me. I reluctantly halted my painful journey and bedded at the edge of a small group of trees. I lay with my head up until long after darkness had settled around me, watching and listening intently as always, for the sound of my approaching mother.

My sleep was again fitful, and I awoke many times to peer wearily into the dark night. Listening carefully, I heard only the soft murmur of the breeze as it moved secretly through the darkness, gently touching the leaves and branches of the rooted ones around me. The stars twinkled brightly in the clear sky above, and the forest at my side was inky black under the moonless sky.

As I dozed again, I walked suddenly with Woslolkia. I followed him as we walked onto the flat ridge toward the mysterious plateau upon which the ancient two-legged ones had grown their tree of life. We walked in silence, save for the echoing sounds of our hooves on the rocks of the secret trail. His huge antlers swayed side to side in the early morning light as he led me into the meadow on the small plateau. Standing finally beneath the tree of life, Woslolkia turned and looked steadily into my eyes.

After a long while he said finally, "You have come to know many hardships in your short life, Tateh. The creator of all, the Great Spirit, has walked at your side often. With you, he has endured your terrible hardships. He has reveled in the joy and love you have known in your heart for your mother and those of your kind with whom you have shared your life."

"Woslolkia," I said, "what is this *Great Spirit*…, this creator of all things? Why does it create wolves and allow them to kill as they did in the valley below? And the cows and calves of my herd that did not stand from beneath the deep snows in the *season of renewal*, did he know of their plight?" I asked.

"Yes, Tateh, he knew," said Woslolkia, "for He *is,* the wolf and the cows and calves of your great herd. He is all life, in all things, Tateh. The Creator is known by many names, but perhaps the name most fitting is, *The Great Mystery.* I cannot say why these things about which you ask me are so. I can only promise, Tateh, that when your life's journey is done… you will know."

"Woslolkia," I cried, "my mother… is she at the safe place? Is she ok?" I begged.

But Woslolkia was gone, and I lay again in my bed staring into the darkness that surrounded me. As loneliness once again settled over me, I wondered about this *Great Mystery,* the one Woslolkia had said "walked with me always." 'Where is he now?' I wondered, as I peered nervously around me in the quiet darkness.

At last, the skies began to lighten, and one by one, the stars disappeared from the sky. I struggled painfully from my bed and started into the basin, anxious to find the big canyon that fell from its far side... the canyon in the bottom of which lay the safe place, and surely, my waiting mother.

I walked steadily into the morning sun through meadows and clumps of timber, as I moved onward through the basin. Most of the snows of the *time of renewal* were gone now, but in the soft, moist soil that lay beside the retreating drifts, I saw no fresh tracks made by others of my kind. And that one set of tracks I wanted most badly to see, I could not find.

The sun was high in the sky when at last I stood looking down the huge canyon in which the spot of my birth, and the safe place, lay hidden far below. As I quietly studied the sprawling chasm, I saw plainly in my mind, the proud cow that was my mother as she led me upward from its depths in the past season of *growing grass.* I turned and watched as the happy pair trotted from view into the great basin behind me. Then as the sad reality of my journey again settled over me, I turned and walked quietly into the canyon.

A soft breeze floated upward, enabling me to scent any danger that lurked below, and I was able to move quickly downward through the many meadows and dense forest in the canyon's bottom. It was still early in the season of *ducks returning*, but in the lower reaches of the canyon, the warming sun had begun already to coax tender green shoots of grass from the soil. The meadows in the canyon's bottom had a smattering of green showing beneath the brown grass, and the fresh smell of the awakening pine trees floated on the afternoon air. The forest was alive with the voices of the many small animals with which I shared this land. I realized for the first time that indeed the harsh *season of renewal* was at last behind me. Somehow, I had survived.

On and on I cautiously walked from meadow to meadow. I crossed small streams and slogged through muddy bogs, then found my way through stands of moss-covered trees. As the sun dropped behind the ridge to the west, I stood finally in the dense timber among the short bushes where I had been born. Here, in the trees there was no hint of green yet, and in the matted brown grass before me was a small, round area that lay pressed flatly to the ground. It was the place, I knew, where my mother and I had lain for a time after my birth. I could easily see her warm, brown eyes as she nuzzled and cared for me there, when that grass was soft and green. I walked slowly forward to the oval depression in the grass and lowered my head to breathe deeply the scent that lay there. Only the scent of dried grass filled my nostrils, but in my mind, I smelled the wonderful aroma of my mother. I stood for a time, bathed in the warmth of the wonderful memories there.

The softening light brought me suddenly back to the present. Realizing how close the safe place was now, I turned excitedly from the place of my birth and moved quickly through the darkening forest.

Trotting, I moved along a faint trail and soon crossed the stream where as a young calf I had first encountered water. Here I turned from the trail and moved anxiously onward into the dense forest.

I stopped suddenly, my heart pounding wildly, as the small knoll of the safe place appeared before me in the fading light. Forgotten were my wounds and the weariness of my long journey as I bounded forward, crashing recklessly through the dense trees toward the small knoll. "Mother," I cried, adrenaline pounding through my veins as I sprang to its top.

An explosion of thundering wings erupted suddenly beneath my feet as grouse burst into the air, startled from their evening roost among the rocks and trees of my safe place. I stood in disbelief, trembling, as the reality before me slowly descended. I stood alone in the gathering darkness. My mother was not here.

The spot among the rocks where together we had lain for so many days was but a small round patch of soft dirt now, surrounded by matted, brown grass. Neither the soft earth of the old bed nor the grass surrounding it showed any recent sign of my mother having been here. I stepped tentatively forward to the old bed and lowered my head, hoping somehow to breathe the fresh scent of my mother, but there was none. Slowly, all hope now gone, I lowered myself onto the soft earth there. I lay looking through the familiar trees that surrounded my safe place as they slowly sank into the blackness of night.

As I had before, I lay for days waiting and listening carefully as my mother had long ago told me to do. I had not eaten or drunk water since the wolf attack. The weakness that now grew rapidly from within, told me I would not go on much longer.

On the fourth day of my lonely vigil the wind began to moan softly through the trees and clouds crept slowly across the sky. As the sun sank from view, snow began to fall from the darkening sky. Not caring about the snow, but waiting faithfully still, I lowered my head to the ground and slept.

Awakened suddenly, I lay peering into the snowy darkness. My heart quickened as I listened intently for that which had drawn me from my anguished dreams. Far off in the forest below the knoll, I heard the muffled, mewing calls of a cow elk. My heart began to pound with growing excitement as I listened intently to the beckoning calls as they drew closer, echoing softly from the trees around me.

Suddenly, my mother appeared before me in the falling snow! I sprang to my feet and in two joyful bounds stood next to her, rubbing her head and neck with mine while shaking and bleating uncontrollably. The joy and elation I felt was overwhelming.

"Mother, oh Mother!" I cried, "How I have missed you! Please forgive me that I did not go under the fence, but instead, tried to jump it! Oh, you were so brave when you broke the fence to free me, then stood alone to face the wolves! Mother, please know that I did not want to leave you, but did as you begged…. I ran and ran, and came here to the safe place where I have waited for days for you to return."

Realizing finally, that my mother stood in silence, I stepped back perplexed and looked closely at her. Curiously, she bore no wounds from the terrible battle she had just fought. She was a beautiful, soft, tan color and looked to me like she had in my earliest memory of her. Looking into her soft brown eyes, I realized they were filled with sadness.

"My son," she said finally, "oh, my beautiful, brave son. I love you, and I will always love you. Walk forward, Tateh, fearlessly, with firm steps on your life's journey, and know I will walk with you always, my son…. always."

Suddenly, I lay alone in the falling snow. "Oh, Mother," I whispered softly…"it was only a dream."

Lowering myself sadly to the ground once more, I saw in the snow near the edge of my bed, fresh tracks where my mother had stood.

Jumping wildly to my feet, I cried, "Mother, please don't leave me!" as I peered frantically into the snowy darkness.

After a long while, I lay quietly again as a strange knowing settled slowly over me. It had not been a dream. My mother's love for me was so great that she had somehow come to me to say goodbye. The wolves had taken her from me.

My head reeled with weakness as I was overwhelmed with grief. I thought sadly about the Great Spirit that my mother and Woslolkia had said created these beautiful mountains and lived within all things here.

'What about this Spirit, this Great Mystery?' I now wondered sadly. 'How could it create such wonderful things and yet let my mother be killed by the vicious wolves in the valley below? And what of me… was this Great Spirit with me now to share yet another terrible hardship? Will he die with me in this dark, sad place all alone? Without the love and companionship of my mother, I do not care to go on,' I thought sorrowfully, and I dropped my head slowly to the snow.

A curious calm began to settle over me, and I was slowly overcome by darkness. I realized suddenly, I was looking downward from above the trees. Below me, in a small bed surrounded by rock and small trees, a helpless calf elk lay starving in the swirling snow. Though the forest was very dark, the scene below me was somehow bathed in soft, white light. I felt a great heaviness in my heart as I clearly felt the hopelessness of the small one as it lay surrendering in the snow. Curiously, I realized that the pitiful one I saw below in the forest was me, and that my life was ending. The soft light under which the calf lay began to dim as I moved slowly upward into the night.

In the shadowy forest below me, I saw a familiar form walk slowly from the trees. A cow elk approached the silent form of the calf and stood quietly beside it with its head lowered. My mother was not gone. I knew then, that indeed, she would walk with me always.

From the darkness around me came a pleading voice that I realized was mine.

"No, no, please, Great Spirit, not this way!" I heard myself beg. "My mother gave all that was hers to give so that I could live. Please, I can't let her final act of love be meaningless... it can't end this way!"

I became slowly aware of a growing warmth that began to build within me. Struggling to consciousness, I raised my head once more from the snow. Looking sadly into the swirling darkness around me, I quietly pondered the vision I had seen in the forest below me. 'Had it indeed been my mother standing next to me? Had the words that rang still in my head been those pleaded by me from in the dark sky above?'

I struggled weakly to my feet, plagued by my troubling thoughts and stood silently staring into the darkness around my safe place.

"Yes, Mother... fearlessly," I promised, then stumbled painfully down the small knoll and into the snowy blackness of the surrounding forest.

Chapter Thirteen

I walked aimlessly onward, tripping and stumbling in the snowy darkness of the forest.

"Yes, Mother… with firm steps," I whispered again into the blackness as I listened to the swishing sound of my footsteps in the snow. I groped clumsily through the dense undergrowth of the canyon's bottom, lurching over rocks and fallen trees, floundering awkwardly into unseen depressions.

At last the sky above began to lighten. I stopped then and watched as the forest around me slowly appeared from the darkness.

Giant, moss-draped trees stood dismally mute in the gray light. The forest floor around me could be seen for only a short distance before it dipped from view, hidden behind a twisted wall of brush. What was once tall grass now lay in a tangled mat beneath the snow. There was no hint of green showing yet among the trees here, where shade almost always covered the forest floor.

From somewhere in the trees the sharp, chirping call of a squirrel echoed. I winced suddenly with fright at the rush of flapping wings as a speeding woodpecker passed closely overhead, its drumming wings carrying it to some secret destination. A few small winged ones, having recently returned to their high mountain home, began to sing and call happily to one another from the thick brush around me. As I listened carefully to the awakening sounds of the forest, I became aware of a soft rumble that echoed from the canyon's bottom. A small stream I was certain, its waters now swollen by melting snow, fell steadily downward beneath the trees there.

The rowdy voice of the brook reminded me again of the burn in my throat and terrible thirst that emanated from deep within me. Wearily, I looked upward into the brightening sky. Slowly, my gaze fell downward to the tops of the massive trees that stood silently around me, then, to the ground where my feet were hidden in the snow. I was suddenly gripped by an incredible feeling of smallness as I realized the insignificance of my being, an awareness I had never before known.

"Fearlessly…." I whispered aloud, forcing the troubling thoughts from my head. Moving forward again, I walked slowly toward the muffled roar of the distant creek.

The canyon bottom was strewn with boulders, and choked by a tangle of downfallen trees that nearly blocked my path. Adding to my challenging trek were a jumble of wiry little trees that grew upward through the maze of fallen timber. My journey became a series of winding turns, a doubtful path that often doubled back and sometimes even crossed itself. My legs were stiff and sore, and the dense underbrush ripped at the fresh wounds on them. The sun rose above the mountains, finally, its welcome light streaming into the dark canyon as I struggled steadily onward.

The dense forest at last began to thin. Ahead of me through the trees, I could see the bright color of a snow-covered meadow begin to slowly appear and in a short time, I stood cautiously at its side. It was quite wide and long and was surrounded by a towering forest. The wall of green trees stood in sharp contrast to the white blanket of snow that covered the meadow.

The grass here, like the grass in the forest behind me, lay buried beneath the snow. But in the openness of the meadow grew many varieties of plants with stronger stalks that stood in defiance of the crushing white blanket. In the center of the opening grew a large thicket of mature trees, and on its far side was a pond surrounded by a sagging wall golden swamp grass. Snow on the pond's surface told of the ice that remained still, from the chill of the recent snowstorm. A light mist rose from the warming meadow and swirled gently at the treetops, pushed along by a nearly imperceptible breeze. Everywhere in the opening, thick frost lay on the brush protruding from the snow and sparkled brightly in the early morning sun.

Certain at last, that no danger was present, I walked into the opening. The cool, moist air in the meadow reminded me again of the throbbing dryness in my throat. Suddenly forgotten was my trek to the distant creek. I walked anxiously, instead, to the little pond at the meadow's far side and lowered my head to the ice that covered its surface.

In eager anticipation of the cold water that lay beneath, I reared with renewed strength and brought my front feet crashing down on the ice. The brittle ice at first refused to break and sent pain shooting through the wounds on my legs. But after repeated attempts, shards of ice slid across the pond's surface in all directions as the ice gave way finally, with a sharp, cracking sound. Gratefully, I lowered my head to the exposed water and sucked the cold fluid greedily into my mouth. The water was stingingly cold and felt foreign in my mouth as I gulped it down my parched throat. I marveled at its chilling progress as the water coursed downward and entered my stomach.

Before my terrible thirst was abated though, my stomach cramped painfully, shocked by my sudden intake of cold water after having gone for so long without. I stood with my head lowered to the ground, coughing and gagging as my parched stomach refused the water I had just drunk. When my gagging convulsions ended finally, I stood with my head lowered and eyes tightly shut waiting in quiet misery for the terrible cramps to cease.

From somewhere across the pond, a gruff voice said suddenly, "You must drink the cold water slowly, Tateh."

I threw my head up in fright, and through anxious eyes stared at a gigantic bull elk who stood watching me from the edge of the timber at the far side of the pond. His dark, brown body was large and muscular, and the antlers that towered above his head were enormous. He quietly watched me as I stood trembling in fright, seeing again the vision of the monstrous bull that had chased me through the darkness.

'If I am to die today, let it be so, but I will die without fear,' I promised myself silently.

A strange calmness settled upon me, then, and void of all emotion I stood silently facing the huge animal.

The big bull came toward me then, but upon reaching the far side of the pond, stopped and lowered his nose to the ice. He drew deeply at the scent of the water beneath, and through flared nostrils, sent billows of steam glancing from the ice as he exhaled. He raised one large front foot and brought it crashing down, shattering ice in all directions. He then lowered his head to drink. The ivory tips of his massive antlers pointed straight at me as he sucked noisily at the cold water in the gaping hole he had just created.

His thirst satisfied, he raised his head from the water and looked again at me. There was a steadiness in his gaze, a look not of anger, but one of knowing. We stood for a time quietly watching one another, then, the big bull turned and retraced his steps to the timber's edge where he disappeared silently into the trees. Only the steaming hole in the ice and a trail through the deep grass where frost no longer clung, remained as proof of the existence of the bull. A bull who had somehow known my name.

I stood at the pond's edge for a bit and pondered this strange encounter. The terrible cramps in my stomach were gone now, but I knew somehow that the words spoken by the strange bull were true. I would have to drink water in small amounts until my stomach began again, to function. With a sigh of resignation, I turned from the pond and walked to the trees at the center of the meadow.

The sun had climbed to a place well above the mountain tops, and as I felt its warming caress on my back, a deep weariness overcame me. I lowered myself stiffly to the snow and was soon asleep.

My slumber was again filled with torment. The purpose of my sleep was no longer for rest and healing, it seemed, but had instead become a time to relive tragedy. I awoke with a start and raised my head quickly to listen for that call or ominous noise that had awakened me. Turning my head slowly as I looked intently about the meadow, brought no clue as to my sudden awakening. The opening was vacant, and to my ears came only the peaceful rush of the distant creek. Try as I might, I was unable to hear the faint mewing calls that I longed to hear. Sadness and loneliness once more settled over me.

The sun was now straight overhead, and as I looked toward the far end of the meadow, I envisioned my mother stepping from the woods. I heard her words of encouragement echo through my mind and wrestled myself painfully to my feet. I drew deeply at the mountain air around me, savoring the sweet scent that now filled my nostrils, and said softly, "Yes, I will remember your words always, Mother." I stepped weakly from my bed and turned toward the pond.

The sun's warmth had turned the snow in the meadow into a slushy wetness, slowly exposing the yellow grass that had lay trapped beneath.

Arriving at the pond, I was pleased to find that my small waterhole had grown larger in the warming sun. I lowered my head to the icy opening and drew the cold water into my mouth. I swallowed tentatively this time, and as before, felt its coolness inside me as it coursed toward my stomach. I raised my head after only a few gulps and stood patiently savoring its wonderful wetness as it soothed the aching dryness in my mouth and throat. My stomach, this time, did not object. Across the pond, I saw the gaping hole in the ice from which the big bull had earlier drunk. Remembering his words, I turned reluctantly from the water to sample the grass growing at the pond's edge.

It had been many days since I had eaten. With my terrible thirst momentarily dulled, pangs of hunger welled within me. I lowered my head with anticipation and drew the wonderful scent of the yellow grass to my nose. The tearing sound of grass as I pulled it from the earth, and the grating sound between my teeth as I chewed, were nearly as satisfying as the feeling of fullness that grew in my stomach as I swallowed.

In fear of my stomach's repeating its rejection of the water I had drunk earlier this day, I reluctantly ended my grassy feast. I returned to the center of the meadow where I rested again beneath the trees and quietly studied the forest around me.

The day passed quickly as I lay resting and healing in my new meadow home. As the sun drew near the far horizon, the small animals in the forest around me shared their thoughts in voice and song. While I quietly listened and beheld the beauty of the meadow and trees in which I lay, a familiar comfort began to settle over me. The water that had abated my burning thirst, and the coarse, yellow grass that rumbled softly in my stomach had sparked a weak glimmer of hope within me.

The sun dropped beneath the mountain finally, sinking the forest and meadow around me into a shadowy world. Only the jagged outline of the treetops at the meadow's edge could be seen against a starry sky. Dreading yet another dream-filled night, I lie awake long after darkness had fallen. I listened to the soft murmur of the breeze flowing gently through the forest and to the ever-present voice of the distant creek. From somewhere in the forest came the reverberating call of owls as they hooted from the darkness, telling one another of their ever-changing location as they hunted.

The traumatic days and nights of my recent past bore in me a deepening exhaustion which overcame me finally. No longer able to deny slumber, I slowly lowered my head. My sleep, as I had now come to expect, was again tormented and plagued by the sounds and visions of the preceding days. My dreams this night, were haunted once more by the shadowy forms of darting wolves and the anguished cries of death that rang through a howling blizzard. Again, I relived the terrible scene at the fence, but now it seemed that I watched from above, as if through the eyes of the great winged one. I awoke gasping for air, my heart pounding in my chest, and my eyes straining to see in the blackness of the meadow that which had existed in my dream. Although I had come to know that my mother would never again return, I lay awake still, as the dark sky began to lighten, listening carefully for her call.

As the stars disappeared one by one from the brightening sky, the meadow around me slowly emerged from the blackness of the surrounding forest. The first tentative calls of winged ones rang from the trees as the day became lighter.

My eyes were drawn suddenly to a hulking form, barely visible, standing in the shadowy grayness near the far edge of the pond. It was the huge bull, I was certain, that I had seen the day before. The bull stood motionless looking my way for a bit, then turned and sank into the early morning darkness that shrouded the thick forest still.

The thirst that I had only started to quench the day before now settled upon me. With the strange bull apparently posing no threat, I rose painfully from my bed and started toward the pond. The night had been cold and calm, and frost again clung in sparkling crystals to the grass. My legs made a soft, rasping sound as they swept the heavy frost from the brush as I walked. My footsteps echoed strangely from the surrounding forest as my feet crunched loudly in snow now frozen hard after having softened in the warm sun of yesterday.

As I neared the pond, I noticed a thin plume of steam that rose from exposed water at its far side where the big bull had again broken the ice to drink. 'Why,' I wondered, 'had this enormous bull chosen such a spot as this to stay? It was now the time when the big ones sought seclusion and privacy, a time during which they shed their massive antlers and began to grow ones even larger for the next season of the bugling bulls. And why would one as large as was this enormous bull share his secret spot with a young bull calf as puny as me?' My urgent thirst, though, drew me from my thoughts, and striding with purpose, I soon reached the pond.

The spot at which I had drunk yesterday was again frozen, but not so thickly as before. A couple of blows with my front feet cleared the new ice from my drinking hole. Lowering my head gratefully to the water, I completely satisfied the thirst that had for so long emanated from within me. My attention then focused on the yellow grass lying at the pond's edge. Unlike yesterday though, I ate until I was full, then walked slowly back to my bedding spot. Once there, I lowered myself to the grass, where for the remainder of the day I rested in the warmth of the strengthening sun. The silence in the meadow and the forest surrounding it told me that the smaller animals languished quietly in the warm sun just as I did.

As the days passed, my legs became stronger, but the terrible soreness in them lingered. The jagged wounds on them had covered over and were healing quickly, but lying for long periods brought on a great stiffness, and walking was still painful upon first rising. I thought often of the healing water that lay deep in the burned forest of a faraway canyon, but the weakness I still felt told me I must stay here until I was strong enough to make such a journey.

This pleasant routine of filling my stomach and resting in my secluded meadow I repeated for many days as the sun grew stronger in this new season of *ducks returning*. Frost seldom lay in the meadow in the early morning light now, and it was no longer necessary to break the ice from the pond before drinking. Everywhere in my meadow home, small rooted ones had begun to rise through the old mat of yellow grass. Now, these new green ones were my food of choice. I had not seen the big bull for days, but on one cold morning, I noticed tracks he had made in the frosty meadow. Strangely, during the night, the huge one had stopped and stood close by where I lay before moving on.

Early one evening as I grazed near the pond, I heard from far away in the sky, the hollow, reedy call of approaching geese. The echoing cries of the *great water birds* became steadily louder as they neared. Suddenly, in the sky above the high canyon walls, they appeared. The geese filled the blue sky above me as the graceful winged ones stroked effortlessly forward. Their numbers were staggering, and yet they flew as one, in patterns of long slanted lines that reached the skyline at each side of my canyon. They called to one another constantly, encouraging each other it seemed, to fly hard and fast to that watery destination where they would soon rest. The haunting sound of their voices awakened within me a curious urgency to move on also. A need to find that place where I too, would rest and stay in the season of *growing grass*.

Chapter Fourteen

I lay quietly pondering the day as I watched the sun drop slowly beneath the ridge tops surrounding my meadow home. My day had gone well. I had drunk my fill of the sweet, cold water at the pond, and I rested now on my grassy bed. My stomach churned softly as it digested the juicy green shoots which I had eaten earlier. The moon appeared above the far canyon wall and bathed my meadow in a beautiful bluish light, enabling me to see nearly as well as I had during the day. I looked up to the starry sky where earlier the flocks of big water birds had flown and wondered in what secret pond they now swam on this moonlit night.

Suddenly, a long, wailing howl shattered the silence. I sprang frantically to my feet facing the origin of the frightful call. Again, it rang across the moonlight meadow. The terrifying call was at first a low, yelping bark that rose quickly to a shrieking wail. The ominous cry echoed from the canyon walls as a wolf stalked the moonlit timber somewhere in the canyon below me.

Shaking with fear, I moved carefully from my bed and hid in the shadows of the big trees at the meadow's center. I strained with eyes and ears toward the opening's lower end, trying desperately to detect any movement there.

Again, the call erupted from below, but closer this time. Adrenaline surged through my body as panic overcame me. I sprang with all my strength from my shadowy concealment and lunged through the meadow toward its upper end where I crashed recklessly into the thick timber. My heart pounded, and I gasped breathlessly for air as I floundered through the trees away from the threatening howls.

Tearing limbs from down-fallen logs as I vaulted blindly across them and plunging through shadowy hollows filled with ponds of mud, I fought my way upward through the forest. But my escape was not to be. The terrible panic that consumed me had robbed what little strength I had and exhaustion quickly overcame me. My feverish flight ended suddenly when I became trapped in the gnarled limbs of a huge fallen tree over which I had been unable to jump. Too weary even to struggle, I gulped at the cool night air in fearful, ragged gasps. My heart beat wildly as I envisioned the ruthless killers stalking silently toward me in the darkness.

In vain, I fought sickening waves of fear that rolled rampantly through me. Tortured by the horrible visions of what I had seen happen to my herd, I readied myself for death. Time stood still as I awaited the snarling assault that I knew was sure to come. But only silence rang through the shadowy forest. There was no attack. Somehow, the wolves had not found me. After what seemed an eternity, my thundering heart began at last to slow, and the burning ache in my lungs diminished.

The night dragged on as I lay ensnared and unmoving. I was certain that any attempt I would make to free myself would alert the sensitive ears of nearby wolves, and the brutal killers would learn of my precarious hiding place. With muscles cramping, I listened fearfully through the night, and watched as dark shadows cast by the moon crept threateningly through the trees around me. I heard no more of the wolves terrible, shrieking voices, and as the sky lightened finally, I dragged myself painfully from the tangled limbs of the downfallen tree.

Free from the big log finally, I stood quietly unmoving as I studied the forest around me for any movement that did not belong. My ungainly entrapment had cramped my legs terribly and I shifted my weight from one foot to the other as I watched. In a short while my cramping muscles relented, and I was able to stand with my weight evenly placed on each of my tortured legs. The increasing light of morning revealed a jungle of fallen trees that stretched in all directions for as far as I could see. The ancient forest had somehow eluded fire and lived well beyond its prime. Barren, weathered trunks of dead trees lie crisscrossed over one another in an endless sea of grayness. In places, they lie stacked to heights much taller than me. The giant rooted ones that stood amongst them still, had scarred and twisted trunks and their tops were already gray with death. The old giants would soon join their fallen relatives on the chaotic forest floor. Water seeped from everywhere it seemed, and trickled secretly away in deep, jagged trenches concealed beneath thick vegetation.

The day slowly became brighter, and finally the sun rose above the canyon sides sending brilliant splashes of light throughout the tangled disarray. Reluctantly, I started forward through the downfallen barrier before me. As the sun climbed slowly overhead, I stood quietly resting, pondering my path through the hopeless maze. I realized suddenly that in the distance, I could hear the muted rumble of water. Somewhere nearby, a stream rumbled downward in the canyon's bottom.

Upon reflection, I remembered the trail upon which my mother had led me from this canyon in the past season of growing grass. I remembered that in places, the trail followed the winding stream closely.

Heartened by the thoughts of easier passage, I resumed my unlikely trek. With renewed zeal, I struggled over and sometimes dragged myself under the tangle of fallen trees that cluttered the forest floor.

When the sun was high overhead, I worked my way at last from the dying forest. I found a narrow trail near the creek that I had heard when still far below in the trees. I was relieved to see that nowhere in the soft earth of the trail were the tracks of wolf. I hoped, that this little-used trail would lead me from this canyon and away from the lurking killers below. I followed the path steadily upward, thankful to no longer be imprisoned in the tangled jungle behind me.

As I climbed higher in the canyon, the path became more defined and merged, finally, with a much larger trail. Cast in the mud of this new trail were the tracks I had made on my downward journey in search of the safe place. Certain now of my destination, I walked upward on this new path with renewed confidence. The thick forest began to thin a bit, and I could see far into the trees at the sides of the trail. It was nearly the season of *growing grass* now, and a smattering of green had begun to appear in even these high meadows through which I now walked. I sampled the short new rooted ones at trail's edge as I remembered my mother had done long ago. There were no flowers here yet, but the myriad plants from which they would spring in days to come, grew everywhere. The sun shone brightly from the cloudless sky, and the heat I felt on my back soothed my lingering soreness as I walked through the treeless openings.

The trail wound steadily upward, and as it did, the canyon bottom became wider and the openings more numerous. Some meadows had ponds while others were covered by fields of large boulders. Both sparked within me memories of the wonderful journey made here by my mother and me, long ago. I stopped often in these meadows and stood sadly remembering. Then, as I had promised my mother, I walked on.

As I entered one large meadow, I noticed at its head, a lone cow elk standing in the trail above me at the timber's edge. My eyes grew wide with excitement, and my heart began to race as I bolted toward her, running headlong across the meadow. As I neared the cow, however, I realized she was not the one that my loneliness had caused me to see. Filled with disappointment, I slowed to a walk and approached where she stood quietly watching me.

She was a large old cow, one I had never seen before, and she traveled alone. The old one studied me carefully as I stopped before her. I saw her eyes grow wide when her gaze fell upon the scar on my shoulder.

After a long silence, the old cow said finally, with sadness filling her eyes, "I was told of the terrible wolf attack in the past *season of renewal*. I was deeply saddened to hear of the death of many in your herd, including their brave leader, your mother, Wakhita. It was not known if her young son had perished with the others," she continued, "the brave one, with the jagged scar on his shoulder. I know now, that indeed, you live."

Interrupted suddenly by something she saw, the old cow raised her head and stared intently over my back toward the direction from which I had just come. Turning, I saw a large bull elk moving slowly along the meadow's lower edge, then, disappear noiselessly into the trees.

"Ksapa" the old cow whispered under her breath.

"Ksapa?" I asked. "Who is Ksapa?"

"Ksapa," explained the old cow, "is a great lead bull, one of the wisest of our kind. He is one of the few great ones left," she said softly, looking again toward the timber where the big bull had disappeared.

I stood looking there for a moment, wondering silently about the mysterious bull. I was certain that Ksapa was the bull with whom I had shared the meadow and pond deep in the canyon below. I looked back to the old cow with questioning eyes, but she answered me only with a steady, knowing gaze. I turned from her then and resumed my journey to the top of the canyon.

Above me, the sun hung low on the horizon, and I felt the first stirring of the downward breeze that signals the end of the day. Nearing the canyon's top, I continued upward in fading light through the natural bowl that formed the great chasm's head. In softening light, I walked at last, into the great basin beyond. I stood for a long while at the basin's edge and quietly beheld the beauty of the rolling land that stretched before me.

The huge drifts of snow that were piled around the groves of trees during my earlier journey were gone now. Rich, green patches of grass marked the places where the great drifts had stood as the moisture from the melting snow still lingered in the soil there. Only narrow lines of white remained near the tops of the ridges now. Gleaming in the retreating light, they stood as icy reminders of the once mighty cornices stacked there in *season of renewal*.

Darkness had barely fallen when a bright glow began to gather above the horizon behind me. I stood quietly watching as the top edge of the moon appeared. It climbed slowly from behind the peaks until it hung bright and round, illuminating the great basin with a flood of soft, blue light. It sent shadows flowing from behind all that it touched. I traveled onward then, able to see all before me clearly in the moonlight.

I came at last to one of many small clusters of trees that grew throughout the basin. The thicket stood at the base of a short ridge and was clearly silhouetted by the moonlight behind them. I drank my fill of cold water from a seep that trickled from a depression near the ridge's base, then ate grass that grew at the edges of the tiny creek.

The urge to travel on was dulled by the grass and water that now filled my stomach. A great weariness reminded me again of the day's steep climb from the canyon and my panicked flight away from the haunting voices in the darkness there. This night, though, was quiet and still, and the ache in my injured legs told me that I must rest. I lay near the trees at the edge of the thicket and slumber soon overtook me.

I awoke long before dawn the next morning but remained resting quietly as I studied the basin before me. The moon had nearly completed its nightly voyage and sat barely above the mountain ridge toward which I would soon walk. I rose from my bed and strode to the small seep that lay glowing softly in the reflection of the retiring moon. After having satisfied my thirst, I turned to the grass at the water's edge and grazed as the moon continued below the far mountains, sinking the basin into darkness. A pinkish glow began to build on the opposite horizon where the sun would soon rise, and as the glow became steadily brighter, I started once more across the basin.

The grass was taller here than in the canyon from which I had just come, as the basin's openness allowed more sunlight to reach the small rooted ones. A dizzying number of bushes growing throughout the grass stood glistening in the morning dew, their sleeping buds still tightly closed. These tiny pods of life, I knew, would explode soon in colorful bloom. Ravens flew in the sky overhead, calling to one another as they searched with keen eye for their morning meal. Their usually black, shiny feathers reflected the red glow of the new day's sun, now peeking from the horizon behind me. As I strode on, the growing warmth of the sun felt wonderful, and my sore, cramping legs began to loosen.

Much of the day was gone when at last in the distance I could see the two small knobs that marked the saddle through which I would pass to enter the canyon of the healing water. When I entered the saddle finally, I stood with a heavy heart and viewed the sweeping canyon below. The canyon was dark and ominous as it had been when my mother and I last climbed from its depths. The great fire that had nearly taken my life at the healing water had seemingly made the big canyon a blackened wasteland.

Strangely though, there were places in its blackened bottom where oddly shaped islands of green timber lived, still. The vibrant green color of these unscathed trees stood in blatant defiance to the fire that had burned the twisted and darkened ones that surrounded them. Upon the jutting cliffs that rose steeply from the canyon's sides, stood enormous blackened trees. They broodingly overlooked yet other narrow lines of green that climbed crookedly from the canyon's bottom beneath them.

From the meadows lower in the great chasm, came the soft glow of greenness in the late day's sun, the promise of lush grass whose growth had been spurred by nutrients left behind by the scorching flames.

As I studied the canyon, memories of my horrible fight to survive the raging flames thundered through my mind. The memory that I saw most vividly though, was that of the dark animal that had strode toward me as I had stood at the pond at the fires end. Her words rang clearly in my mind as I studied the green meadows below me.

"The grass here, Tateh, will grow deeper than ever in the next season of *growing grass*," she had said, "and soon, this forest will live again."

With quiet mind, and in the present once more, I dropped into the shadowy canyon before me with renewed strength.

A trail soon became visible as the natural shape of the canyon funneled me to its bottom, and on this trail I walked downward. I had traveled the path several times before, and the meadows were vaguely familiar to me now. Each held a special memory from the past, it seemed. All familiarity was lost, however, as I passed from the openings into thickets of charred and broken trees. Beneath them on the forest floor were black, sinewy tangles that were once berry-laden bushes, destroyed now by the intense blaze that had ravaged the canyon. My passage through the timber was slow as the once familiar trail was often blocked or hidden beneath fallen trees. The path could only be found again after struggling through a maze of blackened downfall to the next meadow's edge.

Aided by abundant rains, lush grass grew along the crooked brown path in the big openings. Unlike the nearly hidden trails through the charred and falling trees, the path through the meadows could easily be seen far ahead as it wound through the grass.

Many different animals had come to the canyon to feed on the deep grass made lush by the fire of the past year. The many tracks in the soft mud of the trail told of their recent passing. Deer and elk had walked on the trail in both directions. A bear with a small one in tow had traveled up the canyon and turned from the trail into one of the burnt thickets. It was in search, perhaps, of a rotten log from which it might dig a feast of grub worms.

As I passed through yet another charred jungle, I came upon a huge, blackened tree that lay across the trail. It blocked the only passage through a large tangle of fallen trees. The giant tree in its burning had leaned precariously over the trail and broken halfway up its massive trunk, the upper half now lay blocking the trail completely. From beneath the great tree's torn root pad, water seeped slowly into the trail making the dark mud there, soft and boggy.

As I considered my predicament, my eyes came to rest on the trail where it disappeared beneath the huge, dark log. To my horror, my eyes focused on the tracks of a large wolf that had passed not long before me on its journey downward in the canyon. The strange story of its tracks in the mud told of a wolf that had struggled to cross the trunk of the old tree. It had then continued down the canyon walking on only three legs. At times, it dragged its injured fourth leg in the mud as it went.

I stood silently in shock, staring at the ominous tracks. Suddenly gone was my feeling of satisfaction at having arrived finally into this canyon of the healing water. I was filled now with only hopelessness.

"Would these silent killers be everywhere I went now?" I wondered aloud.

I stood shaking, wracked with doubt and fear, terrified at the prospect of continuing down the canyon in the direction the big wolf had recently gone. I fought a growing fear within me that I knew if left unchecked, would turn me forever away from the healing water below.

"Oh mother," I whispered…"I wish you were with me still."

A gentle breeze coursed suddenly through the shadowy forest, whispering softly as it passed through the charred limbs of the huge rooted ones around me. The blackened trees creaked softly as they began to rock slowly back and forth. A large, orange butterfly floated silently from the forest and came to rest on a limb near my eyes at the trail's edge. Its wings pumped slowly as it sat facing me.

As I pondered the little insect's strange appearance in this otherwise dead forest, a curious calmness settled over me. The breeze passing gently by, seemed to speak to my soul in an unknown tongue.

I suddenly sensed life all around me. The trees near me stood dead, but now I clearly understood and saw the beauty each had held in life. As my eyes traveled down one tree's twisted and charred trunk to the forest floor beneath, I was amazed to see tiny green shoots starting through the dead pine needles there. Looking back again at the little insect, I suddenly sensed that the forest was not gone. It was merely in a grand transition. The scorched and shattered trees around me would soon complete their lives' journey. They would return to the earth from which they had first come and become the rich, fertile soil from which their own seeds would soon send new life. Their journey…their great cycle, would then be complete…even as yet another cycle for them began.

Suddenly, I clearly understood confusing words spoken to me long ago by the great bull in my dreams.

"When our life's journey is complete," he had said, "We will return to our Mother the Earth from which we came, but our souls, Tateh, will live forever, and we will return."

As I stood in quiet understanding of his words, I considered the amazing examples of death and life so clearly displayed before me in the burned forest. I realized that the great journey of all living things was much the same. There would be no end, only a "grand transition."

The haunting grief and fear that had filled me at the loss of my mother seemed somehow lessened. I understood now that death was not to be dealt with in angst and sorrow. Indeed, death did not exist. Like that which I now saw before me in the charred and twisted forest, my mother and all of my kind would surely live again and again. My anxiety about tracks that told of an enemy's recent passing began to fade. My panicked mind quieted, and my nerves became calm.

Above the tranquil voice of the forest, I heard my mother's words echo softly once again, "Tateh, there are no enemies here. We are all one."

A wonderful energy surged through me then, and I knew I must go on. With all my might, I jumped and pulled myself painfully over the big tree that lay before me in the trail. With the little butterfly bouncing in the air above me, I somehow felt even closer to my mother as I continued on.

The remainder of my journey through the meadows and thickets of the big canyon was uneventful, and I saw no more of the big wolf's tracks. As I pondered the understanding that had grown within me at the fallen tree, I realized I carried within me now a new strength nurtured by a sense of knowing.

The sun was gone from the sky and only a ruddy glow remained above the mountains to mark the place of its passing when to my nose came the acrid smell of the healing water. I knew that the big meadow lay close below me and with a quickened stride, I soon entered its upper end. The opening was lush and green, rimmed by a blackened forest as all the meadows above had been. Steam rose from the unseen healing water near its lower end, and at its far edge, the great trees under which my mother and I had so often lain, stood twisted and burnt.

My heart pounded as I started toward the pond. I knew my mother no longer walked this land, but as I approached the darkened trees where we had so often bedded, I thrust my nose to the grass and in vain tried to detect her fresh scent there. Though I knew exactly the spot where I had rested so many times against her warm body, the new, green grass that had grown beneath the charred trees now hid any sign of our old bed. Choking down waves of growing loneliness, I turned and strode quickly toward the steaming water.

The pond was exactly as it had been when my mother and I were last here. At its upper end still lay the wonderful, yellow mud. Deep water steamed invitingly at the other. I stood near the edge of the yellow mud in the fading light, seeing plainly in my mind the cow elk who had just led her new calf to the steaming water. As the wide-eyed calf looked on in bewilderment, I saw its proud mother walk confidently into the mud, where she plopped down into the yellow ooze, rolling and kicking with abandon.

Blinking the memory from my eyes, I walked with great anticipation into the soft mud and lay stiffly in the yellow mire. Its warmth felt amazing, and I could feel its healing sinking deeply into my body.

Remembering my mother, I rolled back and forth in the sticky stuff, picturing her as I rolled. I rose stiffly and walked deeper into the pond where I submerged myself in the hot water and lay with only my head above the surface. I soaked in the pond's healing warmth as darkness gripped the meadow around me and slowly plunged all into blackness.

As I breathed the pungent odor of the hot water and peered into the darkness of the meadow around me, the memory of the horrible fire swept over me. I could see again the yellow flames as they twisted and leaped from the tops of the trees around me. I remembered standing in the pond with only my head above the water listening to the deafening roar of the fire as it consumed all in its path.

Forcing the haunting memories back again into the past, I focused once more on the present. I watched from my watery bed as the moon rose slowly into the sky, chasing the darkness from the meadow around me. Though it was no longer fully round, its light enabled me to plainly see the crooked, reaching branches of the towering trees at the far end of the meadow. I lay in the heat of the curing water far into the night, focused idly on the sights, sounds, and smells of all that was now my canyon home.

I considered the burned forest that stood around me in the canyon's bottom. I wondered how old the huge trees were and how long it would be until trees like them stood here again. I thought of the unimaginable age of the huge boulders that had long ago thundered from high on the mountains to sit at the trail's edge. I wondered about the age of the great cliffs that stood looming in the blue moonlight on the canyon's side.

As I looked toward the meadow's edge, I realized that my life's journey would be complete long before green trees stood there again as they once had. And the great rocks that peered from the blackened forest around me would stand as they did now long after my life's end. Mildly surprised by my realization, I thought again about the great cycle that was now playing out in the forest around me and understood more clearly my place in that circle. I felt humbled as I understood the smallness of my being. I was strangely comforted and grounded as I realized the insignificant duration of my problems and even my life in comparison to the age of these natural wonders around me, wonders to which I now felt even more closely related.

The challenges of my day's journey and the warm water of the pond brought a deep fatigue over me. I rose from the healing water and walked to the spot beneath the trees that had always been my bed. I lowered myself gratefully to the grass and looked about the meadow with the tired satisfaction of one who had completed a long, difficult journey.

Lowering my head slowly to the grass, I remembered again the words of the great bull. 'We will return to the earth when our life's journey is done, but our souls will live forever, and one day we will return.'

My thoughts turned then to my mother, and to the little butterfly that had landed at the trail's edge near me. As I felt once again the peacefulness that had settled over me then, I watched in my mind, the gentle pumping of its wings as I drifted into slumber.

Chapter Fifteen

It was good for me to be at the healing water again. I stood from my sleep long before the skies began to lighten. I grazed slowly through the meadow as the first streaks of light appeared in the sky above. The grass in the meadow was covered with a light coat of dew, and only the thought of the warm water in the pond pulled me finally, from it.

Arriving at the pond, I first rolled in the mud, and then as the first gleaming rays of sun spilled over the canyon wall, I stepped into the water and moved slowly toward the deep end of the pond. The water swirled around me as I moved slowly forward, and I was certain I could feel the pond's healing begin within me. I soaked until the sun was nearly overhead, then stepped from the water and resumed my feeding in the grass around the pond. I grazed slowly toward the trees at the edge of the meadow and upon reaching them, I lowered myself to the earth where I lay nearly hidden in the tall grass.

The breeze flowed slowly across the meadow, bringing to my nose the smell of the countless flowers there. The sun's warmth seemed nearly as healing as did the water in the pond. Little winged ones flitted overhead from the forest to the meadow and back again, calling cheerfully to one another as they fed. The sky was as clear and blue as I had ever remembered it to be.

It was now the season of *growing grass,* and all living things here embraced life with great energy, be they animal or rooted one. I rested in the grass until the light began to soften as the sun made its way toward the far horizon. I walked slowly to the water then, where I soaked until well after darkness filled the meadow. This sequence I continued for many days while both my legs and my heart healed from the wounds inflicted upon me in the wintering place at the fangs of wolf.

Often after soaking in the warm water, I would climb once more on the familiar trails worn into the steep canyon's sides during countless trips to the top made by my mother and me. My climbs were slow at first, but I rapidly gained strength, and before long, I was able to run without stopping to the top of the canyon wall. Soon, I climbed the steep canyon's side without benefit of the trail. I was able to leap over large fallen trees in nearly impassable stands of timber as I made my way to the top. I would return after my exhausting climb to soak in the healing water and wash away the ash that had accumulated on my coat.

Other animals also came to the healing water but always in the darkness of night. Often as I slept in my grassy bed at the edge of the meadow, I would be awakened by the splashing of another as they sought healing in the warm water of the pond.

On some nights, after the challenging climb up the canyon's side, I would stay and feed in small grassy openings near the top. I would lie there in the tall grass and enjoy the sweeping view of the canyon as darkness came, then return to the pond in the grayness of early morning to soak.

Time was passing quickly, and the moon had again grown strong. It had now become the season of *ripening berries*. One night, I lay on a small point of rocks a short distance above the big meadow, reveling in the beauty of the silver-blue moonlight as it splashed across the canyon below me.

Suddenly, I heard the soft breaking of limbs below me at the meadow's edge and saw the dark form of an immense bull elk step from the timber near the pond. Its huge, newly grown antlers turned slowly in the moonlight as it quietly studied the meadow. Lowering its head, the bull walked to the pond, sniffing deeply at the grass as it went. It entered the pond and rolled in the yellow mud at its upper end. A short while later, it rose nimbly from the ooze, shook, and disappeared again into the darkness of the forest.

"Ksapa," I whispered to myself.

As I stared at the meadow and vacant pond, I wondered at the strange appearance of this wise one here at the healing water, as he had been earlier at the pond in the canyon of my safe place.

The next morning dawned gray and dismal with rain that fell steadily from dark clouds. Fog hid the canyon below me from view. I stood from my bed and walked slowly down the steep canyon's side toward the meadow, slipping and sliding in the wet mud as I went. I entered the foggy meadow where I fed on wet grass as I grazed slowly toward the pond, hidden in the mist at its far end.

The pond's surface was dappled by falling rain drops as I entered the steaming water. I stood soaking, lost in thought, as I beheld the mysterious world of blackened trees around me that were hidden at times by swirling fog.

Suddenly to my nose came a strangely familiar scent. It brought instantly to my mind again the agonizing scene of my herd as they were killed in the blizzard at the winter range. Whirling in fright toward the far end of the pond, I saw, at the water's edge, a huge black wolf. His scent was that of the huge one who had led the pack of killers in the winter range.

The big wolf stood with its head lowered, glaring at me through yellow eyes that held no emotion. Its mouth was slightly agape, its pink tongue moving slowly between rows of white teeth as it panted quietly. On its head were recent wounds where no hair grew. It stood on three legs, holding one carefully above the ground. As we stared in silence at one another, I slowly realized that the injuries the huge wolf now bore were very probably ones it received beneath the flailing hooves of my mother as she fought to her death in the winter range.

As I stared from the water at the huge one, the terrible fear that clutched at my heart was suddenly gone, replaced by a smoldering anger that grew there.

I heard my mother's voice say softly from the mist around me, "We come here only to heal, Tateh. At this place, we are all one."

But the agonizing rage that consumed me now would not let my heart hear these words. I splashed angrily from the water but stopped as I stepped onto the muddy bank, and I turned to face the wolf.

"One whose life you took taught me that we here at the healing water are all as one," I said as I stared into the sullen eyes of the wolf. "But with you, big one, I will never be as one. I will not share these waters with the murderous one who has dealt such terrible pain to me and my kind, and who walks his journey in life as you walk yours."

I turned and started into the meadow, but the rage pounding in my head stopped me, and I turned slowly back toward the wolf. Our eyes locked for a moment, and I felt the coldness and hate in the big one's stare.

"We will meet again, black one," I promised in a quiet voice. Lightning flashed brightly in the clouds above, and a thunderous boom filled the canyon as I turned and walked angrily away from the pond.

I continued through the meadow to its upper end where I stopped briefly and looked back toward the healing water, hidden now in the swirling mist below me.

"I am sorry, Mother," I whispered. "Would you have me share the healing water with one as ruthless as that one? One who was there to heal from wounds inflicted by you as you fought to your death? So long as he lives, I will never be one with that creature who has taken so much from me," I vowed.

I turned and climbed angrily upward in steady rain through meadows and thickets, racked with guilt and sadness at having for the first time in my life disobeyed my mother.

Late in the day, the rain stopped, and the sun shone weakly between dark clouds before sinking slowly from view behind the canyon wall. I walked steadily upward as darkness engulfed the canyon, driven onward by numbing grief and angry emotions that boiled within me. The moon climbed above the mountains and shone between ragged clouds as I neared the big bowl that lay at the head of the canyon. Soon I stood at the edge of the big basin, staring once again at its wondrous expanse.

The grass here had grown tall since my last passing. It gently brushed my belly and legs as I stood quietly with my nose held high, testing the breeze of the huge opening before me. Flowers stood everywhere in the moonlight, peeking from shadows in the deep grass. The combined aroma of the myriad rooted ones filled my senses, and for a moment, I forgot the anger and sadness that had been suddenly thrust upon me at the healing waters. I looked back at the canyon from which I had just come, and the terrible anger and frustration welled again within me.

Driven by a terrible energy fueled by anger, I burst forward into the basin. Confused and filled with hostility, I crashed across the basin in search of that place where the anger would not exist. I thought about the cows and calves of the great herd as I moved aimlessly through the basin. I heard in my mind their terrible cries as the pack of wolves, led by the one now at the healing water, pulled them to the snow. And I thought about my mother who had fought so valiantly beside her sisters against the black one.

'How could I ever, ever be *one,* with such an animal as wolf?' I wondered as I plodded angrily on.

Daylight found me panting and nearly exhausted, standing on a tall bluff overlooking a steep canyon on the far side of the basin. My wrathful, self-imposed trek upward from the healing water and across the great basin had dulled my anger and frustration. Now only a deep loneliness remained. I turned from the bluff and walked onward in the basin until I crossed a small creek. I satisfied the thirst that had grown in me over the last day and night, then, walked up a small hill and lay beneath the trees that grew on its top. The warming sunlight and gentle breeze did little to appease the emotions that still boiled deeply within me.

I lay unmoving for most of the day, trying to quiet my mind and erase the terrible images of darting wolves in snowy darkness. The scene most vividly playing across my mind though, was the black one glaring at me defiantly from the water's edge. I arose, tormented and angry, as the sun sank beneath the great basin's edge, and walked in fading light toward the spot on the horizon where the great orb had disappeared. When at last the sky brightened and a new day began, I stood at the top of the big ridge down which my mother and I had walked during the past *season of renewal.* My heart told me to go there again, to look, and to see.

But for what, I did not know. As I stood quietly studying the familiar hills far below, my mother's words of warning came to me once again.

"We come to these low hills, Tateh, only when we are forced from the mountains by the deep snows of renewal. During all other seasons we stay as high in our mountains as possible. In these low hills, the two-legged ones are too close," she had cautioned.

"Yes, mother, you are right," I said quietly to myself, and with a sigh of resignation, I sank to the grass near a large rock.

As I gazed downward at the distant wintering ground, I wondered, 'if not here, then where must I go to quiet the anguished voices of my herd and silence the shrieking howls that rang with terrible clarity still, in my mind?'

I lay quietly looking downward as the sun sank and darkness consumed the hills below me. Again, and again, I thought about the great herd and my mother. The image that burned most clearly in my mind, though, was that of the sinister black one now far behind me at the healing water. Our confrontation had ignited these painful feelings that now consumed me.

As the moon rose above the basin behind me, the glowering image of the black wolf loomed again in my mind. I sprang from my bed with emotions tearing at my heart, and whispered into the darkness, "But I must go, mother." I turned, then, and started downward.

As I moved quickly lower the ridge, I remembered my previous journey with my mother. Though it was only in the past *season of renewal,* it now seemed a long time ago. I remembered the excitement I had felt as my mother showed me this new place and the joy that had grown within me at the thoughts of joining the herd again, and seeing my young spotted friends.

After having wandered aimlessly for days in the basin behind me, I walked downward with purpose now, having chosen finally, that destination that I somehow knew would quiet my mind.

As the sun began to climb into the sky behind me, I stood in the place where my mother and I had stood when she first showed me the elk of our great herd. The hills were vacant now, and the grass on these treeless slopes was already a golden yellow color. The many wildflowers that had grown here earlier were shriveled and had gone to seed. In the vast blue sky above, a great winged one soared in long, lazy arcs, but raven and magpie were nowhere to be seen.

Small winged ones flew from the grass around me, scolding excitedly as I started downward again. 'They are the only animals here now,' I thought as they landed and disappeared in the grass at my sides.

Soon I stood on the broad, open hill where the cows and calves of our herd had excitedly gathered around my mother and me upon our arrival. It was the place where I had become reacquainted with my many calf friends. Though I knew I was alone now, my memories were so vivid that it seemed I could hear the happy banter of my spotted friends as we ran through the herd that day.

I walked slowly along the ridgeline at the top of the hills looking carefully about. Familiar voices and sounds rang constantly in my mind as I went. The memories somehow drew me close to my mother and the herd, and it was good to be here again, in this place where I had last walked with them.

I moved slowly across the top of a rock-strewn hill and down into a small ravine whose bottom was choked with trees, then up its other side to the top of yet another open hill. Below me, the hill fell away steeply into yet another small canyon. It was the place, I realized, where Khiza had triggered the snow slide that had nearly killed me and the other calves.

The day passed quickly as I worked carefully along the familiar ridge from hill to hill and crossed through the rocky, overgrown draws that separated them.

As I crossed quietly through a thick finger of timber that separated two large hills, I realized that it was the place where my mother had led me and the herd to shelter during the freezing blizzard that had sprung so suddenly upon us. I stood quietly for a moment as I relived the memory of the terrible howling winds and stinging cold.

"Let the snow cover you deeply, Tateh," I plainly heard my mother say as I walked past the large rock in front of which we had taken refuge during the long storm. As I continued slowly forward, I began to come upon places where many bones lay scattered beneath the trees on the forest floor. These were, I knew, the remains of the cows and calves that had not risen from beneath the snow when the storm had ended.

I stopped and stood solemnly still for a moment when the skeleton of a cow with a calf in front, came into view. Their bleached white skulls lay nearly side by side, staring downward at me as I moved on.

The woods around me were curiously silent. I could hear no squirrels, and even the voices of small winged ones were not present. The only companions that shared my lonely vigil were beautiful, orange butterflies that rose from the grass as if to greet me, then swirled excitedly in the air around me as I moved quietly on.

With a sigh of relief, I walked from the sad forest where so many in our herd had died, then climbed upward onto the sunny face of yet another hill. Looking back at the grim, timber-filled draw, I recalled the look of sadness in my mother's eyes as she led us from those trees after the terrible storm.

As I studied the grassy knob and timber around me, I remembered the great number of us who had walked and fed here, and it seemed impossible that I was alone now.

In the distance, only one more draw yet to cross, was the long, broad hill upon which we fed when the last storm of the season had forced us to the shelter of the trees. In that horrible forest, I knew, was the place where the wolves had attacked us. Filled with dread, I forced myself downward into the draw and climbed slowly to the top of the grassy ridge beyond.

I stood in silence looking across the huge valley, remembering the strange, dark clouds that had crept over the mountains there. I could easily see again the look of concern in my mother's eyes as she led us to shelter on the far side of this hill. The terrible cold and deep snow of that storm seemed impossible now as I stood beneath the sun with deep, yellow grass swaying gently before me in the breeze.

Suddenly from behind a stand of small trees below me, stepped two of the two-legged ones about which my mother had ominously warned. They saw me and immediately began chattering excitedly to one another. Curiously, they then did as the ones had done long ago. They each faced me and held their arms extended toward me, then slowly withdrew them until they were touching their chests. They then sat and quietly watched me. They seemed to pose no threat and remained sitting quietly as I moved nervously away from them along the broad ridge's top.

I stood finally at the ridge's far end. In the distance, in the bottom of the gentle canyon that lay beyond the ridge, I could see the fence that had held me fast in its cutting grip. The place where my mother had so valiantly fought the wolves as I escaped. Below me on the ridge's flank was the timber in which our great herd had lain beneath the snow, struggling to survive the treacherous storm when the wolves attacked us.

Nearly unable to force myself forward, but knowing I must, I started slowly downward with sadness ripping at my heart. I willed myself onward through the trees where we had taken shelter from the blizzard, then, continued slowly toward the small opening in which my herd had made their brave stand against the wolves.

With my heart pounding and emotions raging within me, I stopped at the meadow's edge. The opening and surrounding forest looked exactly as it had then. I stood quietly trembling as again I heard the anguished cries of my dying herd echo through the trees of the now silent forest. As I peered from the trees, I relived the haunting vision of the brave cows of my herd fighting in the snowy darkness. I saw again, their heaving forms in the swirling snow as they lunged and struck, fighting the darting wolves with all they had. I cringed as I heard my mother's voice echo through the trees, "dig deep, sisters! We will beat these demons!"

Barren, white bones were scattered everywhere beneath the trees and in the grass of the small meadow. They lay in solemn testimony to the horrifying fight for survival that had taken place here. As the hills behind me had been, the forest here was deserted also. No animals, large or small, could be seen or heard scurrying through the trees. The horrible sadness here, it seemed, had caused all but the persistent butterflies in the air around me to move on.

Below me through the trees, I could see the gentle canyon down which I had run toward the frightful fence, my mother fighting the wolves behind me as she followed. I had never before felt such loneliness, and with grief clutching at my throat, I forced myself slowly downward toward the ominous canyon below. The stark, white skulls of the brave cows and those of my calf friends, peered from the grass around me as I walked cautiously past them and entered the gentle draw.

With growing angst, I pressed slowly upward toward the fence beyond. The sounds of the attack seemed to echo from everywhere around me.

Suddenly, from behind me I heard the terrible sound of my mother's desperate fight, and then her frantic cries… "run, Tateh, run!"

I wheeled and stood trembling as I stared frantically into the shadowy draw behind me, but the voices were gone. I was alone. Gathering myself, I turned and continued slowly upward.

The sun sat just above the horizon as I stood before the grim specter of the fence. Quivering, unable to move, I stared through unblinking eyes at the terrible apparition before me. Wire still ran between all posts but two, where the wire had been broken and was now curled back and away. Its tangled ends disappeared into the deep grass at their sides.

In places on the wire's thorny barbs, small strips of tan hide still clung. With sadness tearing at my heart, I walked tentatively forward and lowered my nose to them.

I closed my eyes and drew deeply at the faint scent of my mother that each still held. The sadness that sprang from within me was overwhelming.

Though I could see no bones or other visible signs that told of the outcome of the violent struggle that had taken place here, a calm knowing settled slowly over me. I was certain, at last, that life had ended here for my mother. Her journey, I knew, was indeed over.

"Thank you, Mother, for my life," I whispered softly.

From behind me, I heard a deep voice say softly, "Yes, Tateh, this is where your brave mother's life ended."

Whirling with fright, I stood face-to-face with a huge bull elk.

"Ksapa," I whispered breathlessly, my heart pounding in my ears.

"Yes, Tateh, I am Ksapa," the enormous bull said. "I have walked with you and watched over you carefully since the murderous attack by the wolves happened here at the wintering spot."

"But how did you know of the wolves' attack, and why have you followed me?" I asked wide-eyed, my heart still pounding in my throat.

"Your father, Tateh," said Ksapa, "was my lifelong friend. When the wolves attacked your herd in the raging storm during the past *season of renewal*, I was bedded far above on a ridge in the protection of thick trees. As I slept that night buried deeply beneath the snow, Woslolkia suddenly entered my dream world.

" My great friend led me through the darkness to a place where far below, I could hear the frenzied howling of wolves and the anguished voices of your herd as the attack ensued. There were no words spoken by the great bull, but in Woslolkia's eyes I saw a terrible sadness. I awoke from the vision and leaped from beneath the snow listening carefully for the terrible sounds that had filled my dream. Though I could hear nothing in the driving wind, I was certain that the appearance of Woslolkia had not been merely a dream. I plowed through the deep snow of the trees and onto the face of the big ridge. I then moved swiftly downward in the blizzard toward the wintering ground.

"Strangely," Ksapa continued, "I soon stood in the place above the wintering ground where in my dream, I had stood with Woslolkia. As it had been in my vision, I now clearly heard the horrific sounds of the wolf attack below me. I crashed downward to the place in the trees where the cows had formed their defensive circle, but I was too late. The wolves had finished their gruesome work there.

"I then heard your mother's cries as she fought the wolves at the fence in the canyon below. As I moved swiftly through the trees toward your brave mother, I saw the wolves as they darted and slashed at her as she fought. I saw her rise onto her back legs and come crashing down with her hooves, striking the black leader solidly, rolling him limply across the snow.

"The attack stopped for a moment, Tateh," Ksapa continued, "as the other wolves stood in confusion, their leader lying motionless before them. The black one though, struggled to his feet and the horrible attack resumed.

"I charged into the canyon toward the horrible fight, but your mother had given all she had, and could fight no more, Tateh. It was over before I could reach her. As I watched, the black one struggled through the snow as he led his howling pack into the trees amidst a terrifying chorus of screams, the likes of which I have never before heard.

"I had crossed the tracks of a wounded calf as I rushed down the big ridge toward your embattled herd. It had somehow escaped the wolves. The young one had crossed the ridge and entered the timber on its far side. Having been too late to help the elk in your herd, I returned quickly to these tracks. For four days I stood guard on them to ensure no wolves followed.

"I did not know that these tracks were yours, Tateh, until I followed you to the pond in the canyon of your birth where I saw you at the water's edge. I knew then, that you were the brave bull calf of Wakhita and my lifelong friend, Woslolkia.

"I promised my old friend then, that I would watch over you and teach you as you grew to be the leader all elk here know you will someday be."

"You… You saw my mother die, Ksapa?" I asked quietly.

"Yes, Tateh, I did," answered Ksapa. "Due to the injuries inflicted on the black leader by your mother, he did not send his pack to follow her calf. Instead the wolves followed their wounded leader into the canyon below."

"And you guarded my trail so that no wolves would follow?" I asked incredulously.

"Yes, Tateh," said Ksapa. "Then I followed you to make certain you were safe but left you alone to decide for yourself what path you would choose to walk."

"Ksapa," I said sadly, "though I am but a calf, I feel the weariness of one much older than I. I do not understand the misery dealt by animals such as the wolves on the lives of ones like my mother and the others in our herd."

Ksapa listened quietly, then said finally, "Tateh, here in our mountains, that which is known as the Great Mystery works in ways often not understood by us as we endure these hardships. It is hard to understand, Tateh, but like the grouse crouched hiding in the deep grass of our meadows, *gifts* are sometimes concealed in tragedy."

"Gifts?" I asked in disbelief. "Ksapa, how can killing and misery be a gift?"

"Nothing in our world, Tateh, happens without reason," said Ksapa. "The reason is not always known in our mortal lifetime, but the time will come when you will surely know.

"Hidden in the terrible sorrow of your loss is the greatest of all gifts given by our Creator, Tateh, the gift of *knowing*. Knowing, comes only through experience," continued Ksapa. "To your mother, this knowing came as she experienced her ultimate act of love, the giving of her life without hesitation so that you could live yours. She *knew* then, the strength of her own truth. Your gift, Tateh, was to experience the proof of your mother's pure and honest love, her giving for you, all she had to give. Forever, you will carry this most precious of gifts in your heart. You will come one day, to understand that a love so profound is a gift that could only come from a greater power."

"It is easy, Tateh," continued Ksapa, "to walk one's truth in times of goodness. It is in the gift of great hardship such as the one faced by you and your mother, when one truly comes to know the strength of their truth."

I stood blinking, looking first at the broken fence where my mother had died, then back to the knowing eyes of Ksapa. I struggled to hold the meaning of his words, for I somehow knew that in my understanding of what he had said, I would find closure at last.

Again, Woslolkia's words came to me, "It is in the journey, Tateh, not in the destination, that you will find joy."

I knew then that the walking of her truth had indeed been her journey, and in having walked it with such great love, she had known joy.

"Come, Tateh," said Ksapa, "the two-legged ones have drawn close. We must go."

The big bull looked at me for a long moment, then turned and started from the draw.

A golden butterfly floated silently around me as I started upward behind Ksapa. Further up the hill, I stopped for a moment and looked back. The fence stood in the golden grass, outlined boldly now, before the setting sun.

"Yes, with firm steps, mother," I promised softly, as I turned and followed Kasapa over the hill.

The little butterfly, now far behind in the draw, circled excitedly in the breeze above the fence for a bit, then landed on a large, white skull that lay hidden in the deep grass near the broken fence. It sat pumping its wings slowly as the young calf followed the big bull from view.

Chapter Sixteen

For a long time Ksapa and I climbed without talking as we moved steadily away from the draw and the sad memories there. A feeling of well-being settled over me as I followed the huge one upward in failing light. As I listened to the rhythmic clicking of our hooves in the rocky grass as we went, my thoughts returned to my mother and the others in my herd. I thought also of the black one who had so ruthlessly taken their lives in the quiet draw behind us.

"It was Kasota," said Ksapa quietly, breaking the silence and pulling me from the deep thought into which I had fallen.

"The black one's name, Tateh, is *Kasota*. In the language of the first two-legged ones who lived here, Kasota meant, *to kill*. Our kind gave him that name long ago when it became known that even as a young wolf, he often killed without reason, not for survival as most wolves do.

"Kasota grew to be cunning and treacherous," continued Ksapa, "and he became as wrathful and heartless as any leader our kind has ever known. He has ruled the wolves here in our mountains for many years. With unfaltering resolve, he and his huge pack have pursued our herds. The other wolves follow him without question, for to do otherwise would mean a brutal death for them."

As we climbed the ridge in silence, my thoughts remained on the cruel leader of the wolves. Anger seethed within me as in my mind I stood glaring again into his eyes at the healing water.

"We will meet again, black one," I whispered into the darkness, reaffirming my earlier promise to him.

Ahead of me on the ridge I could see Ksapa's enormous silhouette outlined in the glowing horizon. Calmness settled over me again as I watched his antlers swaying rhythmically side to side as we walked.

"Ksapa," I asked, breaking the silence at last, "did any of the members of my herd survive the wolf attack?"

"Yes, Tateh," answered Ksapa. "When the brave cows gave up their fight at last and their defensive circle collapsed, they ran blinded with panic in all directions through the forest. Their numbers were so great that the wolves, crazed by their horrible killing frenzy, were temporarily confused and could not pursue them all. Then, after nearly being killed beneath the lashing hooves of your mother, the black one, wounded and barely able to walk, ended the attack."

Walking silently behind Ksapa once more, I wondered about my calf friends and Wicala. How I hoped that they lived.

We stopped on a small point of rock that protruded from the face of the ridge and turned back toward the rolling hills of the winter range. We stood in silence looking at the broad ribbon of light that shimmered above the far horizon where the sun had long ago disappeared.

"Ksapa," I said, in little more than a whisper, "I should not have left my mother to fight the wolves alone at the fence. Had I chosen to stay, she might be walking with me now."

After a long silence, Ksapa turned to me, his antlers towering on the horizon behind him, and said, "Tateh, though you are a calf still, there are none in our mountains who question your courage. I have long known of the attack of the great silver one on the calves of your herd. It is well known by all of our kind, Tateh, that after having reached safety, you returned to face the great bear and saved the life of your friend Wicala. With wonder they talk of the jagged scar you carry on your shoulder from the huge claws of the silver bear.

"And a story is now told of this young bull calf," he continued, "that during the terrible wolf attack on the great herd, the young one attacked the black leader's mate, again, to save another. In the great confusion caused by your attack, Tateh, many in your herd were able to escape.

"But for your mother," he continued, "it could not be that way. For her, there was no escape. She chose to stand and fight the wolves so that you would live. You have honored your mother greatly, Tateh, by obeying her desperate pleas made as she fought, and because you did, you are here with me now. That the brave bull calf that stands before me is the son of my incredible friend Woslolkia, is to me, no surprise."

Ksapa held my stare for a long moment, then turned and continued upward in the darkness.

Climbing the ridge behind him, I felt a great weight had been lifted from me, and I felt a deep pride in having been called, the son of Woslolkia. My steps up the steep ridge were lighter now as we continued into the night.

Far above the valley and the rolling hills of the winter range, Ksapa stopped on a small bluff that overlooked the valley and stood thinking.

"Woslolkia was my lifelong friend, Tateh," he said softly, breaking the silence at last. "We grew and walked as one, from the time we were calves. It seemed even then, Tateh, that it was me and him against the others when the calves of our herd played our games of life.

"For many years," he continued, "we grew fat in the grassy basins during the time of *growing grass*. Together we survived the brutal storms of the *season of renewal* in secret places near the canyon of the yellow rocks. We were apart only during the season of mating. We would have given our lives, I know, for one another, Tateh." Turning slowly then, he continued, "I miss him greatly, but I know he is still here. He walks with me often in my dreams."

Ksapa lay in the grass then, his looming body outlined by a yellow crescent of moon that had risen above the mountain behind us. I lowered myself to the grass near the big bull, and together we gazed over the valley below. I was deep in thought about my future, while Ksapa, I was sure, was lost in his journeys of the past.

The day had been a trying one for me, filled with emotional turmoil. The closure I had found at last, and the companionship of the bull who lay beside me in the darkness, made sleep come easily this night, and I slept with my head in the grass dreaming peacefully.

As the night slowly passed, my dreams became troubled and were soon filled with bursts of flickering light and booming thunder. Suddenly, in the flashing light, stood my father, Woslolkia. He stood silently looking at me through eyes filled with knowing.

"Walk with me, Tateh," the great bull said quietly, as he turned and strode into the darkness.

Suddenly we were on the rolling hills of the winter range, looking into the broad valley that lay beneath them. Below us on the hillside, I could see a small bull calf as it made its way carefully along. The calf that I watched was me.

Abruptly, from the trees below the calf walked a pair of two-legged ones, as I had seen them do earlier in this day. Again, they were very excited when they saw the young calf on the hillside above them and chattered happily once more. Then, as they had done before, they extended their arms toward the calf and retracted them slowly. Holding their hands over their hearts, they sat cross-legged on the ground and quietly watched him.

Woslolkia stood beside me watching the dark-skinned ones in silence.

"Woslolkia, why are those two-legged ones so pleased?" I asked, as we watched the bull calf continue across the hill away from them.

"When the two-legged ones first saw you long ago with your mother in the winter range, he said, they knew you were a sacred animal sent to them by the mysterious power of *all that is*." These dark-skinned ones found the remains of your slaughtered herd earlier in the season of *ducks returning*, Tateh. They were certain, though, that the young one who wore the sign of the mighty Wakia would not perish. They are now elated to know that their sacred bull calf has survived the wolves."

Woslolkia turned back toward them then, and together we watched silently as the young bull calf walked from sight.

My head shot from the grass as a crackling flash of light shot across the sky, followed by a crashing roar that shook the earth upon which I lay. Woslolkia was gone, and I rested in darkness once more on the rocky bluff as I relived the strange journey that I had just walked with him.

The storm that now battered the ridge around me had approached as I slept. For the remainder of the night, I lay deep in thought beside Ksapa and watched in pouring rain as fire filled the sky.

The storm passed as quickly as it had begun, and as a soft glow began to build in the sky above the mountains behind us, we started upward toward the great basin once more. As we climbed the ridge in the early grayness of this new day, the scent of all that grew on the ridge around us was incredible. The cool mountain air brought to my nose the wonderful smells of the earth, redoubled now by the steady rain of the past night.

The brightness on the horizon built slowly into a fiery red glow, as the sun, below the mountain still, shone through the retreating clouds of the storm. My thoughts returned to my strange dream of the past night as we moved upward, slipping and sliding on the rain-soaked ridge. I thought again about the two-legged ones and about the strange relationship Woslolkia had said I shared with them.

"Yes, Tateh," said Ksapa, suddenly breaking the silence, "I too, was grateful to walk once more with my friend, Woslolkia, last night."

Bewildered by his ability to somehow know my thoughts and wondering about his past night's journey with Woslolkia, I walked in curious silence behind the big bull.

The sun moved overhead and hung at last near the horizon behind us. As the day ended, we stood in softening light at the top of the big ridge, gazing quietly into the great basin that lay before us. The grass in the basin was still green, and we grazed slowly through it toward a small pond as the sun sank from view. Peering contentedly into the blackness around us as we listened to the sounds of the night, we rested in the grass near the pond as darkness overtook the land.

I wondered about this great bull that lay beside me in the darkness, the lifelong friend of Woslolkia. I marveled at the many years he had known my father, and I wondered about the remarkable things that they had seen and done on their journey together in our mountains. I was thankful for his companionship and for the well-being I felt in his presence. I knew though, that Ksapa, like the rest of the big bulls, would soon go to that secret place in the mountains where ones such as he, stay, as they prepare for the coming season of mating. I wondered where I would go then.

"Young bulls leave the herd, Tateh, at different ages," said Ksapa, in answer to my thoughts. "Some stay with the safety of the herd for several years," he continued, "while others strike out at a young age. They wander with other bulls as they grow and learn those aspects about themselves that will define their lives and their roles of leadership in the great elk herds here.

"What are your wishes, Tateh? Where is it you feel you belong?" asked Ksapa.

"Ksapa," I said softly, "I know now that my mother is gone, but I miss the security we knew with the great herd, and I miss my friends there. I long greatly to be with them once more."

"We will find them, Tateh," whispered Ksapa.

He lowered his head to the grass, and with a quiet sigh, said no more. I lay for a long time thinking about the cows and calves of my herd. A wonderful weariness descended upon me as I thought, and soon in my dreams, I was with the herd again.

Happiness filled me as I watched frolicking calves buck and jump and run recklessly between their feeding mothers as they burned the boundless energy within them. But these calves were ones I did not know, and strangely, I did not join their play. I stood alone at the edge of the herd and watched in silence. I awoke then, wondering curiously about the cows and calves in my dream.

'Had I become too old to play,' I wondered? 'Was it now my journey to wander only with the bulls?'

But as I thought about the great herd and my friends once more, I became even more excited at the prospect of finding them.

The day dawned at last, clear and bright, and after feeding in the deep grass and drinking at the little pond, we started along the basin's edge in search of the great herd. As we moved along, Ksapa stopped often at the tops of deep canyons that fell from the huge basin's side. Here, he stood quietly as he tested the wind for their scent and listened carefully for any sound that would tell of their presence feeding somewhere below.

As we stood in fading light above one broad canyon studying the many basins and meadows that lay in its bottom, we suddenly heard the unmistakable sound of cows and calves calling to one another. My heartbeat quickened as Ksapa and I looked at one another knowingly, then looked back toward the source of the sound in the canyon below.

We dropped quickly into the canyon, and after passing through a wide band of trees, entered a meadow where cows and calves stood grazing everywhere. A single bark of alarm echoed suddenly through the meadow as the leader of the herd saw us walk from the timber. All movement in the herd stopped as they stood frozen, ears pressed forward and noses to the wind. Cows and calves alike studied the huge bull and calf that now strode toward them.

As we drew closer to the cows, their eyes grew wide as they recognized the huge bull walking toward them with the small, bull calf behind. The cows and calves surrounded Ksapa, excitedly barking and mewing their greeting, but they became suddenly silent as they saw the jagged scar on the shoulder of the calf that stood at his side. After a long silence, one large cow spoke finally.

"Ksapa, wise one," she said, "it is good to see you. Little one," she said, turning now to me, "it is hard to express the sadness that all here carry in our hearts for the loss of your mother, our brave leader, Wakhita. But now, at this moment, I cannot easily tell you of the happiness that fills our hearts, knowing that her brave son, the bull calf known as Tateh, still lives. Because of the courage shown by your mother and you during the attack of the wolves in the winter range, many here live still. They owe their lives, Tateh, to you and your mother."

Turning again to Ksapa, the old cow said, "We are honored to have you and Tateh, in our herd."

I looked slowly at the cows around us and at their tiny spotted calves that peered nervously from beneath them. I felt once again the incredible oneness that I had known before with the herd.

A small cow stepped from the herd then, and I stared in disbelief as our eyes met.

Wicala had survived the attack of the wolves! I had not felt such joy since the return of my mother at the safe place long ago. Other small elk stepped from the herd then. They were no longer spotted as they had once been, but I recognized each one immediately as they came forward to greet me. My elation at being in their midst again was indescribable.

The cows and calves that had gathered around Ksapa and me slowly began to disperse as darkness gathered, and soon we stood alone, facing each other in silence. I stared for a long moment into his questioning eyes, then turned my head toward Wicala, who stood quietly near me at the edge of the meadow. Turning back to Ksapa, I held his steady gaze for a moment longer. Having understood my unspoken words, he turned with a deep sigh of finality and walked into the darkness.

I bedded near Wicala that night at the edge of the meadow, totally immersed in the feeling of happiness at being with the great herd once more. I lay awake far into the night listening to the sounds of the cows and calves around me, sounds that I had sorely missed. Smelling the wonderful scent of the herd brought a calming peace that quieted the lonely ache that had long throbbed deep within me. Rest came easy this night.

My dreams were filled with playful calves and sunlit meadows. Soon in my dream world, I stood at the grassy edge of a small opening as the sun rose above the trees on its far side. With great joy, I watched the exuberant play of calves as they ran darting relentlessly through the meadow around me. A large cow approached from over a gentle hill at the meadow's side. She was framed perfectly by the rising sun directly behind her as she walked. Standing before me now, I squinted into the bright halo of sunlight that surrounded her, unable to see her face.

The cow said quietly, "I am no longer with the great herd, Tateh, but I will walk with you always. What you knew before as a member of our great herd, you will carry in your heart forever, but you must walk forward now on your journey."

Awake again, I raised my head and whispered softly into the darkness, "mother, are you there?"

Only the sounds of the night now surrounded me. Near me in the darkness, I could hear the even breathing of Wicala as she slept. From the meadow came the occasional bleat of a young calf and the comforting mew of its mother. Feeling the closeness of my mother, and immersed in the wonderful sounds of life that surrounded me, I drifted again into sleep as I pondered the meaning of my dream.

I awoke the next morning and stood from my bed as the sky first began to lighten. I quietly watched in the growing dawn as cows with their young calves entered the meadow. Wicala joined me and began feeding in the grass as the sun began to show above the trees at the meadow's edge. The calves in the herd below us began in earnest, to play their wonderful games of life.

A large cow stood alone on a small knoll in the meadow, encircled by the rising sun behind her. The cow raised her head and turned toward me. Her shadowy figure standing in the brightness reminded me immediately of my dream of the past night. Its lingering message now echoed in my mind.

A strange feeling caused me to turn toward the trees at the top of the meadow. Staring at me silently from its edge, was Ksapa. Our eyes met for a moment, and as I turned back to the cow who stood silhouetted by the glowing sun, I suddenly knew.

"Yes, Mother, it is time," I whispered, and I turned to follow the great bull who had started upward through the trees, away from me. I stopped as I entered the timber where Ksapa had disappeared, and looked back toward the meadow. The knoll where the cow had stood was curiously vacant. Wicala, though, stood quietly at the meadow's edge and returned my stare with a look of knowing. I held her gaze for a moment, then turned from her, and followed the great one from the canyon.

Chapter Seventeen

Ksapa and I walked from the canyon with no words spoken. Soon we stood at the edge of the great basin looking back again into the canyon's depths. No hint of sound or scent was present now of the many cows and calves that grazed somewhere below. Only the feeling of loneliness that I carried within me told of the herd I had been with there.

"Ksapa," I said at last, "I must learn, and there is much I need to know. Will you allow me to walk with you? Will you share with me your journey, and help me to become who it is I will finally be?" I asked.

"My answer, Tateh, was given earlier today, when you turned and looked toward the trees at the meadow's edge, and I was there waiting," he said.

Ksapa turned then, and started across the basin. I looked once again into the canyon from which we had just climbed and realized that one part of my life's journey was now complete. With a feeling of anticipation and wonder, I turned and trotted after the huge one, already well ahead of me in the grassy basin.

Though the days were still very warm, it was far into the season of *ripening berries*, and even the grass in the high basin had begun to form seeds at its top. Few wildflowers bloomed in the deep grass, and white, puffy seeds floated everywhere on the breeze.

Ahead of me, Ksapa's magnificent antlers swayed gently as he walked. It seemed they grew noticeably larger by the day. Though they were massive and imposing, they were still covered by a soft, brown, velvet layer, one that I knew Ksapa would soon remove.

"Your antlers too, have grown, Tateh," said Ksapa, apparently hearing my thoughts.

"What? What antlers, Ksapa?" I asked.

Ksapa strode to a place where a large circle of green stood in the yellow grass and lowered his massive head to the pond hidden there. Beside him, I too, lowered my head to drink. To my astonishment, I saw staring back from the water, a young bull with two short spikes protruding from his head. One antler grew from beside each ear, as did Ksapa's mighty horns.

I jerked my head from the water and looked with wonder at Ksapa, who returned my stare with mirth twinkling in his eyes. I looked cautiously again at the water, and sure enough, antlers stood firmly attached to my head. An unexplained energy filled me suddenly, and I bounded around the pond bucking and snorting, shaking my mighty antlers menacingly at Ksapa. Ksapa lowered his head, and engaging me gently, snorted and mewed indignantly as I pushed him powerfully backward through the grass near the pond.

He raised his head finally, tipping his antlers over his back and bellowed a shrieking bugle that echoed across the basin. Startled by his earsplitting call, I stared at him in awe with mouth agape.

He walked deliberately to the edge of the pond where he pawed with his front feet, throwing clumps of grass and mud into the meadow behind him. He then flopped down into the black, gooey mud he had exposed at the pond's edge and rolled and kicked, covering his light, tan hair with the sticky blackness. He stood from his wallow with mud dripping from his body, and tipping his antlers back once again, sent another bellowing scream across the basin.

Stunned, I stared at him wide-eyed in bewilderment. He looked at me invitingly, then turned and looked toward the muddy spot where he had just rolled. Understanding immediately the big one's unspoken command, I approached the pond's edge hesitantly.

As I smelled the scent of the freshly torn earth though, a strange energy suddenly overcame me, and I threw myself rolling to the ground in the black mud. Thrashing and kicking, I covered my body with black slime as Ksapa had done.

I jumped from the mud with a terrible burst of energy, and tipping my spikes back, I raised my nose into the air and bellowed as loudly as I could. A strange, high-pitched whistling sound, one I had never made before, came from deep within my throat. It thundered, I was sure, far into the basin around us. I attacked

Ksapa then, engaging him once more in a mighty fight, and we pushed each other back and forth, angrily splashing through the pond.

Weary finally, I allowed Ksapa to escape, whereupon we sought restful shelter in the shade of the nearby trees. Lying beneath the big trees that grew at the edge of the pond, Ksapa looked at me still with an amused twinkle in his eyes. I knew, of course, that I had surprised him with my remarkable strength, and I rested near him in the shade feeling quite satisfied with my show of prowess.

The day became wonderfully cool as the sun sank toward the horizon. Ksapa rose from his bed and walked slowly into the trees that surrounded us. He stopped near a small tree whose trunk was the size of one of his huge front legs. He slowly tipped his massive antlers into it and began rubbing them up and down against its trunk. Standing, I watched in curious wonder, this secret ritual of bulls that he now performed before me.

Ksapa ground his antlers methodically against the tree's trunk at first, then pushed more aggressively. Soon he peeled the bark from its trunk with his mighty horns, exposing the sticky, yellow wood beneath. But now, he pushed even harder still, grunting and snorting and grinding his antlers against the tree. Finally, with a groan, he tipped his antlers to the side as he raised his mighty head and ripped the tree angrily from the earth. He stretched his broad neck forward, raising his nose high in the air. As he tipped his gigantic antlers back, he bellowed yet another resounding bugle while glaring angrily at the hapless tree lying before him on the ground. Much of the velvet that had covered his antlers had been stripped by his menacing attack on the tree, and now only shredded strips hung loosely from places on his towering horns. Seemingly unaware of my presence, he strode stiffly past me to the edge of the pond. He lowered his antlers to the earth, raking his tines deeply into the mud, again sending torn clumps of grass flying through the air around him. Raising his head from the mud, he stood before me in savage splendor with ragged strings of velvet and bunches of muddy grass hanging from his rack. His glaring eyes now filled with anger, he bugled furiously once more and with a contemptuous snort, shook his antlers and strode back and stood quietly before me.

Ksapa's eyes softened as he slowly regained his composure. He showed no hint of the enraged bull that had only moments before ripped the tree from the ground that lay destroyed just beyond where we stood. He said finally in a quiet voice, "That is how we bulls prepare ourselves for the season of mating. The tree that you choose to assault and the ground that you rip and tear with your antlers," he continued, "becomes in your mind, a rival bull with whom you are fighting. It is a preparation for not only your antlers, Tateh, but for building within yourself the fierce resolve needed for what is soon to come."

Ksapa turned then and walked to the pond where he lowered his head to the water and made loud sucking noises as he quenched his thirst. I stood trembling in bewilderment looking from Ksapa, who stood drinking at the pond, to the tree he had attacked,

318

lying in tattered pieces on the ground. I marveled at the transformation through which Ksapa had gone in such a short time. In an instant he had gone from a playful bull to an enraged frenzy of raw power in the face of which, any animal confronted, would surely shrink.

As the days of *ripening berries* slipped slowly by, I witnessed many times his secret ritual of polishing horns and his desperate fighting of imaginary foes in his mind. Ksapa's antlers steadily darkened as pine pitch from countless shredded trees and mud torn from the earth grew thick upon them. They had become nearly black in color now, tipped with polished white points.

With each passing day, Ksapa grew increasingly inward. We seldom talked as I followed him through the basin, walking from pond to pond with no apparent destination. I wondered often about this brutal ritual that Ksapa now repeated often, and what frightful challenges were to come that would demand such intense preparation.

"The mating season will be soon," said Ksapa to yet another of my un-spoken questions, as we grazed one day high in a grassy saddle. "Early in the season of *yellowing leaves*," he continued, "the big bulls, dominant ones such as I, Tateh, battle for the right to lead the herds. Only the largest and most powerful of our kind will ultimately lead. The more raging and mighty the bull, the more cows he will have in his herd. The leader will brutally banish all other bulls from the herd during this time of mating. Only the proven strength and endurance of the leader is then carried in the blood of the newborn calves in the coming year. It is in this extremely challenging way, Tateh, that our promise of survival is kept.

"The herd bulls expend a great deal of strength during the mating season," he continued, "running all bulls from their herd night and day. They battle furiously with those who refuse to run. It is at that time, Tateh, when the challengers stand their ground that terrible battles sometimes occur. These fights seldom end in death, though, for the lesser bulls realize finally, the superior strength of the dominant one, and retreat. Still, each fight exacts a heavy toll in expended energy and in new injuries to the leader.

"When the mating season ends at last," continued Ksapa, "the lead bulls, nearly exhausted, abandon the herd to seek solitude high in the mountains where they heal and regain their strength. The great leaders have only a short time to rest before the *season of renewal* again grips our land. The herd is then left to the guidance of wise cows for the remainder of the year."

Ksapa's words of confrontation and battles fought, had brought to my mind again, the image of the dying leader whose enormous herd had followed him to the healing water. I could plainly see the monstrous bull as he struggled forward, fatally wounded, toward my mother and me at the pond. I saw again the wild eyes of the bull that had soon taken the dying bull's cows. I remembered his seething anger as he pushed my mother forcefully into his new herd. And the looming specter of the bull that had killed him later that day in the moonlit meadow, haunted my dreams still.

"Ksapa," I stammered, my voice filled with emotion as the frightful images danced through my mind, "In the last mating season, a huge bull forced my mother and me into his herd in the canyon of the healing water. The bull was immense and easily ran other bulls from his path as we went. There was one bull, though, that was undeterred by our raging leader and pursued us relentlessly.

"To escape the dogged pursuit of the challenging bull," I continued, "our leader drove our herd across the basin and into a canyon on its far side. Deep in the canyon, he realized finally, that flight was in vain and our leader stood his ground. A terrible battle then ensued.

"As the horrifying fight continued, the challenger pushed our leader into the thicket of trees in which I hid, killing him, nearly on top of me.

"The immense bull," I continued, "tried to kill me, too, Ksapa. I am alive only because he could not catch me. The bull's antlers would not fit between the trees through which I fled."

Ksapa stood quietly thinking with sadness in his eyes. He said, finally, "That bull's name, Tateh, is Zomika. He is very large and strong and will gladly kill another bull in battle if he is able. He is one with no heart," said Ksapa.

"The first two-legged ones called his kind, *zomika*. It was their word for *schemer*," he continued, "and we have long known him by that name. Your father and I grew from the time of calves with Zomika. Even then, there was no goodness in his heart. His aim, it seemed, was only to harm others.

"Zomika grew to be an immense bull. He is a ruthless leader who is known to push his herd without mercy. Calves, not yet strong enough to stay at the sides of their mothers, are often left behind his driven herds to fend for themselves. Zomika is one, Tateh, who does not relinquish leadership of his herd to the lead cows at the end of the mating season. Instead, he stays with the herd, and continues to dominate them.

"Long ago, Tateh," continued Ksapa, "your father, Woslolkia, saw in a dream that Zomika had driven his herd into great peril low on the mountain during the white, two-legged one's season of killing. Woslolkia awoke, and knowing the truth of his dream, traveled downward through the night. When the sun rose the next day, he found Zomika and his beleaguered herd far below here near the winter range.

"Your father and Zomika fought then, Tateh. It was an incredible battle. Woslolkia overpowered him finally and chased him far from the herd. Woslolkia returned to the shaken cows and calves and pushed them desperately uphill toward safety. But safety was not to be, for my great friend. The ones who carry thunder had heard the sounds of the bull's terrible battle and had surrounded the herd with their lightning sticks.

"When the killing began," continued Ksapa sadly, "Woslolkia circled the confused herd, trying frantically to drive them away from the white-skinned ones. He returned again and again to gather weaker ones who had fallen behind. When the herd at last reached the cover of the trees far above, Woslolkia was no longer with them.

"It was because of Zomika, Tateh, that your father died."

Stunned, I stared into the wise eyes of Ksapa in disbelief, anger boiling within me. In my mind I could plainly see the bull that I now knew to be Zomika, as he raised his bloody antlers from our dead leader and wheeled in the moonlight toward me.

"Zomika," I breathed, as I turned from Ksapa and walked into the meadow before us, toward the setting sun.

Ksapa had begun already, I realized, to fulfill his promise to me. The magnitude of what he had taught me about the bold journey of the lead bull's, made me feel as though I had aged half a lifetime. I stood in the meadow as the sun sank and darkness surrounded me, my mind brimming with frightful images. I thought of my father Woslolkia, and the scheming one that had caused his death. I remembered the daunting leader that Zomika had killed before turning on me in the darkness. But strangely, most haunting of all in my mind, was the vision of the great wounded one. It almost seemed as though I could feel his pain as he struggled toward my mother and me at the healing water.

Long after darkness fell, I returned to the knoll were Ksapa lay quietly. I stood beside him tormented still, by the thoughts of battling bulls.

"Ksapa," I asked, after a long while, "what was the name of the great dying one whose herd followed him to the healing water?"

Ksapa rose slowly from his bed and for a short time stood quietly before me as he looked into my questioning eyes. Drawing a great breath and then exhaling, he said quietly, "Some things, can be known only through experience, Tateh. Understanding cannot come from the words of another. There will be a time when you will know that great bull's name." He turned from me then, and said no more. He lay down in the grass, and stared quietly into the night.

I stood beside my friend for a long while, puzzled by his curious words, then asked finally, "What is the meaning of your name, Ksapa?"

"*One who walks with wisdom*," he answered softly from the darkness.

When I awoke the next morning, only the slightest hint of light shone in the dark skies above, but already Ksapa stood on our small knoll carefully testing the breeze. For what, I did not know.

We grazed together for a bit before Ksapa broke the silence. "Tateh," he said, "as this time of mating approaches, and I gather my herd, I will at times not acknowledge your presence. I will often do things that confuse and frighten you. However, I ask you stay close, Tateh, and learn."

Ksapa turned then, and with me following quietly behind, walked toward the brightening horizon.

As we crossed a small rise, a group of bulls raised their heads from the grass in surprise as we came into view. There were several in the herd who had antlers of varying sizes, but none nearly as large as Ksapa's. Velvet hung raggedly from some bulls' antlers, others were polished dark with gleaming white tips like Ksapa's.

The bulls watched nervously as Ksapa and I approached, but jumped quickly from his path as the huge one, with me following nervously behind, strode defiantly through their midst without slowing. As we moved past the bulls, I saw their confused glances at one another and the fear that shown in their eyes as they watched Ksapa pass without the slightest acknowledgment of their presence.

As we crossed yet another rise beyond the shaken bulls, a bugle rang from behind us as one of the larger ones found his courage at last.

"That is a bachelor herd, Tateh," said Ksapa from in front of me, as we dropped from sight over the rise. "Those bulls are not yet large enough to lead a herd of their own and will instead follow the large herds closely. At the risk of violent battle with the lead bull, the smaller bulls will try constantly to sneak unseen into the herd and steal a cow to have for their own.

"The herd bulls," continued Ksapa, "become very angry as they expend precious energy without sleep or rest, running smaller bulls from their herd through both daylight and darkness.

"Tateh, there will be a time when you too, will be a part of these bachelor groups," he continued. "When it is that time, walk with wisdom. Many young bulls are foolish during the time of mating and will suffer fatal wounds from horribly tempered lead bulls."

As we walked again in silence, I thought about the group of bulls far behind us now. I pictured again their fearful avoidance of Ksapa as he demonstrated to them his overwhelming dominance by fearlessly splitting their herd as he passed.

A bugle rang suddenly from the basin behind us. Ksapa stopped and turned slowly back, looking carefully in the direction from which the call had come.

"The young bulls follow us now, Tateh," said Ksapa, "for they know I will soon begin to gather cows and will have a large herd. As always, they will test me as they try to steal my cows. Some will pay, as they do each year, with grievous injury."

Ksapa and I grazed slowly in a small grassy bowl rimmed on three sides by tree-covered hills as the day came to an end. The group of bachelor bulls that now followed us had grown in number. They bugled often as they locked horns and pushed one another menacingly on the small hills above us. There were bulls of all sizes, but all stayed well away from Ksapa. They engaged one another in their ritual of pushing and bugling as each one sought to establish a place of dominance in their herd of bulls.

Though I had smaller antlers than any of the bachelor bulls above us, I was equal in size to all but a few of the larger ones.

Suddenly, I saw a bull much larger than the rest standing alone on the hill above us. He had appeared silently from the trees, drawn by the bugles of the other bulls, and stood quietly as he watched Ksapa.

His antlers were wide and dark, and the other bulls around him stayed a respectful distance away. Ksapa, seemingly unaware of the larger bull's presence, continued to graze with his head down in the grass, but as I looked closer, I saw an intense stare in the big bull's eyes.

As the sun's last rays shone between the peaks on the far horizon, a mighty bugle erupted from the bull on the hillside above. My head shot up in surprise, but Ksapa's head stayed to the ground grazing.   In his eyes though, burned a fire, the likes of which I had never seen.

Again, came the shrieking bugle from the mysterious bull above, followed by a series of deep grunts as he started downward toward us. Ksapa stood head down, grazing still, but his fiery eyes bulged so with intensity, that they were rimmed with white.

As the challenging bull, grunting and moaning deeply, entered the small bowl in which we stood, I realized he was comparable in size to Ksapa. I stood fearfully, far to the side, as the bull approached my enormous friend, who stood head down, waiting silently.

The challenger, emboldened by Ksapa's lack of aggression, tipped his huge antlers back and screamed a thunderous bugle. In a blur, Ksapa's head shot from the grass. In a few thrusting bounds, he struck the surprised bull head-on with a mighty crack of antlers, driving him powerfully backward through the meadow. Ksapa shook his massive antlers free from the bull and raised his head in a thunderous bugle.

The defiant bull rushed forward, striking Ksapa's enormous rack with all his might. Ksapa did not give, but instead tipped his antlers to the side, and with a mighty grunt, raised and twisted his head. A resounding crack echoed from the hills around us. The challenger bull's right beam, with its gleaming white tips, broke from his head and flipped end over end through the air, landing near me in the grass.

For an instant, the bewildered bull stood staring in disbelief at Ksapa. Ksapa lunged immediately forward again, striking the shaken bull and sending him rolling across the ground in a cloud of dust. The once defiant challenger, now completely ravaged, sprang to his feet bleeding from his side. He lunged away from Ksapa with all his strength toward the bulls on the hill above, who watched in silent awe.

Ksapa, moaning deeply in his chest, pursued the big bull, rolling him once more to the ground as he entered the trees on the hill above. Ksapa stopped and bellowed a roaring bugle that echoed from the hills around us. Snorting and moaning with rage, he chased the shaken bulls that had witnessed the fight across the opening and into the trees. Finally, alone, he stood motionless on the hillside above me.

Trembling from fright at having witnessed the incredible spectacle, I thought of Ksapa's words of warning earlier in the day. Indeed, what I had seen had confused and frightened me, but like the huge bull who hid now, wounded and humiliated somewhere in the basin, I too, had learned.

Chapter Eighteen

I awoke suddenly in the darkness to the sound of Ksapa's shrieking bugle. The sky showed no sign of light yet, but from the crashing and breaking sounds of limbs as they were torn from trees above me on the hill, I knew Ksapa fought unseen adversaries that loomed again, in his mind.

As the sky slowly brightened, Ksapa's resounding bugle was answered by an echoing call, followed by a series of deep grunts from somewhere nearby in the basin. I could see the huge form of my friend standing in the near light on the hillside above me. He looked with intense anger in the direction from which the answer had come. His giant antlers turned slowly as he read the breeze with his keen nose.

Again, from in the basin, came the resounding bugle of the unknown bull, but even closer now. As I watched nervously, Ksapa strode deliberately from the hill and swiftly past where I stood without the slightest hint of acknowledgement. Shaking with fear, I followed my mighty friend, as he had earlier instructed, toward the bull whose moaning and shrieking bugle grew ever closer now.

The distance between Ksapa and the mysterious bull closed quickly, and soon they stood on opposite sides of a small meadow, studying each other in the growing light. The bull who had so fearlessly answered Ksapa's mighty bugle was enormous, with huge, white-tipped antlers that flowed far over his back. Around him stood a large group of cows that he herded nervously away as he saw the intimidating form of Ksapa.

For the challenger though, it was too late. The mistake had been made. The bull had answered and had come to the call of my great friend, certain he would take Ksapa's herd. With a low moan and a series of deep grunts emanating from deep within him, Ksapa sprang forward, crossing the meadow in what seemed only a few bounds. The fleeing bull turned from his herd and met Ksapa with a mighty crash. They stood for a moment at the edge of the meadow, unmoving, locked in a powerful struggle for the cows who watched anxiously from the trees.

Ksapa's mighty strength soon became evident as he flipped the hapless bull from side to side and pushed him backward through the meadow. They disengaged, and for an instant, stood glaring at one another. Ksapa plunged forward in a mighty rush, but the other bull had had enough and leaped from the path of the raging bull. Ksapa, tipping his towering antlers as he passed, caught the bull high on his rear leg and sent him spinning awkwardly to the ground. The beaten bull jumped to his feet and with Ksapa hard after him, lunged into the timber, relinquishing his herd to the storming one.

Ksapa stood quietly at timber's edge with his head near the ground as he listened to the crashing retreat of the vanquished bull. Knowing finally that the bull would not return, he turned toward the cows that stood nervously waiting in the meadow. He walked slowly through them with his neck extended and head low, learning the scent of each. With an earsplitting bugle, Ksapa then gathered his cows, some with frightened calves beneath them, and guided them onward into the basin. I followed behind the rumbling herd, thinking of the stunning events that I had witnessed in such a short time.

Weariness from the almost constant fear spawned by Ksapa's frightful confrontations began to settle slowly over me as I followed the herd nervously along. I was even more amazed now at the terrible strength and endurance of my enormous friend. I wondered if I would ever be able to match the remarkable feats of Ksapa.

For many days I followed Ksapa closely as he moved his ever-growing herd aimlessly through the big basin. The nights were filled with the echoing calls of angry bulls, and the days were filled with the imposing sight of Ksapa as he vigilantly guarded his cows. Unendingly, the great bull, with head lowered and antlers tipped back, cut through his herd grunting and chucking as he moved carefully from cow to cow. Bulls often answered his booming bugle, but upon seeing the storming one, they sank cautiously back into the trees from which they had come. Cows with calves at their sides often came willingly to Ksapa's bugle now, recognizing him, I was certain, as the immense monarch that indeed he was. As Ksapa had predicted, the smaller bulls that persistently trailed his herd worked him at times into an angry frenzy as he ran them night and day from his cows.

The shrieking bugles, that rang from the trees around Ksapa's herd slowly diminished finally. I realized, at last, the mating season would soon be over. Although the days were still warm, the nights had become cold, and now, frost often lay in the meadows in the early morning light. The grass throughout the basin had turned yellow, and the incredible numbers of flowers that had grown there earlier were now shriveled and gone. I had followed the herd closely as Ksapa had said to do. Though I was certain he had seen me more than once, I had not seen the slightest sign of recognition in his eyes. I wondered if I were to venture too closely to his cows, if I too, would suffer the terrible wrath of the mighty bull.

Ksapa's herd was very large now, but still he cut constantly through the cows, head lowered, chucking and mewing softly as he studied the scent of each. I doubted I would ever be able to endure such an astounding display of frightful strength and tenacity as that which I had witnessed during this season of mating.

Ksapa's tremendous energy, I knew, had begun to dwindle as the ferocious fighting and constant attention to his cows had begun to take its toll. He moved his herd less often now and for shorter distances when he did move. Still, he guarded his cows with unyielding devotion and dealt severe punishment to those bulls foolish enough to challenge him.

This day was unusually warm, and the alluring scent that had come less and less often from the cows of the herd seemed strong again on the soft afternoon breeze. The many bulls that had grown silent in the surrounding basin smelled the intoxicating scent also, and the forest around us was alive once again with nearly nonstop bugling.

Ksapa had just unceremoniously run a younger bull from his herd when a thunderous bugle rang from far off in the basin. Ksapa seemed to recognize immediately the bugle of what was an immense bull. He stood suddenly motionless, glaring intensely toward the direction of the unknown bull. The roaring bugle again echoed through the basin, but closer now. Ksapa, weary from lack of rest and the many life-threatening battles he had recently endured, declined the confrontation. Rather than stand his ground, he instead circled his herd and moved them quickly through the basin away from the approaching bull. I followed the herd closely, wondering about the outcome should this unseen challenger overtake Ksapa and his huge herd.

Ksapa forced his herd aggressively onward, thundering through the basin toward its far side. Each time he stopped, the shrieking bugle would echo again, even closer behind us.

My giant friend drove his cows toward the deep canyons at the basin's far side as the sun dipped slowly below the horizon. The young calves of his herd had begun to tire. Some, unable to endure the relentless pace, now lagged far behind the herd and would soon be lost. Ksapa saw the increasing struggle of the young ones and circled his herd at the edge of a small meadow where the great basin dropped into a huge canyon beyond. He quickly returned and gathered the exhausted calves, then guided them hastily forward into the nervous herd. He walked quietly to the center of the meadow then, and stood silently awaiting this bull that had so untiringly pursued him.

The screaming bugle of the bull erupted again from the trees near the far side of the meadow. Ksapa slowly lowered his head to the yellow grass. A profound, reverberating moan erupted from his throat as he waited unmoving, in the meadow. His cows and calves watched nervously from the side as the great one stood alone before them.

With a terrible breaking of brush and crashing of limbs, the challenger burst suddenly into the meadow. It seemed that the bull, though he had no cows, was Ksapa's equal in every way. Glaring with furious eyes, the enormous bull stood at the edge of the trees shaking his antlers and screaming earsplitting bugles across the meadow toward Ksapa. Ksapa stood unmoving with his great head lowered to the grass, a deep, rumbling moan emanating still from his throat, as he studied the bull before him.

Fear choked the wind from my throat as Ksapa's huge opponent charged suddenly forward. The giant bulls met with a resounding crash of antlers that echoed back from the hills surrounding us. The bull pushed Ksapa backward through the meadow, their antlers grinding loudly as they grunted and moaned from the tremendous exertion of their battle. They disengaged for a moment, but the challenger sprang immediately forward, hitting Ksapa even harder than before, driving him backward again.

Ksapa lost his footing as the daunting bull overpowered him, pushing him backward through a fallen tree. I stood in horror as I watched the challenger topple Ksapa backwards in a tangle of limbs and small trees. I remembered the bull I now knew as Zomika, as he toppled our huge leader backward in the moonlight.

As Ksapa rolled awkwardly backward, he lifted his mighty antlers with all his strength. With a terrible groan, he pulled the huge one over the top of him as he rolled backward, sending the challenger twisting and kicking through the air, crashing to the ground in the trees behind him.

In a dust-filled explosion of breaking brush and flying limbs, the two monsters sprang to their feet and stood once again glaring with hatred at one another. The indignant rival screamed a thunderous bugle at having been thrown to the ground and denied his victory. In a blinding rage, the huge bull lunged powerfully forward again at Ksapa.

As the driving bull lowered his head for impact, Ksapa twisted suddenly sideways. As the onrushing bull's antlers swept past him, Ksapa tipped his antlers hard into his side, sinking them deeply into the ribs of the charging bull as he thundered past. A resounding bellow erupted from deep within the stunned bull as he stumbled sideways in agony, then, regained his balance. Ksapa met him immediately with a head-on, all-out charge that sent the dazed bull lurching backwards and onto his side.

His huge opponent kicked and lurched and struggled finally to his feet to face Ksapa. Ksapa stood quietly, though, and struck him no more. He knew the fight was over. The beleaguered challenger stood teetering before him with blood streaming to the ground from gaping wounds in his side.

Ksapa, his head lowered to the grass, stood silently watching the wounded bull before him. Gone was the terrible moan from his throat, and sadness filled his eyes that only moments before had brimmed with rage. My great friend watched quietly as his huge adversary turned from him and stumbled weakly into the trees from which he had come.

The cows of Ksapa's herd stood in stunned silence at the meadow's edge, their calves quivering with fright beneath them. Ksapa slowly raised his head from the grass and walked to the path in the trees upon which the defeated challenger had departed. He lowered his head to the ground and breathed deeply the scent there, then stood quietly listening in the direction the bull had gone. As darkness gathered, a mournful, quavering wail echoed eerily from deep in the timber beyond where Ksapa stood. The cry was like that of a helpless calf calling to its mother. This call, though, was deep and resonant.

Darkness had long filled the meadow when Ksapa turned at last from the trees where the bull had fled. I watched as my great friend returned to his herd and circled his shaken cows, gathering them in the murky blackness. I followed nervously behind them as he guided them downward into the deep canyon that lay behind us.

Later that night, as I lay resting in the canyon's darkness, I listened to the troubled sounds of Ksapa's still, unsettled herd. The bleats of shaken calves and the soft, reassuring mews of their mothers floated in the darkness around me. The sounds most remarkable to me though, were the relentless footsteps and the soft, clucking sounds made by Ksapa as he moved unendingly through his herd.

The night was warm and still, and the sky was filled with stars from horizon to horizon. Strangely, the mountains around us had become quiet. Gone were the calls of frustrated bulls that only hours before had echoed from all sides of the herd.

Sleep was difficult as I pondered the brutal happenings of this day and the many recent days during this time of mating. As I thought about the enormous challenger and the terrible battle of earlier, I remembered the remorse in Ksapa's eyes as he watched the dying bull disappear into the forest. The cry of death that had rung from the darkness, I knew, was etched forever in my memory.

As the skies became light, I stood in the forest at the edge of the narrow meadow where Ksapa had chosen to stay the previous night. Cows, one by one with anxious calves at their sides, entered the small opening and began feeding in the deep grass there. Ksapa, though, for the first time since the season of mating had begun, continued to lie quietly at the meadow's edge. He seemed indifferent to the presence of bulls who lurked in the trees near his feeding herd.

The sun rose and shone brightly on the gathering herd, highlighting their tanned bodies against the golden grass in which they fed. Small groups of calves, tentatively at first, began to bound playfully through the herd. Soon they were cutting through the feeding cows with reckless abandon, kicking and jumping as they had before this season of mating had begun. As I watched the leaping throng of miniature elk, I, too, felt the relief that had begun at last to settle over the herd.

The days remained warm and calm, and the bugles of bulls were now seldom heard. The cows and calves of Ksapa's herd seemed to feed and rest as if it were again the season of *growing grass*. Ksapa even rested quietly, tolerant now of smaller bulls that had joined his herd.

One evening, as the sun fell below the mountain tops, Ksapa stood from where he lay at the edge of the meadow and strode deliberately to the middle of his feeding cows. The cows and calves raised their heads from the grass and gathered around him, ears forward, watching him intently.

He stood quietly among them for a short time with respect shining in his eyes. Then, carefully meeting the gaze of each cow, he turned until he had acknowledged each one. He walked slowly through the herd, and without looking back, strode uphill through the meadow to its upper end. He stopped as he entered the trees, and turning back toward his herd, tipped his great antlers back and sent a thunderous bugle echoing downward to his quietly watching cows. He turned then, and disappeared into the trees.

I stood intently watching from the trees at the bottom of the meadow, confused by the big bull's actions. Realizing that Ksapa had abandoned his herd, I ran hastily up the edge of the meadow and entered the trees where he had disappeared. Ahead of me, I saw the looming form of Ksapa. With his head lowered, and great antlers tipping side to side as he walked, the huge bull moved steadily uphill in the gathering darkness. With great trepidation, remembering the many bulls he had so angrily rebuffed, I assumed a place far behind him and followed him from the canyon.

Darkness fell, and without the slightest acknowledgment of my presence, Ksapa continued upward toward the basin above. I plodded quietly behind him in the blackness, pondering fearfully the wrath of the great bull should he suddenly sense my presence.

Long before the light of the new day, we climbed from the canyon and entered the basin. Ksapa stopped finally, and turned toward me. Fearing the worst, I stared nervously at the towering silhouette before me. He stood quietly for a time staring at me through eyes clouded with emotion. Then, without a word, he turned away from me again, and continued into the basin. Relieved at his unspoken acknowledgment of me and seeming permission to again be in his presence, I followed him more closely as we moved through the night.

As the sky began to brighten, we walked through the saddle and into the grassy bowl that I knew lay above the canyon of the healing water. We moved steadily downward on the trail that coursed through the blackened trees and the meadows of golden grass in the canyon's bottom. As I plodded quietly along behind Ksapa, I wondered if we would ever talk as we had before, or if this violent season of mating had changed my great friend forever.

As the sun grew weak on the far horizon, we at last entered the meadow of the healing water. My heart quickened as I saw this place I had come to love, and I followed Ksapa closely as he walked without hesitation into the yellow mud at the pond's upper end. I watched respectfully from the pond's edge as he rolled and squirmed in the gooey mud. He then stood and walked into the steaming water and lay with only his head and antlers above the surface. I then rolled in the mud as Ksapa had done, and joined him in the pond. At a careful distance from the great bull, I watched as darkness fell over the canyon and consumed the meadow around us.

Late in the night, I stood and walked from the hot water, cooling myself as I fed in the grass that surrounded the pond. Ksapa, however, continued to soak. I watched from the grass beneath the blackened trees at the edge of the meadow as the new day dawned. In the gray light of morning I could see the familiar profile of the great bull who lay unmoving, still, in the healing water. Ksapa seemed unaware of me as I cautiously approached the pond and entered the steaming water again. His gaze was fixed on something far away, something I knew only he could see. After soaking for most of the day in the warm water, I grazed again in the meadow that evening. Still, Ksapa lay quietly in the water of the healing pond.

Watching from my bed as the first light of a new day began to grow slowly in the sky above, I saw the dark forms of two huge bulls facing each other in the meadow near the edge of the pond. One, I recognized immediately to be Ksapa. The other bull, to my amazement, had only one huge antler. The two bulls stood quietly facing each other for a time in the near light, then both lowered their heads in respect of one another and walked in separate directions. Ksapa returned to the pond where he lowered himself into the warm water, and the other bull disappeared into the trees below him.

For many days Ksapa did not speak as we soaked together in the healing water, nor did he speak as we filled our stomachs browsing in the yellow grass in the surrounding meadow. We rarely made eye contact, but I could see deep fatigue and a storm of emotion boiling in his troubled eyes when we did.

As the first days of the season of *leaves falling,* slowly passed, Ksapa's strong and muscular body, so severely diminished by the trials of the mating season, began at last, to strengthen. The wounds he had suffered in his many violent battles were nearly healed. Ksapa, it seemed, lived now in a world that existed only in his mind. As the days wore on, I came to believe that my magnificent friend, my teacher of life, would never again talk to me.

Early one evening as the light softened and shadows crept across the meadow where we stood grazing, Ksapa raised his head from the grass and turned to me.

Staring into my eyes, he said quietly at long last, "Tateh, when I was young, I walked with steps that were strong and firm. I felt wise and knew that with my great strength, I could overcome any obstacle that stood before me on my journey. I was certain that with my prowess, I could control all that was around me.

"But as I have grown older and wiser, I have realized that my steps are not as firm as I once thought them to be, and the great knowledge I have gained seems only to define how much I do not know. I understand, finally, Tateh, that in life we are in control of nothing.

"The ways of our kind," he continued, "are very difficult. During our season of mating, only the mightiest of the bulls will control the herd, and they must battle with all their might, often against brothers they have known for many years, for the right to lead. The bull, Tateh," said Ksapa, "that I battled last, at the edge of the basin, was my lifelong friend. He was the last bull still living with whom I had played my first games of life. As calves, we often played the joyous game of fighting bulls, as we pushed and butted heads under the watchful eyes of our proud mothers.

"How could I have known that those wonderful games we played would end in such terrible reality?" he said sadly.

His voice choking in his throat, Ksapa turned from me, his words unfinished. With his knowing eyes filled again with emotion, he walked into the meadow where he lowered his head once again to feed.

My years passed quickly as I followed the great bull through the seasons of our land. Ksapa was fulfilling the promise of what I had long ago asked him to do. He was teaching me not with words, but by the example of his life, a great love and understanding of our mountains and of those with whom we shared them. He demonstrated to me and to all others around him his great respect for life, as well as the acceptance of not only our kind, but of all four-legged and rooted ones.

During the season of mating, I was continually filled with awe of not only his great intensity and endurance, but also of his compassion for the cows and calves of his herd. In shocking disbelief, I witnessed many times, his incredible display of skills and strength as he battled with bulls equal to him in size and strength, but ones, who could not match the unyielding will that filled the heart of Ksapa.

Chapter Nineteen

As the seasons passed, I grew larger and stronger. I continued to learn of our unending cycles of life under the watchful eye, and by the example of Ksapa. I followed him through the hills and meadows of the great basin as we rested and grew fat through each season of *growing grass*. I trailed respectfully behind the huge bull and his herd as he led them through the remote canyons that fell from the basin's side during each season of mating. Ksapa led me upward to open, rocky plateaus during the season of killing where we stayed in safety and solitude until its end. Most of our *seasons of renewal* were spent on the open ridges above the rolling hills of the winter range. The cows and calves of Ksapa's herd fed far below us in the valley. But sometimes as the harsh season approached, the great bull led me downward to the strange land near the thundering canyon of the yellow rocks. There, we spent the snowy season in a mysterious land dotted with hot pools of steaming water. We shared this mountainous world with shaggy bison and many other four-legged ones as we grazed on the tender grass that grew in all seasons around the warm ponds of bubbling water.

We foraged often near the side of the immense canyon, unable to hear or speak above the thundering roar of its cascading water. At times in very cold weather, the mist from the falling water froze in the air on its downward journey, and rising ice crystals sparkled so in the sun that I could not see through them to the other side of the canyon. Many times, I walked behind Ksapa as he led me downward on trails across sheer, rocky ledges into the depths of the huge chasm. There, in the canyon's bottom, we fed on abundant grass that was exposed along the churning water's edge.

When the harsh season ended at last, and the sun became warm again during the season of *ducks returning*, we patiently followed the retreating snow line up the mountains toward the great basin above. Our strength quickly returned as we fed on tender young grass that grew beneath the warming sun.

Early in each new season of *growing grass*, I watched many times with sadness as the cows of the great herd rebuffed their nearly grown calves born in the previous year. They pushed them sternly away to join other herds as the mothers-to-be made themselves ready again for the new lives they would soon bring to our mountains. Ksapa and I sought solitude then, and journeyed high into the basin. We spent the warm seasons in green, abundant meadows and readied ourselves for the coming season of mating.

We had lived this past *season of renewal* near the canyon of the yellow rocks, and though there had been little snow, the severe cold had been bitter and long lasting. The scant snowfall had enabled us to begin our journey toward the great basin much earlier than in past years. Now, under a warming sun, we fed on hillsides only recently bare as we followed the rapidly retreating snow upward. My appreciation of the sun now glaring brightly down was many times greater than in years past. The bitter and biting cold of the *season of renewal* had been more severe than any I had ever known. Though the season was very young, the snow line had receded already to a place higher in the mountains than I had ever known it to be in the season of *ducks returning.*

I had grown much during the seasons through which I had followed Ksapa. I now stood shoulder to shoulder, nearly equal in size to him, but I doubted I would ever possess antlers as enormous as were his.

As we grazed day by day on rooted ones on the greening mountainsides, my growing excitement to enter the great basin and explore again the mysterious canyons that fell from its side, was nearly overwhelming. I wondered if perhaps this would be the year when I too, would gather a herd.

Around us on the hills were many bulls of varying sizes, ones I had come to know as I followed Ksapa and his herd during the season of mating. Many, as did Ksapa and I, stood feeding while others lay relaxing in the sun. We moved ever higher in the mountains following the receding snow as the days of *ducks returning* passed slowly by.

One afternoon as the sun sank toward the far horizon, Ksapa and I stood overlooking the great basin at last. The grass before us lay flatly pressed to the earth from the weight of recently melted snow. No hint of green showed anywhere as far as we could see across the sprawling landscape. Missing though, were the deeply piled drifts of snow at the downwind side of huge tree clumps. The rapidly disappearing snow that did remain was

347

darkened by myriad tiny, black, snow fleas. At the rims of the rolling hills throughout the basin, cornices of snow, much smaller than in years past, stood glistening in the afternoon sun. Small flocks of little winged ones flitted nervously around us, and the warm afternoon air was heavy with the smell of waking trees that stood gently swaying in the breeze.

Ksapa stood quietly for a time studying the brown grass and rolling hills that stretched before us in the basin. Then, without a word, my huge friend started forward. Walking directly away from setting sun, we moved steadily onward, the shadows we cast danced strangely before us as we walked side-by-side through the dry grass. A light brown trail of dust stirred from the earth by our passing, glowed softly behind us in the setting sun.

We walked without stopping through the night, and as light began to grow in the sky above, we stood in the small basin that lay above the canyon of the healing water. It was wonderful to stare again into the deep, broad canyon, but in the gray light of dawn, no hint of green showed yet in the meadows that lined its bottom. Without hesitation though, Ksapa led me into the blackened canyon.

The day slowly brightened as we walked downward, and as the sun started above the steep canyon's side, we began to notice small, green rooted ones reaching from beneath the mat of brown grass along the trail's edge. The timber through which we passed stood black and gaunt. There was little growing yet beneath the ghostly trees, but the height of the new grass growing in the meadows between the blackened stands, increased as we dropped lower into the canyon. We moved steadily downward, and when the sun had climbed to a spot directly overhead, walked at last, through meadows of lush greenness. We fed gratefully on the tender rooted ones as we passed.

As the sun sank toward the top of the canyon's side, the acrid smell of the healing water came to my nose, and soon we entered the broad meadow where the pond lay steaming at its lower end. With a series of barks and half-bugles, Ksapa and I broke into an excited run as we happily loped through the green meadow toward our steaming destination. Without slowing, we lunged through the sticky yellow mud and splashed loudly into the wonderful, warming water beyond. The soothing feeling of the pond's water was indescribable, and we lay for a long time without speaking. We were both silently recounting, I'm sure, the bitter cold and howling blizzards of the season we had just endured.

Looking into Ksapa's eyes as I soaked in the warm water near him, it was evident that the great bull was deep in thought.

After a long while, Ksapa said at last, "Tateh, in the seasons during which you have walked with me, you have grown large and strong, and the wisdom you have acquired will serve you well. During the coming season of mating, you will dominate, I am sure, the herd of bachelor bulls that will follow my herd. As you walk near my cows, Tateh, remember carefully the words that we have shared. Remain patient, for I know your time to lead will soon come."

He stood then, and walked from the water into the meadow where he lowered his head and began to feed.

As I lay near Ksapa in darkness that night at the edge of the meadow, I thought again about the big one's words of earlier. Disappointment filled me as I remembered his words, "be patient." I hoped that the strange excitement that now grew stronger within me by the day, would not cause me to deny Ksapa's request.

When sleep came finally, it was fitful and without rest. In my dreams, I walked anxiously among fighting bulls and snuck quietly through herds of nervous cows and calves. Strangely though, the herd through which I passed suddenly became difficult to see as blinding clouds of smoke filled my dream.

Waking suddenly, I raised my head quickly from the grass and stared into the blackness of the burnt forest around me. As I lowered my head once more to sleep, I thought curiously about my strange dream and wondered how long it would be until my fiery nightmares of the past no longer returned.

The days remained warm and sunny, and no rain fell from the skies as the days of *growing grass* passed swiftly by. The streams in our mountain home, though flowing still, did not rumble through our forest as they had in years past. The runoff from the light snowpack had not filled them to the tops of their banks. The small clumps of green trees that had survived the fire in our blackened canyon had little new growth at the ends of their limbs, and few flowers grew in the meadow around the pond.

As in years past, Ksapa's velvet-covered antlers grew larger by the day. The softening light of the sun as it traveled ever lower in the sky on its daily path, told me that the mating season would be soon. My antlers too, had grown large and thick. Ksapa and I spent much time on opposite sides of the great meadow now, grinding and polishing our horns against the trunks of small green trees that had grown amidst the blackness there.

The days of *growing grass* were quickly behind us it seemed, and it was now the season of *ripening berries*. Ksapa grew increasingly quieter and more inward each day. We seldom made eye contact or spoke now. I knew that soon I would follow my immense friend from this canyon, and the mating season would begin.

It was the dark of the moon now, and as I lay each night in my bed at the meadow's edge, I could see nothing but blackness around me. But from the darkness at the far side of the meadow came the grunts and moans of Ksapa as he battled unseen foes in the darkness below the pond.

Early one morning, as the first hint of light began to show in the sky, I heard heavy footsteps that I knew to be Ksapa's, approaching in the darkness. As the great bull drew near, he stopped and without a word, turned toward me. Even in the near darkness, I saw burning in his eyes, the intense fire that I had seen many times before. I knew immediately to follow.

I moved nervously behind him at nearly a trot, as we climbed the side of the canyon where long ago the great herd bull had pushed my mother and me angrily toward the top. We reached the top of the canyon's side near a large outcropping of rock that overlooked the healing water far below. Ksapa stopped and walked to the small cliff where he stood for a moment surveying the beauty below him. Tipping his head slowly backward, he bellowed an earsplitting bugle that echoed downward through the meadow and returned from the canyon's far side. He turned then, and with me following cautiously, continued upward on the ridge where we soon entered the great basin.

The skies became brighter as we skirted along the edge of the huge opening. As the sun rose above the mountains behind us, we dropped into a steep canyon where I had never been. The canyon was narrow with an angry creek that boiled crookedly down its bottom. The grass that grew beneath the trees was scant, but in its many small meadows, stood lush and green. The sides of the canyon rose gently at first, then turned to towering cliffs that formed an impassable barrier far above the canyon's bottom. Large trees grew widely spaced throughout the gorge and up its sides to where the rocky cliffs loomed suddenly above them.

Ksapa's thundering bugle had been answered earlier in the day as we moved through the basin above. Now the shrieking replies from that bull and others that had followed us, echoed from the cliffs of this strange new canyon. The explosion of crashing and breaking limbs in the forest ahead, often told of a bull that had come to Ksapa's bellowing challenge, but upon seeing the great one, had made a hasty retreat.

Behind me, I could hear the heavy footsteps of other bulls as they crashed noisily through the timber, following us ever closer to that place where Ksapa would gather his herd.

One large bull ahead of us in the timber met Ksapa's shrieking bugle with a thundering challenge of his own, and promptly paid a terrible price for his brave stand. Ksapa immediately engaged him with a violent charge that sent him crashing to the ground, breaking the top two tines from the bull's massive rack. Ksapa rolled the beaten bull twice more to the forest floor as the beleaguered one attempted to escape the wrath of my mighty friend.

The canyon below us widened into a large, grassy meadow rimmed by thick trees standing at its lower end. Its sides were lined with towering spires of rock that stood among sheer cliffs. A huge herd of cows and calves milled nervously around a large pond that shimmered at the meadow's center. Ksapa, as if he had known they were there waiting, walked without hesitation to the center of his new herd.

I could see bulls of all sizes walking anxiously through the timber around me, enviously eyeing Ksapa's herd. As the day passed, the bugling from the trees at all edges of the meadow increased, but no bulls were foolish enough to challenge my great friend.

As the season of *ripening berries* continued, the days remained sunny and warm, and no rain fell from the cloudless skies. The once bright, green grass in the meadow quickly turned yellow.

The bugling from the forest around Ksapa's herd had become nearly nonstop, and my days and nights were filled with constant denial of exciting new urges that grew steadily within me. My rapidly growing frustration made me intolerant of the bulls that moved continuously around me, bugling as they circled Ksapa's herd. After many violent encounters, they rarely came near me now. They had quickly learned that I dealt fiercely with those who ventured too close.

As the days of the mating season wore on, the pond over which Ksapa ruled, was growing quickly smaller, but still, he did not move his herd from his large meadow home. Grunting and mewing softly, he walked constantly through them, leaving them only briefly to wallow in the mud at the edge of his pond. Bulls that became brave enough to approach his herd were easily seen sneaking through the open meadow and were quickly chased back into the timber at its edge.

During one such encounter, Ksapa angrily pursued a foolish bull into the timber near me, punishing him severely as they crashed through the trees past me. As he returned from his violent chase, our eyes met briefly as he walked past me at the meadow's edge. He stopped and stood for a moment looking intently into my eyes. To my wonder, Ksapa dipped his great antlers, respectfully acknowledging me for the first time during the season of mating. The great bull returned to his herd and walked slowly through them.

He soon guided a small cow from their midst and pushed her into the meadow toward me. In disbelief, I walked stiffly forward to stand proudly beside Wicala. Looking past her at Ksapa, my gaze was met by knowing eyes that were filled with pride. He turned from us and rejoined his herd.

The hot, dry days passed more quickly now, and it seemed that I, like Ksapa, spent the days and nights angrily chasing other bulls who ventured too closely to Wicala. The loneliness and frustration I had felt earlier was gone finally, and it was good to walk once again with her.

Early one morning, shortly after the sun had risen above the steep canyon walls, Wicala and I peacefully grazed near the edge of the meadow. The silence was suddenly broken by the strange droning call of what I had come to know was the talk of two-legged ones. It echoed from the timber in strange bursts of garbled chatter at the meadow's lower end.

Ksapa, upon hearing the approach of the two-legged ones, quickly drove his cows and calves rumbling into the timber at the meadow's upper end. As the dust settled in the vacant opening, we stood nervously watching from the timber as several white-skinned ones appeared at the lower end of the meadow.

The two-legged ones were unaware that only moments before, a great herd of elk had grazed there. They chattered excitedly to one another as they walked slowly through the meadow and past the pond. Without stopping, the two-legged ones made a wide circle in the opening, then returned to the timber from which they had come. Soon their strange, chattering talk could no longer be heard, but Wicala and I remained hidden at the edge of the meadow. Ksapa continued to circle his herd and held them nervously in the protection of the timber where they had taken refuge.

When darkness again filled our canyon home, Wicala and I walked cautiously into the meadow and began to graze. As the moon rose above the canyon's wall bathing the opening around us in its bluish light, I led Wicala cautiously toward the meadow's lower end where we had seen the two-legged ones disappear earlier. Their scent hung heavily in the warm night air, and we easily followed their odor downward through the trees there.

In a short while, we emerged from the forest into a broad opening, where above a gentle rise in the meadow's center, we could see a strange glow. Walking to the top of the rise, we looked cautiously below. At the bottom of the meadow where the forest once again filled the canyon's bottom, burned a small fire. We could see the shadowy silhouettes of the two-legged ones as they moved about in its flickering orange glow. As Wicala and I stood nervously watching the odd movements of the two-legged ones, their strange voices echoed occasionally from the wall of trees at their bedding place. Their awful scent was everywhere in the night air around us.

In a short while, I turned away from the peculiar scene below and walked quietly from the rise. We retraced our steps through the timber until we were safely again in the meadow where Ksapa and his herd grazed in the moonlight at its upper edge.

When the moon had traveled halfway across the night sky and shone from straight above our canyon, Wicala and I walked from the opening and lay in the grass beneath the trees at its edge. A warm, dry wind began to move slowly through the forest around us and built gradually in strength as the night progressed. Soon the trees around us began to groan and creak loudly in the stiffening wind.

Suddenly, a dreadfully familiar scent filled my nose, and I jumped from my bed, startling Wicala. I stood quivering in the moonlight as I stared toward the lower end of our meadow and the origin of the frightful odor. From somewhere below in the canyon, the scent of smoke floated upward toward us in the gusting wind. Wicala, having now smelled the smoke also, stood at my side as we gazed anxiously downward. As we watched, a strange orange glow began to build rapidly in the sky above the trees at the meadow's lower end.

The thundering hooves of Ksapa's herd drew my attention from the glowing sky. I watched with growing apprehension as Ksapa circled his nervous cows in the meadow across from us and pushed them quickly into the trees and upward in the canyon. Dark, billowing clouds of smoke rolled silently toward us as I stood paralyzed with uncertainty in the timber at the meadow's edge. Panic clutched at my chest as I was suddenly a calf once more, trapped in the water of the healing pond as the forest around me was consumed by a raging blaze.

The smoke quickly hid the meadow before us in a churning wall of brownness. Tearing myself from the past, I lunged recklessly forward, crashing through the forest away from the opening with Wicala following desperately behind me. Jumping downfallen trees and leaping across small ravines, we tried franticly to overtake Ksapa and his fleeing herd. The boiling haze of smoke quickly engulfed the forest around us, making it nearly impossible to see in the grayness of the early morning light. The thundering roar from the rapidly approaching fire hid the crashing sounds of Ksapa's retreating herd.

I stopped and whirled anxiously looking, trying in vain to see my great friend and his fleeing herd through the blinding smoke and growing shower of embers.

Suddenly, in my mind I heard words from long ago. "Never flee uphill from a fire, Tateh, it will almost always overtake you."

But the large cliffs that lined both sides of the canyon left only one route. We were left with the impossible task of outrunning the speeding flames uphill in the canyon's bottom.

A small group of bulls thundered suddenly from the churning wall of smoke and stood fearfully beside Wicala and I. Horror-stricken, we watched as searing flames thundered upward in the canyon toward us. A huge black bear crashed suddenly from the burning trees below. His eyes were unseeing and filled with panic.

Smoke curled from the scorched hair on his back as he lunged past us and disappeared again into the wall of boiling smoke ahead.

Suddenly, Ksapa's thundering bugle echoed ominously through the smoke from the far side of the canyon. A shiver coursed through me as I heard the terrible, distressed cries of his cows and calves. I realized in horror that the towering cliffs at the canyon's side had blocked their flight. The terrible blaze had overtaken the great bull and his herd.

Frozen with fear, I stared into the terrified eyes of Wicala and the other bulls that stood near me as flames erupted, twisting and dancing in the trees at our sides. Suddenly a strange calmness settled over me. The terrible pounding of my heart slowed, and my ragged, gasping breath became even and measured. The dreadful roar of the fire seemed distant as I watched the smoke and glowing embers churning through the trees around us. Ahead of us, in the swirling smoke, suddenly stood Woslolkia.

Without a sound, he turned and disappeared into the boiling haze. Torn from my trance, I quickly ran to where the great bull had disappeared. With Wicala and the terrified throng of bulls close behind, I followed Woslolkia through the blinding smoke.

Ever upward away from the raging flames he climbed, until without warning, his shadowy form disappeared into the towering wall of rock that stood high on the canyon's side. With adrenaline pounding in my veins, I charged through a sea of smoke and embers toward the place where I had last seen him. Choking and gasping for air, we stood finally, at the base of the towering cliff.

Before us was a tall, reaching crevice in the wall of rock. The fissure, whose steep bottom was strewn with a river of small, loose stones, hid an ancient trail that was barely wide enough for us to enter.

With the thundering flames leaping into the sky from the trees below us, we entered the crevice. Tripping and sliding in the loose rock on our unlikely path, we struggled upward between soaring walls of rock, blistering heat washing over us from behind.

Our hearts pounding, and gasping for air, we stood finally, at the top of the cliff looking downward at the burning gorge. The canyon's bottom was entirely engulfed now. The twisting and curling flames had climbed far beyond the spot where we had entered the ancient trail.

Embers from the raging fire floated upward on the heated wind, and the drought-stricken trees that stood at our sides exploded in a roar of swirling flames.

With my small herd pounding anxiously behind me, I lunged upward toward the top of the canyon. With smoke boiling thickly around us and flames exploding in the trees at our sides, we crashed from the forest into a small meadow. Suddenly, above the rushing sound of the advancing fire, we heard the screeching cry of a great white-headed eagle.

Looking upward as we rumbled across the opening, I saw two of the great winged ones flapping frantically in the sky above a large nest at the top of a huge tree. Two small heads bobbed anxiously within the nest, while yet another young one perched nervously on its edge. Its neck was stretched skyward and its immature wings pumped frantically at the sky. The huge birds screamed excitedly as they circled the nest, encouraging the young ones to fly. The young bird, clutching at the air with all its might, sprang suddenly from the nest, and for a moment, hung suspended in the sky above the burning forest. Then, flapping furiously, it descended into the boiling smoke. A cry as ancient as the earth itself erupted from the great birds who circled tightly in the smoky sky above the nest. It was a cry, I knew, of anguish.

As we thundered past the tree, I saw the larger of the two eagles descend and land on the nest, crying wildly as it spread its great wings to cover and protect the remaining two. As we reached the top of the opening, I looked back and watched in horror as the smoke engulfed them, and their screeching calls became silent.

Suddenly, ahead of me, I saw the shadowy form of Woslolkia as he disappeared again in the writhing billows of smoke near the top of the canyon's wall. I led my anxious herd relentlessly upward through the burning trees to the spot where I had last seen the great bull. Engulfed again in blinding grayness, I stood peering helplessly through the smoke, unable to see even the panic-stricken bulls that I knew stood behind Wicala and me.

I became slowly aware of a strange, rhythmic sound nearly hidden by the chaotic roar of the thundering fire. The sound became louder as I led my unlikely herd steadily upward. As we stumbled through the smoke onto a narrow, rocky saddle at the ridge's top, I remembered a dream from long ago. A trail, nearly hidden in the blinding smoke, fell from the far side of the rocky ridge. It led, I knew, to the mysterious plateau where the ancient two-legged ones had grown their tree of life. It was the drums and mysterious song of the ancient ones, that I had heard.

With Wicala and the others following closely behind, I scrambled through the saddle and onto the ageless trail. We emerged from the boiling wall of smoke into clean, fresh air as we worked our way carefully along the rocky hogback toward the plateau. Soon, covered with soot and ash, we stood trembling in the grassy meadow beneath the great white tree. The stench of our singed hair hung heavily in the air around us as we watched the raging fire consume the main ridge at the far end of the rocky hogback. Angry, twisting flames now leaped into the sky from the trees where we had stood.

The meadow, encircled by a dense forest, and the tall spires of rock that lay at the plateau's edge were exactly as they had been in my dream. The great tree of life that towered above us, was as beautiful as I remembered it to be. With pounding hearts, we looked nervously back at the ridge and wondered if the spiraling orange flames that roared through the trees there, would follow us to the small plateau on which I knew we were now trapped.

The driving wind persisted for many days, pushing the fire through the mountains and often out of view, leaving only towering columns of smoke to tell of its progress. The wind would turn then, and bring the angry flames roaring suddenly back to leap once more, from the ridge near our small sanctuary. Endlessly, it seemed, we watched from the meadow as the mountains around us burned. The skies were constantly filled with dark clouds of smoke. At night, a burning sea of embers floated on the wind, but amazingly, always in a direction away from our plateau home. We slowly came to believe that unlike Ksapa and his herd, our lives would be spared, and that our meadow and the forest around us would not burn.

Chapter Twenty

I was haunted in the darkness of night by the memory of Ksapa's besieged bugle as he called to me from the scathing smoke of the burning canyon. The anguished cries of his entrapped herd echoed often in my mind. With great sadness in my heart, I thought often of the great bull and his herd of cows and calves. It did not seem possible that one with such incredible strength and will, could be gone forever from these mountains. I wondered often about the mysterious circumstances under which Wicala and I and the small herd of bulls had survived the horrific firestorm.

The passing days brought us finally to the season of *falling leaves,* but still the mountains around us smoldered, and smoke hung thickly in the valleys. On days when the dry, blustery winds returned, flames soon leaped from the ridges throughout the mountains, and the firestorm would begin anew.

The grass in the small meadow beneath the tree of life was dry and yellow, but our small herd ate well as we anxiously watched the burning mountains around us. At the edge of the forest where the trees gave way to jagged cliffs at the lower edge of the plateau, water seeped from the base of a towering rock spire. It dripped onto a basin-shaped ledge where it formed a small puddle of water before disappearing into the ground at its side. We easily emptied the tiny basin each day, but each morning the basin stood full and ready to quench our thirst once again.

There were seven bulls in our herd, some nearly as large as me. The top two tines on one side of the antlers of the largest bull had been broken off by a ranting Ksapa earlier in the time of mating. That troubling time having passed, I was no longer angered when he or the other bulls fed near Wicala and me in the meadow.

One evening as the sun dipped below the horizon, dark clouds began to build in its softening yellow glow. Before darkness settled, the clouds had fully overtaken us and filled the skies overhead. We stood grazing in the meadow when the first drops of rain fell gently from the sky. It soon became a steady downpour. We all stood in the dark meadow enjoying the wonderful wetness as we listened to the patter of falling droplets and smelled the wonderful scent of the wet earth around us.

When it became light the next morning, the rain still fell steadily from dark, threatening clouds, but the choking brown smoke and ash that had filled the skies for so long was now gone. Thin wisps of white smoke still floated mysteriously through the trees on the far ridge, but gone were the towering columns of smoke that had endlessly risen from the mountains around us. The rain continued for several days. It fell with greater intensity each day, and the air became cooler as each day passed.

As we lay beneath the trees at the edge of the meadow early one evening, the steady drumming of rain slowly ceased, and we felt the first cold flakes of snow land on our sensitive noses. Soon we lay covered in a growing blanket of snow, staring quietly into the meadow as a glowing mantle of whiteness grew deeper around us.

When the skies at last became light the next morning, we stood in snow that was halfway to our bellies. We stared nervously across our meadow whose far side was hidden behind a wall of swirling white flakes driven by a pounding wind. For several days, the raging storm persisted as we watched from beneath the protection of the trees.

One evening as we stood in the driving blizzard digging patiently for grass, the large, broken-horned bull raised his head suddenly from the snow. In a voice edged with fear, he said to the others, "We must leave this place where the snow is so quickly deepening. We must journey to the winter grounds where we will survive this *season of renewal*."

I whirled angrily and stared into the nervous bull's eyes. "No," I said, "we will not leave this plateau. The grass here beneath the snow is abundant, and it is here that we will stay during this *season of renewal*. To do otherwise would be foolish."

I knew that such a journey would be perilous. The snow had become too deep. It would be nearly impossible to cross the ledges and hidden crevasses on the rocky trail that led from our plateau to the mountains beyond.

As I looked into the anxious eyes of the other bulls who had gathered around us, I said, "The fire has surely burned the grass for a great distance through the mountains, and there will be no food with which to sustain yourselves on such a journey.

"Our only chance is to stay here in our plateau meadow where the grass is plentiful. That way, we will surely survive to see again the season of *ducks returning*."

During the night of the storm's sixth day, the clouds parted finally, and stars stood twinkling coldly in the inky blackness above. The next morning as we dug in the meadow for grass beneath growing drifts of snow, the broken-horned bull turned to us and said, "It is now time that I lead us from this place of deepening snow. Follow me to the wintering ground where we can join the many others of our kind and survive this *season of renewal*. He turned then, and started across the meadow, lunging through the deep snow toward the ancient trail that crossed the rocky ridge. The remaining bulls looked anxiously at me, then toward the laboring bull that drove steadily forward through the snow.

"Tateh," they begged, "lead us to the wintering grounds."

"No, brothers," I said. "It is here that Wicala and I will stay. You must follow your hearts though, and go where they lead you," I said, looking into their pleading eyes. "Whether you choose to go or to stay, walk with firm steps and go fearlessly, brothers."

Reluctantly, one by one, the bulls turned and followed the deeply furrowed path of their new leader. The laboring line of bulls soon disappeared among the rocky spires on the ridge. Wicala and I turned back to our digging for grass, occasionally raising our heads from the snow to look at the deep trench made by the departing bulls. We wondered about not only their uncertain futures but ours as well.

As the days passed by, it seemed that the skies were always filled with angry, gray clouds, and that we dug for grass in a relentless blizzard of driving snow. The snow had accumulated to a depth halfway up our bodies. I dug and exposed the grass beneath the snow for not only myself now, but for Wicala as well. She struggled greatly, and was growing weaker by the day. I no longer sought the grass beneath the deep snow in the meadow. I labored now, in the shallower snow beneath the trees at its edge where the wind had swept the snow away from the great tree's bases.

After countless days of storm, the skies above our plateau home cleared at last. The sun emerged to shine weakly as it passed through the sky each day barely above the horizon. The days had become incredibly cold, and we lay this night huddled together beneath a glowing moon. In silence we listened anxiously to the cracking report of trees in the forest as their trunks splintered from the growing pressure of frozen pitch within them.

Sleeping finally, I was suddenly in the small meadow far above the pond of the healing water where Ksapa often circled his herd during the time of mating. Below me, on a point of rocks overlooking the canyon was my mighty friend. His head tipped slowly back as I watched, and a thunderous bugle erupted from his throat and echoed into the canyon below him. I awoke suddenly from my dream, certain that I had been drawn from sleep by his haunting call. I listened carefully for its resonating echo in the moonlit opening before me. The meadow, though, lay silent, sparkling in the moonlight before me. I stared quietly over the sleeping form of Wicala at the glowing white silhouette of the tree of life whose frosted branches glistened brightly in the center of the meadow. It seemed a sad mix to stare at the beautiful symbol of life while thinking of the passing of Ksapa, and wondering if Wicala would rise from her bed when the sun rose once more.

I slowly became aware of a growing sound. It was the same haunting music I had heard when lost in the smoke of the great fire. Soft, chanting voices and a rhythmic pounding rumble seemed to echo from somewhere around me in the moonlight. The drumming became louder and louder, until an almost deafening thunder seemed to come from below us in the earth.

We sprang from our beds as the ground began to shake violently. Blinding torrents of snow fell in luminous cascades from the trees around us as the heaving ground freed the snow from their heavily laden limbs. The snow in the meadow was churned and thrown into the air by the intense rolling and shaking of the earth. Amidst the thunder and nearly hidden in the swirling snow, I saw the shadowy forms of two-legged ones as they danced and pounded their drums in the moonlight beneath the tree of life.

After what seemed forever, the dreadful shaking ceased, and the thunderous roar that came from the earth, quieted finally. We trembled fearfully in the moonlight as the last of the snow falling from the trees behind us sifted quietly to our feet. The deafening silence that now filled the night made the piercing cold air seem even more biting. Though I knew it was my imagination, it seemed that I could smell the acrid odor of the wonderful hot water of the healing pond. The tantalizing memories of its steaming warmth were redoubled by the intense cold that Wicala and I had for so long endured.

We remained anxiously standing through the night. Listening carefully for growing sounds in the earth beneath us, we watched nervously as shadows from the trees crept slowly across the sparkling snow of the meadow. At last, a pinkish glow began to build above the mountains, signaling the coming of a new day. When the sun rose at last, shining through sparkling flakes of frost, I saw a glistening white plume of smoke rising from deep in the trees at the far edge of the plateau. Excitement grew quickly within me as I remembered the clouds of steam that rose from the strange ponds near the canyon of the yellow rocks. I lunged excitedly forward through the deep snow, breaking a trail for Wicala. Our progress was slow as I labored through the forest toward the place in the trees where the white smoke shimmered upward into the cold sky.

A jagged wall of rock appeared slowly in the trees as we struggled forward. Between two immense boulders was a narrow opening in the cliff, nearly hidden by brush and small trees that grew in front of it. On the enormous rocks, the ominous forms of large animals had long ago been etched. On the craggy face of one, was the mysterious form of a strange, standing bear. On the other rock was the silhouette of a gigantic winged one, a kind I had never before seen.

Carefully working our way through the wall of brush, we found an overgrown trail that entered the narrow opening between the towering rocks. The sound of our passage echoed eerily from the rock walls as we toiled slowly upward through the crevasse. The crack was so narrow in places, that I was forced to turn my head so that my antlers would pass.

The old trail led us into a small opening surrounded by towering rocks, in the center of which lay the ancient bed of a small, dry lake. Near the middle of the old lake, a churning plume of steam boiled into the air. Hot water, awakened somehow by the frightful events of the past night, had begun to churn from the earth there, and now slowly filled the ancient pond.

On tall, flat rocks at the base of the rocky spires around the mysterious pond were more of the strange drawings. Four-legged ones of my kind, pursued by two-legged ones, were etched there, and in places stood the enormous, hulking figures of bison. There were drawings of strange, dancing two-legged ones. A shiver coursed through my body when I saw that on one rock overlooking the secret pond was etched the likeness of a huge black wolf.

I walked slowly to the edge of the steaming water and lowered my nose carefully to its surface. The water's heat on my lips felt like that of the healing water that lay in the canyon now so far away. I waded into its steamy warmth to my belly, then turned beckoningly to Wicala who watched anxiously from the edge.

Wicala walked cautiously to me in the steaming water, and together we stood with our eyes closed as we felt the marvelous warmth sink slowly to our very cores.

As the cold day gradually passed, we remained in the pond's relaxing warmth, watching as the rising water melted the snow in the tiny lakebed. It overflowed finally into a small opening in the rocks at its edge, where it disappeared silently into a steaming fissure.

Wicala and I lay quietly warming as darkness settled over us and the moon shimmered through the steaming sky that night.

The next morning, warm and rested, we climbed from the pond and made our way again through the narrow crevasse. We followed the deeply furrowed trail we had made the day before and were soon in the meadow. With renewed energy, we dug beneath the trees at its edge and gratefully filled our stomachs.

We spent each of our days as before, grazing beneath the trees near the edge of the meadow, but now, each night we rested peacefully in the steaming water of the secret pond. As the *season of renewal* progressed, we often lay in the warm water at night and watched as the pulsing sky above us was flooded with waves of mysterious color that burst across sky from the northern horizon.

The sun became stronger as this most brutal of seasons slowly released its icy grip on our plateau home. Ragged clumps of brownish grass began to appear in the snow beneath the trees at the edge of the forest, but still no grass showed above the shining white surface anywhere in the meadow.

The snow had receded far from the edges of the pond, and now we dined daily on short grass that had begun to sprout in the warm soil there. Exposed from beneath the snow among the rocks and ledges around the pond were the bones of many animals that had come here to die. Huge, white skulls of bison and the great antlers of elk lay among the rocks. On small ledges beneath mysterious drawings lay the smaller bones and strange round skulls of two-legged ones partially wrapped still, in the ancient hides of bison.

As the days became longer and the sun traveled higher in the sky on its daily voyage, our relentless quest for grass became easier. The warmer days were less taxing, and we spent less of our precious energy fighting the bitter cold around us. I thought often about my great friend and teacher, Ksapa, and his herd. I often relived that terrible day in the fiery canyon and thought sadly about how my journey in life would be so much less without him.

I did not see again, the shadowy figures of two-legged ones chanting in the moonlight beneath the tree of life, nor was I visited in my dream-world by Woslolkia during the remaining days of *the season of renewal*. As I thought about the mysterious events that had brought Wicala and me to this remarkable place, and had enabled us to survive, I came to know that indeed there was a wondrous force at play in our mountain home.

Chapter Twenty-One

The meadow in our plateau home had at last, become almost completely bare. Totally exposed now, were large areas of matted brown grass that only a short time ago we had labored endlessly to uncover. Green grass peeked everywhere from beneath the brown mat, and only slender fingers of snow remained where deep drifts had piled high during the *season of renewal*. The smell of the awakening forest drifted heavily around us, and small, green buds now shown throughout the limbs on the tree of life. Having finally returned, flocks of small winged ones flew nervously around us in the meadow, and the forest was once again alive with their wonderful calls.

One evening as Wicala and I fed, we suddenly heard the approaching calls of the great water birds. Soon, large flocks of the noisy winged ones filled the sky above our meadow as they flew onward in the sky. When the geese had passed from view and we could no longer hear their haunting calls, I resumed grazing once more. Wicala, though, stood quietly looking into the sky beyond the blackened ridge where the great flocks had disappeared.

When she turned at last from the ridge, she looked into my eyes with a knowing gaze. I realized that it was time that we leave this place and journey upward into the great basin. Wicala, I knew, would travel alone into one of the deep canyons that fell from the basin's side where she would find safety and seclusion. There, she would bring new life to our mountains. I would travel alone to the canyon of the healing water where I would spend the season of *growing grass,* and in quiet ritual, would prepare for the coming season of the bugling bulls.

When the sun rose the next day, I led Wicala from the plateau and started carefully along the ancient trail through the rocky jumbles and jagged spires to the burnt ridge beyond. As we rounded an enormous stack of rocks on the ancient trail, a large flock of ravens flapped noisily into the sky, squawking their disapproval of our unseen approach.

In a narrow crevasse beneath a spot where the trail crossed on a slender ledge of rock, the skeleton of a bull elk hung ominously from its horns. The hapless animal had somehow fallen from the trail into the fissure, and hung now from its antlers wedged firmly on each side of the narrow gap. In my mind, I suddenly saw the pleading look in the eyes of the nervous bulls who had gathered before me in the snowy meadow. As we crossed the rocky ledge above the hapless bull, I noticed the top two tines on one side of the bull's antlers were missing.

We worked our way carefully through the remaining cliffs and crevasses on the rocky hogback and came finally to the blackened ridge where we had seen the fire rage so long ago. The trees on the ridge stood hauntingly before us, gnarled and burned. The ground beneath them was blackened and bare. The heat had been so intense from the blaze that even the seeds hidden in the soil had been destroyed.

We started upward on the charred ridge, and as we entered a small opening that fell from its far side, we heard the piercing scream of a great winged one. Looking downward into the greening meadow we saw at its center, a large, crooked tree where a huge eagle sat on a limb near its top. Below the great bird was a large nest where three small heads bobbed curiously as they watched our approach. The fire had miraculously split in the meadow beneath them and had left the great tree untouched. In wonderment, I realized that the forsaken winged ones we had seen while fleeing the fire had been spared.

The sun sat low on the horizon when we came to the top of the burned ridge and walked into the basin that lay beyond. The fire had not burned into the great opening, and we stared in wonder at a gently flowing sea of green grass that lay before us in the breeze. We lay that night with full bellies near a small pond, staring at the hills around us in the soft light of the full moon.

Early the next day, as we crossed above the head of a deep canyon that plunged from the great basin's side, Wicala stopped and gazed into its mysterious depths.

After a long silence, she turned to me and said quietly, "It is time, Tateh. I must go alone now, into this canyon." The emotion that I saw burning in her eyes as she stared into mine, told me of her great strength and resolve. I knew then, that she would return from the challenges she would face there, and we would walk together once more in the coming season of *ripening berries.*

She turned from me then, and disappeared into the gorge below. I stood for a long time above the canyon, remembering the knowing look she had held in her eyes. I remembered soft, brown eyes like them, the first into which I had ever looked, deep in a canyon far from here.

I came at last to the saddle that lay above the canyon of the healing water. As I stood in the rocky depression staring into the canyon, the memory of my great friend Ksapa washed over me. I thought about the many times we had stood in this very spot and gazed into the drainage below. As the sun moved lower on the horizon, I started downward, filled with a terrible loneliness as I moved through growing shadows in the canyon's bottom.

Blackened trees stood as before in bands of timber that separated lush, green meadows in the broad canyon's bottom. I nibbled constantly at the green rooted ones in the openings as I moved quickly on in the failing light.

The moon was high overhead when at last I entered the meadow above the healing water and saw the familiar plume of steam glowing in the moonlight at its lower end. As I walked through the meadow toward the steaming pond, a strange, lonely feeling gripped me, and I turned away from the healing water. I climbed instead, up the canyon's side above the trees where I often bedded.

Driving upward, I came finally to the meadow where Ksapa had many times held his herd of cows and calves during the time of mating. The meadow stood vacant and silent in the bluish light of the moon. I stood in the trees at its edge and relived the memory of the many cows and calves that I had seen there. I could hear the storming one's bugle that had echoed so many times from the opening.

I walked across the empty meadow to the outcropping of rock at its lower end where I had seen Ksapa stand in my dream as he roared his frightening call into the canyon below. Remembering sadly, I slowly raised my head, tipping my antlers over my back and bellowed a mighty bugle. I stood quietly listening as my booming scream echoed again and again from all sides of the canyon beneath me.

As I turned from the cliff, a shrieking bugle erupted from above me on the canyon's side. I stood frozen near the point of rocks, staring intently across the meadow as heavy footsteps crashed toward me from the timber above. With disbelieving eyes, I watched in astonishment as the enormous silhouette of Ksapa emerged from the shadowy timber into the moonlit meadow above me. We lunged to the center of the opening where we stood silently facing each other in the moonlight. Our gaze was locked, and for a short time there were no words spoken.

Then, we erupted suddenly, in a bugling, barking, rush of emotion as we crashed dizzily down the canyon's side toward the pond of the healing water. I was nearly overcome with joy as Ksapa and I charged onward, leaping and kicking through the air as we thundered across the meadow toward the rising plume of steam. We ran full speed through the pond to the yellow mud beyond. We slid to a stop with mud flying in all directions and rolled and kicked in the moonlight as if we were calves.

When resting quietly at last in the soothing water, Ksapa broke the silence as he said, "Tateh, I was certain that you and Wicala had lost your lives in the burning canyon. When I was unable to find you in the place of wintering, I knew truly, it was so. After the *season of renewal*, I climbed the mountains where I wandered for many days in the great basin, only now coming to the canyon of the healing water."

I told Ksapa about the mysterious events that had saved Wicala's and my life. Ksapa listened intently as I explained how Woslolkia had mysteriously appeared in the fire and led us upward from the burning canyon. Chills coursed through me as I told him of our unlikely survival on the mysterious plateau. It was a place, I told him, where the earth had trembled and shook, and the spirits of ancient two-legged ones danced in the moonlight beneath their tree of life.

Ksapa studied me quietly through the rising steam, and after a long while, with knowingness shining in his eyes, said in barely more than a whisper, "My old friend Woslolkia, walked beside me too, Tateh, as I led my herd from the burning canyon."

As we grazed in the rich grass of the meadow and rested during the heat of each day beneath the trees at its edge, Ksapa's antlers grew quickly, as did mine. One day as we rested in the shade near a point of rocks at the meadow's edge, Ksapa lay deep in thought in the warm grass at my side.

379

Turning to me, he said, "Tateh, you have shared my journey for many years and have grown to be a magnificent bull. Your antlers are broad and imposing and are the envy of most bulls here. Your wisdom has become equal to your size. You have walked patiently in my shadow, and you have demonstrated your understanding of our ways as you traveled with the other young bulls near the herds of the mighty leaders here. You have grown to be the equal of any of the great bulls who now walk our mountains, and when it is again the season of mating, your greatest challenge will be suddenly before you. Remember what I have taught you, Tateh, for soon it will be your time, and you will lead the great herd. When it is again the season of mating, we will walk separate paths. Our journey will no longer be as one, Tateh."

Ksapa stood from the grass then, and walked into the meadow where he lowered his head to feed.

As the season of *ripening berries* came at last, the time of mating drew nearer. With great excitement, I thought often about Ksapa's curious words and his prediction of my leadership. I wondered about his words of caution, though, and the knowing they seemed to hold. The excitement and energy that grew within me at each passing day was astounding. As I had seen Ksapa do for so many years, I now ripped at the earth and ground my horns against the trees as I battled imaginary foes into submission for the right to lead.

Ksapa and I no longer spoke, and as we did each year at this time, we chose to live solitary lives on opposite sides of the meadow. We filled the night with the sound of battle as we crashed noisily in the darkness. We ripped violently at trees and screamed frustrated bugles that were often answered by the other's angry, bellowing reply. Several other bulls hid in the trees around the meadow, having been drawn into our canyon by our resounding calls, and they often joined the echoing fray as we filled the night with our angry rant.

Late one day, dark clouds boiled across the sky as the sun sank toward the horizon. As darkness slowly settled, Ksapa and I stood in the fading light glaring at one another from opposite sides of the meadow. Bright flashes of light began to shoot from cloud to cloud in the sky above us. After each blinding streak, came a thundering boom that was answered immediately by Ksapa's roar as he furiously punished the trees in the darkness. As the storm's fury grew, so did Ksapa's shrieking bugles, and I soon heard the soft rumble of approaching footsteps as he crossed the meadow toward me. With no outward acknowledgment of me, Ksapa trotted angrily past, and continued up the side of the canyon toward the rocky outlook above. Realizing that this was Ksapa's unspoken signal that he was leaving the canyon to begin his search for cows, I quickly followed him upward.

He climbed steadily through the trees on the steep canyon's side and entered the small meadow near the rocky point above the healing water. He walked quickly to the cliff that overlooked the canyon, and as the light flashed in the sky above him, roared a shrieking bugle into the dark meadow far below. Ksapa turned, and with me following a respectful distance behind, continued along the canyon's top toward the great basin above. We entered the huge opening as the light of a new day began to build in the stormy sky. Ahead of me, the great bull walked with his head low, his antlers swaying rhythmically as he went. From behind us came the echoing bugles of bulls that had followed us from the healing water.

Golden rays of light streamed between thinning clouds as Ksapa continued past the head of the blackened canyon in which we had nearly perished in the last season of mating. When Ksapa came at last, to the canyon where years ago my mother had led me in search of the great herd, the sun shone brightly from a cloudless, blue sky. My huge friend stood with his head held high as he tested the wind and listened carefully into the canyon below. Finally, with his head lowered to the ground, sniffing carefully as he went, the great bull dropped quietly into the canyon.

Ksapa's bugle was met by shrieking replies from all sides of the canyon as we walked downward. He moved quickly toward any bugle he thought to be that of a herd bull, and upon finding him, promptly took his cows and sent the startled leader crashing frightfully away. As in years past, most bulls, upon seeing Ksapa, wisely relinquished their cows and sank back into the woods, but some stood bravely and paid a terrible price. Cows often came willingly to Ksapa's resounding bugle, and his herd grew rapidly as we dropped farther into the ever-widening canyon.

As we entered one big opening, a large herd of cows and calves looked nervously toward us from its far edge. The large, green meadow fell steeply away into several rocky ravines. An enormous bull stood in front of them, his head lowered to the ground, a deep, growling moan coming from within his chest as he watched through glowering eyes, the purposeful approach of Ksapa.

The bull was Ksapa's equal in size, but as they met in the meadow with a thundering crash, Ksapa drove him backward, and together they toppled from sight into one of the ravines. Dust boiled from the tiny gorge as the sound of thundering hooves, grinding horns, and the grunts and moans of the battling bulls filled the air. I stood with wide eyes at the meadow's edge as I listened to the echoing crash of the terrible battle below. All became quiet finally, and all ears and noses were turned toward the ravine as the anxious cows listened carefully to heavy footsteps approaching from below.

An enormous set of antlers rose slowly above the horizon as Ksapa climbed from the draw, and with eyes filled with intensity, gathered his new herd of cows in the meadow above it. One cow though, with a small calf at her side, refused to join his herd and stood stubbornly alone near the center of the meadow. I bugled excitedly as I recognized the defiant cow. Ksapa watched with seeming approval, as Wicala and her calf ran to where I stood at the edge of the meadow. The happiness that shone in Wicala's eyes as she approached me, was equal, I knew, to the joy that now brimmed in mine. I was filled with wonder as I carefully studied the young calf that stood nervously beneath her. Wicala and I stared into one another's eyes for a long time. There were no words needed saying.

Ksapa stayed in the meadow for many days. Wicala, her little calf, and I, grazed along its edges. There were more bulls circling Ksapa's herd this year than in any year I had seen, and he worked harder than ever, night and day, chasing the would-be thieves. As he chased bulls from his herd in one direction, several would sneak from the other, and often cows were stolen and pushed away in the darkness. Ksapa's screaming bugle rang nearly nonstop in both darkness and light as his frustration and anger steadily grew.

One day, after thundering past me in the timber, brutally punishing a pair bulls, Ksapa stopped as he returned to his herd and stared intensely into my eyes. As I held the great bull's gaze, I saw in his eyes a storm of emotion.

"Prepare yourself," he said quietly. "Your time is soon, Tateh." He dipped his great antlers to me then, and trotted back toward his herd to resume his angry rant.

The young bulls' torment of Ksapa was relentless. Late one day when the sun hung low in the sky above the canyon's edge, an enraged Ksapa could stand no more. Bellowing angrily, he gathered his cows and pushed them upward into the timber away from the thieving bulls that skulked brazenly at the edges of his herd. Screaming as he went, Ksapa worked upward through the heavy forest toward the great basin above. As I followed him and his herd from the canyon, I was stunned at the number of bulls that answered each of Ksapa's ferocious bugles.

Darkness had long settled when the canyon above us became silent. I knew then, that Ksapa's herd and the many excited bulls that had followed them, had entered the great basin beyond. My huge friend's bugle could barely be heard when Wicala and I at last walked into the dark basin, and we moved quickly in the direction of the great one's fading call. When the first streaks of light began to fill the sky, the basin ahead of us became quiet, and I knew that Ksapa had dropped from its side into the canyon of the healing water.

When at last we entered the canyon behind them, we could hear Ksapa's resounding bugle high above us on the canyon's side. Crashing and breaking timber told of the place where Ksapa dealt brutal punishment to the thieving bulls that plagued him.

When the sun was nearly straight overhead, Wicala and I came to the great meadow where the healing water lay beneath a plume of steam at its lower end. Far above us, we could hear Ksapa's screaming bugle. My great friend, I knew, was near the point of rocks in the meadow near the top of the canyon's wall. For several days, he defended his herd there, and his angry bellows that echoed through our meadow were nearly constant.

One morning, as the sky first began to lighten, dark clouds boiled over the canyon wall and filled the sky above us. Soon, rain fell steadily from the threatening clouds, and rumbling peals of thunder followed bright flashes of light. From far above, Ksapa's bugle answered each flash and booming report as he unrelentingly guarded his herd.

The rain worsened as the day slowly passed, but still, Ksapa's bugle echoed unceasingly from above. Suddenly, from the dense timber on the side of the canyon below the pond, came a roaring challenge to Ksapa's intimidating screams. The mysterious bugle was much deeper and louder than any of the bulls that I had heard answer Ksapa during the season of mating. An unsettling feeling drew over me as I pondered the sudden arrival of this bull that had bugled from the canyon below us.

Standing from the grass, I waited nervously at the edge of the meadow for the appearance of the approaching bull. The bull though, stayed above us in the trees on the canyon's side as he climbed quickly upward toward Ksapa. As his crashing footsteps faded in the rainy forest, I struggled to clarify a troubling memory borne from the resounding bugle of this stealthy one.

Ksapa grew suddenly silent as he heard the bellowing call of the bull that rapidly approached him from below. He now waited, I knew, with his head lowered to the grassy meadow's floor and watched quietly through wild eyes for the arrival of this challenging bull.

Over the din of the deepening storm, I heard yet another thundering call from the mysterious challenger. I reeled with confusion and inexplicable dread as obscure memories danced with greater clarity behind my eyes. Overcome finally by angst, and consumed by unjustified fear, I sprang forward, leaving Wicala and her calf startled and confused beneath the trees at the healing water. I crashed upward through the forest, lunging with all my might toward Ksapa and his herd in the meadow above.

I heard the first thundering smash of antlers when only halfway up the mountain, and I knew that Ksapa now battled the challenger in the meadow at the canyon's top. Above the sound of my crashing approach, I could hear the grunts and groans and the mighty smashing of antlers. The fight for leadership was quickly intensifying.

An incredible scene appeared before me as I exploded into the bottom of the meadow, where near its top, the two behemoths battled for supremacy. With heaving chest and legs burning from my lunging climb upward, I watched in awe, mesmerized, as the drama above me unfolded.

The huge challenger and Ksapa were equals as they brutally pounded each other. Colliding again and again with shuddering impact, they drove one another grunting and moaning through the meadow beneath the thundering sky. They ground their horns against each other, flipping and turning, struggling with all their might to gain advantage. Their fight had become a violent struggle for life. As the vicious battle continued, cows and calves became scattered through the meadow as the straining bulls, with antlers locked, crashed and twisted through their midst.

As I started forward once more, the enraged bulls parted, and stood for a moment gasping for air. With antlers lowered still, they glared with hatred at one another. A young calf, driven from its mother by the frightful battle, ran suddenly between the huge bulls. The cunning challenger saw his chance at last, and sprang forward toward Ksapa with a mighty charge. Ksapa quickly tipped his horns and turned to sweep the imperiled calf from the path of the charging bull. The sly one, lunging forward at full speed, hit Ksapa squarely in his side. Sinking his enormous antlers deep into his ribs, he drove my great friend sideways, and to the ground. In a fit of unbelievable rage, Ksapa kicked and twisted painfully, wrenching himself free from the antlers of the scheming bull. He whirled to his feet and charged the devious one with such heart and ferocity that the resounding collision drove his immense opponent halfway across the meadow and onto his back.

The sly one though, had fooled Ksapa. He had struck a fatal blow. Stunned, I stood transfixed, watching, as my great friend fought valiantly on before his disbelieving herd. The storm exploded overhead as Ksapa lowered his mighty antlers for yet another charge, and thunder reverberated through the meadow as his knees buckled, and he sank to the ground. The fire that burned within the great one though, brought Ksapa twisting and staggering once more to his feet to stare with seething anger at the treacherous one before him. The life, though, was nearly drained from my mighty friend, and he could fight no more. His immense opponent glared with hatred as he quietly watched Ksapa sink to his knees and with chest heaving, roll onto his side.

As if in a dream, I watched as the victor, snorting with contempt and shaking his mighty antlers menacingly, gathered Ksapa's confused herd. Any cow or calf that refused was immediately knocked from their feet, then upon rising, was pushed roughly into the herd. In an instant, it seemed, the ranting leader had gathered Ksapa's cows and calves and had driven them upward from the meadow. Blinking my eyes, trying desperately to wake myself from this nightmare, I forced myself forward, lunging toward where a lone cow stood quietly near Ksapa. The old cow raised her head as I approached, and the sadness in her pleading eyes told me it had not been a dream. Ksapa lay in the grass at her feet.

My great friend's eyes stared blankly at the sky, and his legs pumped gently in the grass, as if he loped across some faraway meadow. Deep wounds in his side bled slowly still. Unwilling to believe what I knew in my heart to be so, I lowered my nose to my huge friend. From his body rose not only his familiar scent, but also the strange scent of the mysterious bull that he had so brutally battled.

A fury of wrath washed over me as the ominous memory that had so drawn me toward this terrible battle became suddenly clear. With clarity I saw the angry, flashing eyes of the bull that had long ago raised his head from our lifeless leader and whirled in the moonlight toward me.

"Zomika!" I breathed. Blinding light throbbed in my head and blood pounded at my temples as I was consumed by blinding rage. As if driven by a will not my own, I wheeled from Ksapa's lifeless form, and crashed from the meadow toward the ridge top above.

I could barely hear Zomika's bugle ahead of me on the ridge as I charged upward through the soggy forest. Soon when I

389

stopped to listen, I could hear only the steady patter of rain around me. Knowing that the silence meant that Zomika had driven Ksapa's herd into the basin, I drove upward with all my strength toward the top of the ridge.

The light had begun to soften in the dark clouds when at last I entered the great basin. Far ahead of me, I heard the faint, echoing bugle of the treacherous one, and in a burst of anger, I lunged forward in the failing light.

As I pounded feverishly forward on the muddy, churned trail of the enraged bull and his fleeing herd, I began to pass young calves standing exhausted and confused, left behind by the coldhearted one ahead of me. As I bolted into a small meadow near the top of a rolling hill, I passed an old cow that lay on her side with mouth agape and sides heaving as she gasped for air. Her eyes suddenly focused and widened as she saw me. As I thundered quickly past, the dying cow raised her head and whispered my name.

Darkness began to settle over the basin as I drew closer to the fleeing herd. Finally, on a rise in the distance, I could see the ghost-like shapes of elk as Ksapa's herd climbed the small hill in near darkness. A great flash of light suddenly filled the sky, and I saw the enormous form of Zomika, his head held high as he stood in the pulsing light.

A deafening bugle filled the darkness around me. Startled, I realized that the bellowing call that now echoed across the basin had come from deep within my own chest. Upon hearing my thundering challenge, the great bull whirled in disbelief and stared with contempt in my direction. As I crashed wildly forward, Zomika quickly circled his herd and drove them over the rise and out of sight. The great bull knew now that he was pursued. Charging violently from the basin, he pushed his exhausted herd furiously into a steep canyon that fell from its side.

Having seen the object of my pounding rage finally, I charged forward with strength I never knew could be mine. Zomika no longer bugled as he fled downward in the stormy canyon. As I lunged ever nearer, though, I could hear the steady rumble of hooves and the stressful cries of cows and calves as they crashed fitfully downward in the darkness below me.

Realizing that escape from the one who so doggedly pursued him was not possible, Zomika stopped in a meadow below me and brutally forced his exhausted herd into the trees at its side.

Hearing the nervous barks and mews from the cows and calves below me, I knew that Zomika no longer fled. I had caught my quarry. He waited now, with seething fury for the appearance of the brazen one that he knew he would soon punish.

With fury pounding in my head, I slowed to a walk, and with a growling moan rumbling deep from within my chest, I moved downward.

Lightning sizzled across the sky as I walked toward an opening in the trees. In the pulsing light, I saw Ksapa's shaken herd as they stirred anxiously, eyes wide with fright, at the edges of the meadow below me. As I entered the opening, I realized that it was the meadow in which my haunting memories of Zomika had long ago been born.

Zomika raised his head and screamed furiously in my direction as I walked slowly forward. The bull was even larger than I remembered, with wide, towering, white-tipped antlers, the last two on each side stained with the blood of my great friend. I stopped for a moment, glaring with hatred at him, inwardly curious at my strange lack of fear. I silently savored the rage that now emanated from every fiber of my being. I walked forward, trembling with anger, toward the huge one who stood waiting in the center of the meadow.

As I neared the monstrous bull, the hate and anger that boiled within me burst like fire within my head. In blinding rage, I sprang forward. We met in the center of the opening with a thunderous collision that sent us both staggering to our knees. We sprang immediately to our feet and crashed violently together again, grunting and straining as we fought furiously to knock one another to the ground.

The rain fell harder, and lightning and thunder filled the sky nonstop as we fought on and on in the muddy meadow. Frightened cows and calves jumped nervously from our path as we grunted and groaned, straining with all our might, locked in a brutal battle that I knew would end in death. We parted for a moment, and as we stood gasping for air, lightning crackled through the sky above. I saw in Zomika's glowering eyes a terrible hate and anger that I knew shone also, in mine.

My lungs ached and my legs burned as we collided again with a resounding crash and ground our antlers against one another as we twisted and grunted in the darkness. Zomika was cunning and wise, but he knew now that my strength and size was equal to his. He soon began to use the deceitful tricks he had learned during the violent battles of his many years.

As he pushed me backward on one gut-wrenching, straining drive, I suddenly felt the rake of small trees at my back legs. I realized in horror that the cunning one had pushed me into the short, gnarly trees where years ago he had killed the great leader of our herd. Stiff, wiry branches grasped at my feet in the darkness. Zomika, realizing he had fooled me, drove even harder against me as I lost my footing and began to roll backwards.

With my horns engaged in Zomika's, my head was tipped awkwardly forward as the huge one, moaning and grunting, rolled me powerfully backward in the trees. I suddenly felt Ksapa's presence beside me, and then I remembered.

I no longer resisted the charging antlers of Zomika, but instead, with all my strength, I pulled suddenly against them as I had seen Ksapa once do.

Grunting and moaning, with every muscle in my body screaming with pain, I pulled Zomika from his feet. With tines snapping from our straining antlers, I hurled the massive bull

kicking helplessly over me in the air. The deceitful one landed in
the short trees behind me with an agonizing gasp. I twisted to my
feet and whirled with head lowered to lunge again at the Zomika,
but strangely, he did not rise. The raging one lay kicking and
grunting helplessly on his side. Lurching weakly to his feet, finally,
he stood for a moment looking at me, confused and dazed. With
blood pouring from his side, Zomika staggered slowly sideways and
crumpled to the ground.

Lightning again filled the sky. In the pulsing light, I saw lying
in the grass near Zomika's heaving body, the haunting white skull
and towering antlers of the huge leader that Zomika had killed here
long ago. The tines on the enormous, bleached antlers of the old
bull gleamed wetly with Zomika's blood in the flickering light. The
old leader had reaped his revenge.

Gasping for air and with my heart beating wildly, I stood in
the crashing light with my antlers lowered, watching the cunning
one through eyes seething still, with rage. After a long, ragged
gasp, Zomika lay quietly in the grass, and moved no more.

I stood for a long while facing the motionless form of the
huge bull. The pounding in my chest quieted finally, and the terrible
rage that had consumed me slowly dwindled. A great fatigue
settled over me as I realized that the battle had ended. I had won. I
had avenged the death of my friend, my teacher, Ksapa.

The world around me began to focus once more, and I became aware of movement in the meadow around me. I raised my head slowly from the lifeless form of Zomika, and in bewilderment, studied the cows and calves that milled nervously in the rain at the meadow's edges.

Ksapa's confusing words earlier in the season of *growing grass* sprang into my mind. "When it is again the time of mating, Tateh, you will lead," he had said.

Realizing that his dire prediction had come true, I walked to the edge of the meadow and moved quietly among the cows and calves that chirped and mewed nervously beneath the trees there.

A deep sadness filled me as I walked slowly around the edges of the meadow gathering my herd, but as I started them slowly up the canyon in the crashing light, I was filled with a wonderful new excitement. I had at last earned the right to lead.

I stopped and turned back to look as I moved my herd of cows and calves into the timber at the meadow's upper end. In the flashing light of the terrible storm, I could see that the grass in the small opening was churned and torn with rutted tracks from the violent battle I had fought there. Lying at the meadow's far edge, I could see the enormous antlers of Zomika. Staring at his lifeless form from the grass beside him, was the ghostly skull and towering white antlers of the old herd bull.

There was little talk shared by the weary cows and calves as we moved quietly through the rainy darkness toward the basin above. Having witnessed the terrible life struggle in the meadow below, bulls that we met on our way upward moved quickly from my path and sank nervously into the trees. They were unwilling to risk the ire of the great bull that had won the terrible battle.

Light had begun to grow in the sky when we climbed from the canyon and entered the great basin. The rain began to slow as the day grew brighter, and the sun shone between ragged clouds when it climbed at last above the horizon.

As we retraced the steps of the previous night's crashing flight across the basin, jubilant mothers were once again reunited with wayward calves that had fallen from the herd during the terrible journey. The happy sound of cows and calves began to erupt from my herd as we moved onward through the great opening.

We came at last to the ridge above the healing water and moved downward from the side of the great basin on a wide, rutted trail that had been pounded into the earth just one day before. The sun was nearing the far horizon when we entered the small meadow at the top of the ridge above the healing water.

As we walked from the timber, there was a great rush of wings as birds flew excitedly into the sky from the body of my great friend. There were no ravens or magpies though. Only the white-headed winged ones sat watching from the trees around us. Ksapa's herd, in a display of respect, walked single file past where the great bull lay. I stood to the side of my passing cows, looking toward the point of rocks at the edge of the meadow. In my mind, I could see Ksapa standing there again as he bellowed his thundering call into the canyon below. I remembered his troubled eyes on that day not long ago when he had told me, "Ready yourself, Tateh, soon you will lead."

Darkness was gathering over the canyon when at last we entered the meadow at the healing water. Wicala and her small calf ran excitedly from the timber and stood at my side, looking with wonder at the huge herd standing before us in the meadow. My exhausted cows began immediately to feed, and their weary calves were quickly asleep laying beneath them. Wicala quietly studied the fresh wounds on my shoulders and neck. After meeting my gaze with emotion brimming in her eyes, she turned and joined the feeding cows.

I guarded my herd in the meadow at the healing water for the remainder of the season of mating. As the days slipped by, I came to know the great frustration of Ksapa as I worked night and day to chase would-be thieves from my precious herd. The story of my brutal fight with the treacherous one traveled quickly among my kind. Few bulls found the courage to challenge this wild one who guarded his herd with such anger, the one upon whose towering antlers were tines ravaged and broken from battle.

The great white-headed eagles flew often in the skies above our meadow. I knew when they sat in the trees nearby, that the spirit of Ksapa still guarded his herd.

Often, as I walked among my cows and calves, I thought sadly about my great friend. I now understood the ominous words he had spoken to me earlier.

'Indeed Ksapa,' I thought often, 'in this season of mating, I did face my greatest challenge, and now, sadly, forevermore our paths will indeed, be separate. Our journey will never again be as one.' "Yes, great one," I would then say aloud, "I now understand your words, but never, will I understand how you knew."

Chapter Twenty-Two

After the death of my friend and teacher, Ksapa, my life became a secretive, solitary existence. Each of my seasons of *growing grass* were spent near the healing water, where I strengthened myself after the long *seasons of renewal*. I lay each morning in the warm water as daylight came to the canyon, then climbed the canyon's steep side where I rested in the seclusion of the dense forest as the sun traveled slowly through the sky. When darkness fell once again, I would descend to the meadow to feed, then enter the healing water once more. This routine was my daily custom as I readied myself both physically and mentally, for the brutal challenges I would face in the season of mating.

When at last the season of *ripening berries* arrived, I would leave the healing water and travel impatiently upward into the great basin in search of cows. I always found them in the deep canyons that dropped from the great basin's side where they had gathered after having brought new life into our mountains earlier in the season of *growing grass*. Often, I stayed for the remainder of the season of mating in the canyon or timbered basin where I had gathered my herd, moving only if the pressure from competing bulls became too great.

As the years passed quickly by, I grew larger and stronger, and my antlers became enormous. It was now said that my strength and size rivaled the greatest bull ever known to walk our mountains, my father, Woslolkia.

My herd became larger each year, and the task of guarding my precious cows became immense. As the numbers of my herd swelled, my brutal reputation during the time of mating grew as well. I was soon known by the other great bulls in our mountains to be a seething tyrant, a bull whose leadership should not be challenged by any bull not prepared to die. It became rare that I was forced to battle for the leadership of my herd, but when I did, it was with such anger and ferocity that the challenger was quickly overwhelmed and dispatched to stagger weakly away, and to my great sorrow, sometimes to die.

When the time of mating was at last finished, I was always exhausted from the relentless torment of sneaking bulls and would return to the canyon of the healing water. Over time, it had become my sanctuary. Here, I rested and healed my weakened body in the warmth of the healing pond and strengthened myself while grazing in the meadow around it. When the time of killing came again to our land, I climbed to safety in the high plateau above the great basin where Ksapa had long ago taught me to hide. As the snows became deep, I dropped from my windswept refuge long after all others had traveled downward to the wintering grounds. I plowed through the snow of the great basin, descending to the thundering canyon of the yellow rocks where in solitude, I endured the *season of renewal*.

This most bitter of seasons was lonely without Ksapa as I grazed in driving blizzards and terrible biting cold around the pools of boiling water. During the most challenging days of the brutal season, I journeyed downward on narrow rock ledges where Ksapa had led me long ago to the bottom of the thundering gorge, and there fed on grass that stood exposed at the edges of the churning river.

Though I walked alone now, I remembered the words that Ksapa had shared with me, and I pondered often, the teachings of my father who came to me in mysterious dreams during the darkness of night. And on those cold nights when the chilling winds tore at my sleeping body, I found warmth in the memory of the kind, brown eyes of my mother.

It was now early in the season of *falling leaves* in my fourteenth year, and the white-skinned ones' time of killing had begun. The moon had risen into a cloudless sky, and I lay sleeping on a narrow, grassy shelf of rock, high on an open plateau. Here, I was safe from the killing one's sticks of thunder.

My dreams were suddenly filled with the anxious mewing and troubled calls of my herd. In my tormented dream, a crazed, angry bull drove my cows and calves through a meadow low in the mountains beneath the great basin. The frightened cows and calves refused the bull's harried attempts to drive them on, but with his great antlers lowered, he drove them brutally downward. On the ridges and in the timber surrounding my besieged herd were many two-legged ones who snuck carefully forward toward the frightened herd. I awoke with a terrible start as the white-skinned ones stood suddenly from the timber at the edges of the meadow and the killing thunder began.

Springing from my bed, I stared intently into the darkness with my heart pounding in my chest. The opening before me, though, lay empty and silent, bathed in the moon's soft light. I lay awake far into the night listening carefully to the mountains around me, as a troubling feeling grew within me. After a long while, I lowered my head once more to the ground to sleep, but the killing thunder erupted again in my dreams. My cows and calves mewed and barked in fright as they milled in confusion, unsure of which way to run. Dust filled the air around them as cows and calves began to fall to the earth before the thundering sticks of the killing ones.

I sprang again to my feet fully awake, and stared anxiously through the meadow reliving the frightful scenes of my dream. Though there were no cows or calves insight, the haunting cries of my embattled herd echoed still, from the moonlit opening before me. I was certain now, it had not been a dream. I knew I must find them.

I lunged across the meadow and crashed into the forest beyond. Soon I came to the edge of my plateau sanctuary and crashed downward in the darkness toward the great basin below. The moon was low on the horizon as I pounded through the basin, and the sun had just risen when at last I stood at its far edge staring into the huge valley that lay far below.

As it had been in my dream, I could see the killing, two-legged ones as they climbed slowly upward in the early morning light. From somewhere below me, I could hear the haunting calls of cows and calves. With my heart pounding, I bolted forward with all my might and crashed downward toward the ominous cries.

I exploded from the timber into a large meadow where an enormous bull worked feverishly to push my frightened herd toward the trees at its lower end. I saw the first two-legged ones appear from the trees as I neared the cows and calves. The storming bull that drove them, whirled immediately to face me. To my astonishment, the enormous bull was my oldest foe, Khiza.

With haunting memories of long ago crashing across my mind, I lowered my head and lunged toward him. The killing thunder erupted from the edges of the meadow as we collided with a mighty crash. I drove him backward across the opening, rolling him onto his back. As he rose, I sprang forward and drove him again, to the ground. Staggering to his feet, the fight in him now gone, Khiza spun away from me and bolted toward the trees below us. As I gathered my panicked herd, the killing thunder roared from the timber where Khiza had disappeared.

"Run, sisters," I yelled above the booming roar of lightning sticks. As my terror-stricken herd rumbled upward in the meadow toward the trees above, cows and calves confused by the terrible thunder, turned and ran in all directions.

Turning back, I ran frantically to the terror-stricken cows and calves yelling, "run, sisters, run," as I gathered and pushed them desperately upward toward the fleeing herd above.

Buzzing sounds like that of angry bees sizzled through the air above us…and then I felt a terrible pain in my side.

"Run, sisters," I screamed again, as my strength began strangely, to wane.

A blinding pain exploded suddenly in my shoulder, and my legs crumpled beneath me. Helplessly, I rolled to the ground, unable to continue.

As I lurched and kicked, trying desperately to gain my feet, I screamed yet again to the fleeing cows, "run, sisters, do not stop."

As my head settled slowly to the grass, I saw the last of my herd disappear into the trees at the top of the meadow and knew they would escape.

The sound of the killing thunder became distant as I lay in silence with my heart pounding and my chest heaving. A curious, sleep began to settle over me and I stared blankly upward into a cloudless, blue sky. Suddenly to my horror, I heard the approach of footsteps. Forcing my head from the ground, I saw several white-skinned, two-legged ones, chattering excitedly as they moved closer. A terrible surge of energy coursed through me, as they neared, and though I lurched and kicked, fighting furiously to gain my feet, I could not. A curious silence fell over the two-legged ones, as one slowly lifted his lightning stick and pointed it toward me.

Yelling and screaming erupted at the edge of the meadow as more two-legged ones burst suddenly from the forest.

Dark skinned ones clad in clothes the color of deer, screamed furiously as they charged through the meadow toward the white-skinned ones who surrounded me.

A great battle ensued as the newcomers crashed into their midst. I watched through frightful eyes as the long-haired ones seething with rage, rolled across the ground locked in furious battle with the ones who carry thunder. The newcomers overpowered the white-skinned ones, finally, and yelling and screaming still, chased them into the woods.

Because it was the time of killing once more, the dark-skinned ones had come to the mountains in search of me, the one they knew to be their sacred bull elk.

They had heard the terrible thunder erupt, and had run frantically to the meadow. They had seen me trying desperately to gather my herd and push them to safety. To their horror, they had watched me fall to the ground, kicking and lurching, to die. In angry rage, they had attacked the killing ones, and after destroying their lightning sticks, had chased them from the meadow. The dark-skinned ones then returned to me, hoping somehow to save my life.

With my strength draining quickly, I lay in the meadow fighting the darkness that settled steadily over me. The long-haired ones knelt in the grass by my side, calling softly to me with sounds I had not before heard. I stiffened at their touch, but was unable to move as they gently stroked my neck and lightly touched the huge scar on my shoulder as they whispered anxiously to one another.

Soon I heard a soft, rumbling sound, and with strength born from terror, sent two-legged ones rolling in all directions as I jerked my head from the earth trying desperately to escape. I saw a strange craft drawn by huge beasts moving slowly toward me. My terror grew when from the craft climbed yet another two-legged one who walked quickly toward me, knelt down, and poked me in the neck with a small, stinging stick. The soft chatter of the long-haired ones grew quickly distant, and as the world around me began to spin, I succumbed to the darkness.

I stood suddenly on a ridge above a large meadow beside the towering form of my father, Woslolkia. We stood in silence as we watched a group of two-legged ones in the meadow below us gesture anxiously to one another. An enormous bull elk lay motionless before them in the grass. Beside them in the meadow was what Woslolkia had long ago shown me to be a wagon, drawn by two large horses. The horses stood pawing the ground restlessly as they squirmed against their harnesses. With eyes wide and necks straining, they looked nervously toward the huge bull that lay near them in the grass. I watched with curiosity as the two-legged ones strained and groaned, working furiously to drag the enormous elk onto the wagon. After tying the bull securely into place, the long-haired ones guided the wagon slowly through the meadow and disappeared into the trees below.

When the blackness in which I slept turned slowly to light, Woslolkia was gone, and I was lying on strange, hard ground that had no dirt. I was in a very small opening that was surrounded on all sides by walls of flat, white rock. Above me was a cloudless, white sky against which my horns would touch if I could stand. In the strange sky hung a tiny, weak sun.

My ribs were now wrapped with a peculiar white material, and my leg was bound so tightly with the strange stuff that I could not move or bend it. White-coated two-legged ones hovered above me and called with sounds of happiness as I awoke. In panic, I kicked and strained to fight my strange two-legged assailants, but my world began again, to spin, and darkness settled over me once more.

I was suddenly again, standing beside my father, Woslolkia. We stood on a small hill, where below us small groups of the dark-skinned ones sat quietly on the ground around a large, square structure.

I turned questioningly toward Woslolkia. The great bull looked at me with knowing eyes, then turned toward the strange scene below us. "The dark-skinned ones," he said, "have taken you from the mountains to this place of healing in their valley. Special ones of their kind have worked feverishly for a day and a night to remove bullets shot into your body by the lightning sticks of the white ones. Your shoulder was broken by the bullets, Tateh. It is not known by them if you will live or die. There is much doubt in their hearts, but none of them knows the amazing fire that burns within you. The long-haired ones who sit quietly on the ground around their place of healing, wait patiently now to see."

Suddenly the dark-skinned ones, who only moments before, had been waiting quietly, sprang to their feet yelling and screaming, filled with joy. They had been told of my awakening.

Woslolkia turned to me then, and said, "You must go back now, Tateh, your journey is not yet complete. There is more that you must do. Go fearlessly, son."

When I awoke once more, I was in yet another strange opening. My ribs ached terribly, and my shoulder throbbed with pain as it had long ago after the attack by the great silver bear. I stood suspended barely above the ground by what seemed to be large, thick vines that passed beneath my belly and chest. These were held fast at each end to white walls of rock that stood at my sides. My shoulder was bound so tightly I could not force its slightest movement. Waves of sickness passed dizzily over me, as my world continued to slowly spin. I kicked helplessly at the ground, heaving painfully to escape the clutch of the vines as I fought the darkness that sought again and again to settle over me.

For countless days, I stood in the strange meadow racked with pain, hanging helplessly entrapped by the vines, held captive by the two-legged ones. The sickness within me continued to grow, and I became so weak that my head hung helplessly forward with my antlers pressed to the ground in front of me. The pain in my shoulder and neck was agonizing, and sharp, stabbing pains shot through my ribs with each breath.

The days and nights passed slowly as I endured the pain and torment of my terrible captivity. I longed for the warm waters of the healing pond and knew I would quickly heal if only I could escape and go there. The wound in my side, and my tightly bound shoulder throbbed nonstop. I hung for countless days in a strange world of dreams, held fast above the ground in the small opening in which the dark-skinned ones held me torturously captive.

The long-haired ones who had fought in the meadow to save me, came each night and sat cross-legged on the ground near my strange opening. They sat quietly in the darkness while making soothing, birdlike sounds when they blew their breath into strange sticks that they held to their mouths. Sometimes, the curious ones chanted and danced as I had seen the ancient ones do long ago beneath their tree of life on that cold snowy night when the earth had trembled and shook.

As the days dragged slowly by, I began to grow stronger. One day, the two-legged ones lowered me gently to the ground to eat and to drink water. Often, when the healing ones came, I was poked with a small, sharp stick and soon entered a dark, dreamless sleep. It was after one such visit that in a groggy stupor, I felt myself settle slowly to the ground in my small opening, and the vines that for so long had held me fast, sank slowly from my belly and chest and were pulled away.

As my world settled slowly into place once more, I realized that I stood teetering feebly on all four legs.

My first steps beneath the full weight of my body were shaky and weak, but I walked tentatively forward, grateful to be free. When I reached the far side of my tiny opening, I turned back to glare angrily at my captors. My leg and shoulder were no longer bound, and the strange, white material that had covered the wound in my side was gone. There was a surprising lightness to my head and neck as I looked around, and to my great dismay, I realized that the two-legged ones had somehow taken my antlers during my dark sleep.

'How can I possibly survive the *season of renewal* on legs so badly weakened?' I wondered anxiously. 'And with no antlers with which to protect myself from the murderess wolves, I will surely perish.'

Many days passed, and it seemed a lifetime that I had been so unmercifully held captive by the dark-skinned ones in my strange, small meadow. I longed to see the sky and to smell the wonderful scents that floated on the breeze, and even to know in what season I now walked. I thought often about the cows and calves in my herd and wondered who would lead and guard them when the season of mating came once more to the mountains.

The long-haired ones came one day and removed the barrier at one end of my tiny white meadow, then, prodded me gently through the small opening they had created. I stood in a much larger opening now where the sun shone brightly down on me, but I was captive still.

The unfamiliar opening was encircled entirely by a peculiar fence of limbless, skinny trees that lay on their sides, suspended from short, limbless trees that stood upright. The trees that comprised the walls of my opening were spaced evenly apart to a height above my head. Though I could not jump over this strange fence, I could easily see through my enclosure in all directions. A fresh breeze carried the wonderful scent of green grass and wild flowers, and I could smell trees that I knew must be standing somewhere nearby. I stood with my head held high and nose pointed upward, savoring the wonderful smells as I felt the heat of the sun on my back. It seemed I had not felt its warming touch for many seasons. An incredible energy coursed through my body as the scents that came to my nose and the intensity of the sun told me that the *season of renewal* had passed. I was certain it was now the season of *growing grass.*

My antlers had begun to grow again, and I was increasingly nervous at the attention they now drew from the long-haired ones. It was with great apprehension that I stood one day at the edge of my small opening as an unfamiliar group of odd, white-skinned ones covered in coats of black, walked quietly toward me.

They stopped near the edge of my opening and stood on the far side of the wall of trees pointing excitedly toward me. They spoke in hushed tones to a gray-haired one who stood watching me quietly from in their midst.

Hearing their strange talk and seeing their odd mannerisms, I began to pace nervously through my opening as the black coated ones continued to mumble and point. The gray-haired one, the apparent leader of the strange group, saw my growing anxiety and spoke to the others who then turned quietly away, leaving him alone at my meadow's edge.

The old two-legged one came slowly closer, then stopped at the side of my opening and stood staring quietly at me from behind the wooden wall. Gray hair grew on not only the head of the old, white-skinned one, but grew also beneath his nose and hung from his chin. A long-forgotten calm settled over me as I saw the knowingness in his eyes and heard the gentle strength in his voice when finally, he spoke.

"I know, great one," he said finally, "that you do not understand my words, but you have awakened in me something that has long been asleep. I know in my heart that you are a leader of your kind. I am humbled by the scars that you carry on your shoulders and sides – scars that bear witness to the many battles you have fought as you have walked your journey and led your herd. I, too, am a leader, great one," he continued, "and like you, have known much battle. Unlike the scars that you wear proudly, the scars that I bear are in my heart. My scars, like yours, are from battles fought against my own kind. But unlike your battles, mine are ones about which I am not proud. By your very being and in your wonderful grandeur, that which you have awakened in me, huge one, you have begun to awaken also in my people.

"My kind has grown apart from that which we once were, and we no longer walk in harmony with your kind, big one. Forgotten is not only the oneness that we once shared with you, but also with the great land in which you live. Huge one," he continued, "I understand much about battle and now understand also the siege under which your kind and others like you have long been. I will make it so, great one, that the land in which you live will be set aside for all of time. It will be a land where your kind and my kind will discover each other once more and live forever together in oneness.

"In honor of the mighty canyon of yellow rocks that courses through the center of your great mountains, this land will be known for evermore as the land of the Yellowstone. Never again in this land, big one, will your kind or any other animal ever again be hunted.

"Soon you will be made free again to roam the land in which you were born. Grow strong, great one, and lead your herd fearlessly once more, as you have for many years. Certainly, you have earned the right."

The gray-haired one stood for a long time then, and spoke no more. Turning finally to walk away, he stopped and turned slowly back toward me.

"Great one," he said quietly, "I wish there was a way that I could make you know that because of your fearlessness and strength, and your relentless will to live, you have brought a great peace to your kind and to the land in which you live. To my people, you have brought a stillness, the beginning of an enduring calm. Indeed, huge one, you have shown us the way home. I have been

413

given your amazing antlers," he said, "and I will cherish them always."

Long after darkness had settled around me, I lay with my head up thinking about my strange encounter with the old gray-haired one. I heard again his soft reassuring voice and saw the kindness in his eyes as I drifted into sleep.

My sleep was tormented this night, as in my dream, I stood again near the old two-legged one hearing over and over the soft drone of his voice. Suddenly I stood beside my father, Woslolkia. We stood on a small rise in a meadow in which I had never been before. Below us in the opening, was an enormous bull, held captive in a strange enclosure. A gray-haired two-legged one stood near the great bull quietly talking. Recognizing the bull below, I turned with questioning eyes to my father. "Yes, Tateh," he said, "the great bull is you. The gray-haired one is the leader of all the two-legged ones in this land. The dark-skinned ones who saved your life," he continued, "traveled throughout their land pleading with all other two-legged ones to create a place in the mountains in which you and the rest of our kind could live forever free from the ones who carry thunder. They traveled far away to the place where this great leader and others like him dwell. They told this great one the story of their bull who now grew stronger at their place of healing in their mountains far away. As a gift they gave the great antlers they had taken from you to this old gray-haired one. This white-skinned, two-legged one is the greatest leader of all his kind, Tateh. He is known by the two-legged ones as… Grant."

I awoke the next morning long before the skies began to lighten above my enclosure. I stared into the darkness remembering my odd dream and wondering about the strange two-legged one called Grant.

The days drug slowly by as I paced endlessly back and forth across my small enclosure. One morning when the skies first became light, the long-haired, healing ones quietly approached my small meadow. To my absolute terror they pointed a small lightning stick at me, from which suddenly flew a small object that stuck in my hip. As they watched, a strange dizziness overtook me, and though I fought with all my strength to stand, my legs buckled beneath me, and I settled slowly to the ground. Though fully awake, I lay paralyzed, unable to move even my eyes. The long-haired ones quickly created an opening in the wooden wall at the far end of my meadow through which there suddenly appeared horses pulling a wagon. Long-haired ones poured over the wooden walls surrounding me, and together, they dragged me into the wagon. They carefully bound me inside a small enclosure over which they placed a large cover that completely hid the sun.

Lying helplessly in the dark, I felt the wagon lurch suddenly forward, creaking and groaning as I began to move, pulled along by the plodding beasts. With all my strength I fought to gain my feet, but try as I might, I was unable to induce even the slightest movement from my legs.

I bounced along in my darkened prison for what seemed a long time. Finally, my enclosure came to a creaking halt. I felt a subtle shake and heard the squeak of the wagon as the two-legged who had guided it, jumped to the ground. The horses snorted impatiently as they were disconnected in a rush of strange clicking and rattling sounds from the wagon in which I lay. All became quiet then around my darkened cage as the heavy footsteps of the horses faded in the distance.

I lay paralyzed still as I listened to the soft footsteps of two-legged ones approaching me quietly once more. Sunlight burst upon me as the veil that covered my strange enclosure was suddenly drawn away. I lay squinting in the brightness at a green, mountain world that now surrounded my prison. My cage had been placed beneath a huge log arch that stood in a meadow near the foot of a towering mountain. Through my enclosure floated a soft breeze that carried to me the unmistakable scent of my beloved home. Still unable to move, I lay quietly in my cage, lost in the wonderful smells that caressed my senses, listening carefully to the wondrous sounds of the mountain world around me.

As darkness began to gather, I was able to move my legs and raise my head from the floor of my prison. The wonderful scents flowing downward from the mountains in front of me, were intoxicating, and I longed for the days when I had journeyed freely through them.

When the moon had climbed high overhead and brightly illuminated the small basin, I was able at last, to stand. A strange feeling settled over me as I peered from my cage. A chill flowed through my veins when suddenly I recognized the place where long ago, my nightmarish life struggle with the wolves had taken place. Just beyond the draw where I now realized the terrible fence had once stood, loomed the towering ridge upon which I had escaped the wolves to the great basin far above. Anxiety welled within me as I relived the terrible scene, and my head was filled once again with the shrieking cries of attacking wolves.

But the terrible, wailing cries that roared in my mind turned to soft, birdlike calls. I became slowly aware of the familiar sounds coaxed from the wooden sticks of long-haired ones as I emerged from the clutch of my haunting vision. They had gathered around me in the moonlit darkness. I stood quietly through the night in my small enclosure, listening to their songs echo through the darkness. Wonderful memories played in my mind as I smelled the tantalizing aroma of my nearby mountain home and watched the shadows creep slowly across the grassy basin in front of me.

The sun was high overhead the next day when the long-haired ones appeared again and carefully replaced the veil over my small cage, plunging me once again into darkness. As the day passed slowly by, the activity near me in the small basin steadily increased. Soon, I heard the heavy plodding footsteps of horses and the voices of two-legged ones mixed with the creaking sound of wagons as they rattled past where I stood anxiously in my darkened prison. The excited voices became a steady rumble as more two-legged ones than I had ever known existed, gathered somewhere beyond the protecting shroud that covered me.

Suddenly, the familiar voice of the gray-haired one boomed near me in my captive darkness, and all others fell silent. The gray-haired one called steadily to the many others who had gathered around my darkened prison. I remembered the steady gaze of the old, black-coated one, and his calming voice as he had spoken to me from the far side of the strange wooden wall.

In a short while, the gray-haired one spoke no more, and I heard only the soft shuffle of feet, and an occasional cough or muffled word from the many who stood quietly around my strange enclosure.

I heard footsteps approaching my cage from somewhere beyond the veil and then heard the kind voice of the old gray-haired one as he stood near me. "Great one," he said quietly, "as I promised, it is at last your time."

The shroud that held me in darkness was removed, and the far end of my enclosure slowly opened.

I stood unmoving for a moment, blinking in the brightness, staring into the knowing eyes of the gray-haired one. Then with all my might, I spun from his gaze and exploded forward through the gaping end of my prison.

As I leaped from my cage and lunged forward beneath the huge log arch, a deafening roar erupted from the enormous throng of two-legged ones that had gathered around me there. The feeling of the mountain beneath my pounding feet as I surged powerfully forward was wondrous. The deafening roar of the chanting two-legged ones fell quickly behind me as I crashed across the opening and lunged upward on the great ridge beyond it.

"Run, Tateh, run," I heard from somewhere in the past as I leaped across downfallen trees and bounded over jagged rocks on my head long run toward freedom.

Bolts of stabbing pain shot through my wounded shoulder as I bound upward. My pounding heart and burning lungs quickly told me that my long captivity had robbed me of my once abundant strength. With my heart thundering in my chest, I soon stopped, gasping for air, and turned to look back into the valley. The two-legged ones, no more than small black dots now, scurried about beneath the log arch where I had finally escaped them. None of the two-legged ones had attempted to follow me, but as I watched their movement far below, memories of my agonizing captivity loomed in my mind. With renewed energy, I whirled and sprang upward once more.

As I climbed higher on the ridge, I began at last to feel safe, and with my fear diminishing, became slowly aware of my surroundings once more. The scent of grass, sagebrush, and flowers, and the tangy aroma of trees filled my nose. I realized that the air around me was filled with butterflies, companions that had joined me in the celebration of my upward flight to freedom.

Far below me in the valley, a long procession of horse-drawn wagons now moved slowly along a dusty trail that began beneath the log arch. Like a long line of ants, they meandered along a trail that disappeared into a large canyon from which a shimmering river flowed.

Darkness had begun to settle when I stood at last at the top of the ridge looking into the great basin. The grass was tall and green as far as I could see. On unsteady legs burning with fatigue, I moved forward across the great expanse. Chomping greedily at the grass, I refused rest as I continued across the basin toward the canyon in which I knew lay hidden the mysterious pond of the healing water.

The moon rose above the mountains in front of me as I continued through the rolling hills. The wondrous exhilaration that I felt after my long confinement made the openness of the great basin seem tenfold to any journey I had experienced before. The happiness that I now felt drove me ever onward with increasing anticipation toward its far side.

The sun was high overhead when at last, I stared into the wondrous canyon of the healing water. Though weary to my core, I started without hesitation into the depths of the blackened canyon. I moved steadily through the darkened stands of timber, feeding in the lush meadows between them as I travelled downward.

As I entered the large meadow where the tall plume of steam rose as always near the trees at its bottom edge, I stopped and for a long time stared quietly across its green expanse. I could easily see my great friend, Ksapa, as he circled his herd in the meadow before me, bugling his thunderous warnings to those bulls hiding in the trees at its edge. And I could see also my mother and her spotted calf as they fed with the herd in the deep grass near the mysterious pond.

I entered the meadow but turned when halfway across the grassy expanse and began climbing the far side of the canyon above the healing water. The sun was nearing the horizon when on legs weakened from my long journey, I stopped at last in the small opening at the canyon's top. Ksapa's sun-bleached skull and towering antlers lay glowing softly in the deep grass of the meadow that for so many years he had ruled.

Walking quietly to his antlers, I lowered my head and gently engaged them with my own. Carefully raising my head, I carried Ksapa's antlers and skull to the rocky point where he had so often stood, and carefully laid them in the rocks overlooking the meadow and healing pond far below. As I walked from the meadow, I stopped and turned back. The setting sun shone brightly in the clouds above the horizon, and the silhouette of my great friend's skull and mighty antlers gleamed boldly in the fiery sky behind them. From deep within my chest, I screamed a thundering bugle toward my old friend who stared solemnly into the valley below. As my bugle echoed through the canyon, I was sure I heard the roaring bugle of Ksapa echo once more through the small meadow around me.

The moon had risen above the canyon's steep side when again I entered the meadow above the healing water. Quivering with anticipation, I walked to the steaming pool that had for so long filled my torturous dreams, and flopped stiffly into the yellow mud at its upper end. Remembering the joyous reunion that Ksapa and I had shared here what seemed only yesterday, I rose from the mud, and feeling his presence, splashed thankfully into the moonlit water of the steaming pond.

I lay in the healing water for days, climbing from the pond only to eat at the succulent grass at its side. Then, with my hunger satisfied, I would return to rest in the healing water once more.

When at last I began to climb the canyon's steep sides on trails I had come to know well, I was forced to stop often and rest. My shoulder ached and throbbed with pain and my lungs burned as if on fire. I was once the grandest bull to walk my mountain land, but now I wondered if I would ever again command the fierce strength that had once been mine.

Often, late in the night as I lay soaking quietly in the healing pond, the terrible thunder of lightning sticks would again fill my mind. Again, I would stare into the cold eyes of the white-skinned one as he slowly raised his lightning stick. The nightmare would vanish though, as the memory of the soothing sticks blown by the long-haired ones would echo hauntingly through the darkness. Their soft, birdlike sounds would fill the night around me as they had when they gathered near my cage beneath the huge log arch. The wondrous feeling of freedom that was again mine would then settle mercifully over me.

As the time of *ripening berries* drew closer, I began to prepare myself once again for the season of mating as I polished my antlers and battled trees at the meadow's edge. But strangely gone, was the desire that had always burned within me to dominate all other bulls as I led my herd. I was filled instead, with doubt and anxiety that had grown strong within me. My strength and stamina had withered before the terrible lightning sticks and long captivity by the two-legged ones.

As the season of mating approached, I lay one night, soaking quietly in the warm water of the pond. Suddenly, a thundering bugle erupted from the timber below me in the canyon. With adrenaline pounding through my veins, I splashed from the pond and lunged into the meadow where I stood waiting angrily as the bull drew nearer. But as the approaching bull sent yet another shrieking bugle ringing through the canyon, I was suddenly overcome with doubt, and sank quietly into the trees where I stood until he had passed.

The season of mating came finally, and the mountains around me were alive with the resonating sounds of bugles. Still I lay soaking at night in the healing water and rested quietly in the thick timber on the sides of the canyon during the day. Mine had become an endless battle now. Adrenaline and anger pumped through my veins at the sound of each roaring bugle, but uncertainty and dread cooled my great fury and numbed my once relentless will to lead.

One night, as I lay in the warming water of the pond, Woslolkia appeared at its edge. He stared silently into my eyes for a long time, then turned and looked upward across the big meadow. Following his gaze, I saw a large herd of cows and calves standing at the meadow's upper end. I was nearly overwhelmed with anxiety when I realized that there was no bull in their midst. The cows and calves milled in confusion at the meadow's edge, they had no great bull to lead them. When I looked questioningly back to Woslolkia, he was gone, and I lay alone in the steaming water. As I stared through the darkness at the vacant meadow where the mysterious herd had been, I wondered if ever again I would possess the will to lead.

I remembered the terrible fear that I had fought to overcome after the death of my mother and the numbing dread that I had at last conquered after my confrontation with the great silver bear. I thought anxiously again about leading my herd in my weakened condition. Filled with frustration, I wondered how many times in my life the mysterious power that caused all things to be, would put before me the choice to turn and back away, or to stand fast and look bravely into the eye of death.

As the days of the season of mating slowly passed, the battle within me grew. The rage that filled me at hearing each screaming bugle sent me crashing in uncontrollable anger to the top of the canyon, hurdling logs and jumping through small ravines, but always away from the approaching bull.

The season of mating passed finally, and the mountains became quiet once again. The roaring bugles of bulls no longer echoed from the walls of my canyon home. Still, anger and doubt raged within me. The season of *falling leaves* came quickly to the mountains. Snow fell from churning, gray skies and was driven through the meadow by a stinging wind that roared constantly through my canyon. Still, I soaked each night, strengthening my shoulder in the healing pond.

During the day, I climbed high on the canyon's side where I lay quietly watching for the ones who carry thunder. Pride would not let me admit to myself that it was fear, not injury that had kept me at the healing pond through the season of mating. I knew the truth though, on those dark nights when I lay alone in the steaming water beneath the falling snow. Indeed, the fear of death had kept me here. Sadly, I realized, 'the ones who carry thunder cannot kill me. Fear had already taken my life.'

As the snows became deeper during the season of killing, curiously missing was the sound of lightning sticks echoing from the mountains around me. The tracks of the killing ones that had always been present in the snow in seasons past, never appeared.

With the snow now nearly to my belly in depth, I realized at last that the killing ones had somehow been unable to find my canyon. It was now time for me to leave the healing water and travel to the canyon of the yellow rocks.

I stood from the steaming water early the next morning and started through the snow as the skies began to lighten. Twisting spirals of snow rose from the floor of the meadow, driven by a stiffening wind as I plowed through the snow toward its upper end. Though the day had become fully light, there was no hint of sun behind the gray sea of clouds that boiled across the sky. I thought about my friend Ksapa, whose bleached skull and antlers now stood lonely vigil on the rocky cliff far above me on the canyon's wall. I remembered the many times we had climbed upward in this canyon, taking turns breaking trail as we lunged through the deep snow on our yearly journey to the canyon of the yellow rocks. As I came to the edge of the timber at the upper end of the meadow, the sky above me was filled suddenly with the screeching call of a white-headed, winged one. Looking up, I saw the great eagle as it spread its mighty wings and sprang from its perch in the top of a tall, dead tree. It glided silently from sight upward in the canyon.

The day passed quickly as I labored upward through the meadows and dark stands of timber through increasingly deep snow. As I plowed through drifts in the last dark stand of timber below the great basin's edge, the snowy silence was suddenly shattered by the bellowing roar of a great silver bear. The monstrous one reared to his hind legs from behind a huge rock at the trail's edge.

For an instant, I stood as a calf again, staring into a snarling, silver one's eyes as an enormous paw sliced through the air toward me.

The feelings of anxiety and fear that had grown strong within me, suddenly disappeared. I was consumed by a long-forgotten rage, and an exquisite feeling of tension quivered from every muscle in my body. Slowly, I lowered my massive horns in anticipation of the enormous bear's attack. The bear lowered himself to all four feet and walked quietly into the trail where he stood facing me.

"We meet again, great one," said the enormous bear, glaring angrily at me now. "Your brave actions and the scar you bear on your shoulder are solemn proof of your courage. I see that you would die today before you would turn away from me in fear. I have seen you many times as you led the cows and calves of your herd. You have long walked with fearlessness and wisdom on your journey through the canyons and ridges of our mountain home.

"The courage that is yours, is equal to your size, and like me," the great bear continued, "you know no fear. I know that if I choose to kill you today, we will die together in this canyon. Though my kind knows no fear, we know that life is a gift that is not to be wasted in meaningless battle. Today, and for many more days, huge one, we will live," said the great bear.

Slowly, I raised my head. For a long time, I returned the intense gaze of the great bear. When he turned finally and walked into the burned trees at the trail's edge, I saw an old, jagged scar etched deeply in the silver fur of his leg. It ran from his shoulder to his enormous paw where two of his long, white claws had long been missing.

I stood for a while on the trail, quietly looking at the huge tracks in the snow where the bear had stood. A long-forgotten strength settled slowly over me as I remembered again the silver one's words. Indeed, I had felt no fear as I had stared into the eyes of the great bear. I would have died before turning away from him.

As I turned to plow forward once more in the deep snow, I realized that the mysterious power that causes all to be, had put before me once more, the choice to flee or to stand.

My decision had shown me that I was again, ready to lead.

Chapter Twenty-Three

The sun had fallen to a place barely above the far horizon when at last I stood at the great basin's edge. A surging wind drove billows of snow from the direction of the setting sun as I plowed forward through the deep snow. At each powerful lunge, I sent jagged shards of snow sliding across the wind-crusted surface before me. When finally, the sun dropped from view, the crimson sky left behind in its fading light bathed the basin in a gleaming, reddish glow. The wind became calm, and stars slowly appeared in the clearing sky as I moved without rest toward the basin's far side. I chose to travel near the tops of small ridges where the snow had been blown off by the relentless winds that rule this land during the *season of renewal*.

When the sun rose the next morning, I stood at the great opening's far edge, looking downward into an enormous expanse of low, rugged mountains. Huge stands of dense timber covered the craggy terrain where the immense canyon of the yellow rocks lay crookedly etched in the stretching, snow-laden land. Tiny pockets of steam billowed into the frigid morning air from places where hot, bubbling ponds lay hidden in mysterious canyons. Forests stretched for as far as I could see. It seemed long ago when I had last descended from the great basin with Ksapa, and now with growing anticipation, I started downward.

For a day, I moved lower on a steep, broken ridge, skirting huge outcrops of rock and working through thick timber toward the canyon below. As the sun dropped from view, I stood at last, gazing into the rumbling canyon of the yellow rocks. In snow only to my knees, now, I quietly studied the amazing gorge and the many bison that grazed on the windswept bluffs at its side. Some of the shaggy behemoths lay near steaming pools quietly resting as they nibbled methodically at grass that grew from the heated earth at their edges. Though it seemed long ago when I had last stood at the canyon's edge, it had been only two years. Still, I looked into the canyon with much the same feeling of awe as when I first viewed its thundering depths beside my mother, long ago.

I stood quietly gazing for a long while, remembering the many times my friend, Ksapa and I had stood in this very spot and had grazed beside the boiling pools of water that lay around me. When darkness began to fall, I turned from the canyon and walked to the steaming edge of a nearby pool. With a feeling of satisfaction, I lowered my head and began to browse on the green grass at the warm water's edge.

The *season of renewal* dragged slowly on. The snow did not stack as deeply as it had in years past, but the biting cold that gripped the land was relentless. Each day, several of the shaggy ones did not rise from their beds. The nights were filled with the haunting calls of wolves that stalked the darkness, feeding on the unfortunate ones that had succumbed to the cold.

Remembering the brutal *season of renewal* that I had endured with my mother long ago, I wondered about the cows and calves of my great herd.

Late one day, thick, gray clouds crept ominously over the mountains where the sun had just dropped from sight. They soon filled the sky above my frigid home. Snow began falling steadily from the sky as I lay resting near a pond of boiling water.

All at once, the sky was lit by a brilliant flash of light. The deafening boom that followed, echoed eerily through the steamy darkness around me. Again, and again, the lightning hissed through the ragged sky, illuminating the swirling snow in a luminous, pulsing light. I had never seen lightning during the time of renewal, and I lay awake pondering nervously the meaning of the mysterious light that now exploded in the snowy darkness above me.

Sinking finally into a restless sleep, my herd was suddenly in my dreams. My cows and calves called anxiously to me from the night as they stood tightly circled in deep snow. The darkness around them was filled with the dreadful wailing of wolves.

I awoke with a terrible start, and peered through the snowy darkness around me, almost certain I would see the darting forms of wolves, but there were none. With lightning crackling through the snowy skies, I tried to push the haunting visions from my mind. Lowering my head, I sank once more into a troubled slumber, but the wolves, appeared again in my terrible dream.

The frightful vision that filled my slumber was suddenly cloaked in darkness. I could no longer see my beleaguered herd or even hear their fearful cries. The wolves had left them, and now in my tormented dream-world the wretched hunters circled me. I was unable to see them in the darkness, but I knew of each wolf's location as they stalked and snarled menacingly from the night.

A great flash of light lit the snowy skies above me, and I saw the ruthless black leader staring coldly at me in the lightning's bluish glow. Suddenly, the night was filled with a thunderous, whistling wind, and crashing from the sky was an enormous white-headed eagle.

The winged one, larger by far than any I had ever seen, swept the snarling black one from the snow. Clutching the wolf tightly in its enormous talons, it climbed upward into the flashing sky. The gigantic eagle suddenly released the wolf to fall twisting and spinning helplessly toward me from above. The black one struck the earth near me with a terrible thud, sending an explosion of snow flying into the air.

Struggling from my fitful dream, I sprang to my feet, peering anxiously into the darkness. The terrible flashing light and storm were gone. Snow no longer fell from the sky, and stars now shone brightly above. Gone, too, were the wails and haunting calls that only moments before had filled my mind. The soft thunder from the nearby canyon was now the only noise that came from the darkness. Nervously, I lay once more in my bed, but each time I slept, the lurking wolves were there.

I remained awake, anxious, and unrested, until the skies at last began to lightened. Suddenly from the trees behind me, came the resounding screech of a great winged one. I leaped from the snow remembering my dream, and spun toward the direction of the startling call. In the top of an old gray tree sat an enormous eagle, and to my astonishment, at my feet lay the bleached skull of a wolf where the black one had landed in my dream. As I looked again toward the giant bird, it leaped from the tree and circled close in the air above me. Then, with cries that strangely beckoned, the eagle flew upward toward the ridge upon which I had descended earlier from the great basin. My eyes fell again, to the snow at my feet where the weathered skull of the wolf lay staring coldly back at me. I now understood the meaning of the pulsing light of last night's storm. My haunting vision of the previous night had not been imagined. My cows and calves had somehow called to me in my mysterious dream. I knew I must find them.

A journey across the mountains to the winter range that lay on the far side, seemed an impossible undertaking in the *season of renewal*. But without hesitation, I started forward through the deep snow. The eagle circled silently above me as I pressed steadily onward through ravines and over small hills toward the towering ridge that I would climb to enter the great basin.

The sun had traveled halfway across the sky when I started upward on the huge ridge. Near a jagged outcropping of rock far above me, the great bird sat in the top of a twisted old tree and watched as I toiled slowly upward in the deep snow. I thought again about the strange vision I had seen during my restless sleep

433

and realized that it was not to me that my frightened cows and calves had called. Certainly, they knew me to be dead.

'To whom, then, had they called in their time of peril, and what mysterious entity then,' I wondered, 'had caused me to hear them?'

As I approached the dead tree in which the great bird sat, it sprang once again from its perch, and in a clatter of flapping wings swooped barely above my head in the air, then circled upward toward the great basin.

My grueling struggle through the deep snow quickly sapped the strength from my legs. I stood often with my head lowered to the snow and my chest heaving as I painfully drew the cold mountain air into my burning lungs. Looking back at the great expanse from which I had just climbed, it was good to see that the canyon of the yellow rocks had grown distant.

Darkness had long fallen when at last I stood wearily at the edge of the great basin. The wind howled across the open expanse before me, and clouds of snow whipped angrily at my face as I started forward.

I traveled when I could, on the tops of plateaus and ridges where the wind had nearly blown their rocky surfaces clean, as I labored toward the great basin's far side. When I was forced to cross through ravines and small basins that separated the wind-swept ridges, the snow was above my head in depth. I lunged and wallowed as if swimming, to pass through them. I often became trapped in snow that was past my shoulders in depth, unable to touch anything solid beneath me. I would lie with my head and neck outstretched on the snowy surface before me, gasping and wheezing with my eyes squeezed tightly shut against the hissing, wind driven snow. I would think of my beleaguered herd then, and struggle to rise. Each time, the cry of the great winged one would come from somewhere above the swirling snow, and I would stand again, and battle forward.

For a day and night, I fought through the windswept basin. At times I could not see the ground in front of me through the blinding snow. Late in the night on the third day of my perilous journey, I realized that I had become lost in the sea of blowing snow. As dawn approached on the fourth day of my trek, I struggled forward on legs that had grown numb with fatigue.

As I moved slowly along in the driving white-out, the snow at my feet shuddered suddenly, and with a resounding crack, fell from beneath me. I tumbled helplessly downward in a churning torrent of snow. Blinded by the blizzard, I had ventured too close to the edge of a huge cornice, and the cliff of wind-stacked snow had broken beneath my weight.

I rolled, choking and gasping in a dizzying wall of snow, as I plummeted ever downward. I came to a crunching halt, at last, buried to my shoulders, so firmly bound in the snowy mass that I could move only my head. Kicking and twisting with all the strength I could gather, I freed myself finally, and stood gasping hoarsely as I struggled to gain my senses.

I had tumbled downward in the river of snow to a place on the mountain now far below the clouds that enveloped the ridge top from which I had fallen. Gone was the relentless wind and swirling clouds of snow through which I had labored. I walked carefully between gigantic chunks of snow and lunged over huge pieces of broken trees as I struggled through the rubble that had fallen with me from the mountaintop. As I looked over a strange, new valley that lay before me, I realized that my death slide had placed me on the face of the huge ridge above the hills of my herd's winter range.

From in the vast openness above the valley came the screeching call of the great winged one that had guided me. The eagle appeared suddenly in the sky flying directly toward me. Our eyes met for an instant as the eagle passed close overhead and soared upward into the air behind me. The great bird twisted gracefully in the sky and dove at me again from behind. Bathing me in a rush of air, it soared outward into the valley and was gone.

"Thank you, Ksapa," I whispered to the now vacant sky. "Indeed, our great leaders live forever in the hearts of the mighty winged ones."

Turning anxiously toward the rolling hills, I moved quickly downward in snow barely above my knees. The plaintiff cries of my frightened cows and calves now filled my mind with such intensity that I was no longer certain if they were real or imagined.

The morning sun had just risen when at last with pounding heart, I burst into the top of a long, narrow meadow. As in my terrible dream, the embattled cows and calves of my herd stood bravely circled in the center of the opening below me.

Surrounding them, were many wolves. Some lay panting in the snow, tearing at the carcasses of cows they had dragged from the herd. Others, paced menacingly around the terrorized cows and calves circled tightly before them. As I watched, I saw the huge black tyrant, Kasota, rise from the snow. As his head tipped slowly backward, I heard the terrorizing wail that had plagued my dreams for countless nights.

At the black one's screaming signal, his shrieking pack charged forward once more, ripping and tearing with vengeance at the circle of battling cows. For a moment I was again in the past, cringing fearfully in the darkness, surrounded by the cows of my terrorized herd. In my mind I saw the shadowy figures of my mother and the others as they reared and lashed relentlessly in driving clouds of snow.

Seething with rage born of my horrific memories, I laid my head back and from deep within my chest came a resounding bugle. As my bellowing roar echoed through the meadow below me, all movement ceased. The wolves stood frozen in place, as all eyes, both wolf and elk, turned in amazement toward me. A low, rumbling moan boiled within my chest as years of anger welled to the surface. With adrenaline pounding in my veins, I started downward.

"Tateh!" I heard my stunned cows yell in disbelief, as the wolves, snarling menacingly, turned toward me.

The piercing cry of Kasota rang ominously through the meadow. Immediately his murderous pack was behind him, snarling and wailing with rage as they charged upward.

The pack hit me in a pounding wave of snarling and twisting bodies. They tore viciously at my shoulders and flanks and ripped at my neck. The black one, remembering me now, sprang onto a large rock before me. Glaring through eyes that sparkled with hatred, he waited for his chance to finish what he had started long ago.

The wolves sprang at me from all directions, slashing and ripping at my legs and belly. The air was filled with the primal sound of battle. From around me came guttural wails, snapping teeth, and the tearing sound of my hide as the wolves sought to overwhelm this strange bull elk that had challenged them. I reared and kicked, sending yelping wolves rolling painfully through the snow, but again and again they rose and attacked me. As I turned my head, feigning to strike at wolves who tore at my flanks, Kasota saw his chance at last, and sprang through the air toward my exposed neck. I tipped my antlers and whirled with all my might toward the black one. With the sound of piercing flesh, I caught the wolf in midflight, penetrating him completely with the tips of my antlers. With a powerful flip of my head, I sent the sinister one careening awkwardly through the air to land amidst his shrieking pack. Kasota struggled to his feet, but staggered only a few steps toward me before collapsing in the snow.

The startled wolves became immediately silent and their attack stopped. The bewildered pack stood in dismay, looking anxiously from me to their dead leader who lie motionless before them in the snow. Whining and yipping softly, the wolves sank fearfully away from me as I stood shaking my antlers angrily, still, at their dead leader. Glancing fearfully back toward me, the shaken pack disappeared into the timber at the edge of the meadow. I walked slowly forward to where the black one lay in the snow.

Lowering my head, I said quietly to the lifeless form before me, "I have now taken from you, Kasota, that which long ago you took from my mother. Now finally, black one, wolf and I, will walk as *one*."

Slowly, I became aware of movement around me in the meadow. The frightened calls of calves and barking replies of anxious mothers filled the air. My herd gathered nervously around where I stood with my head lowered still, near the dead wolf. I raised my head as I saw Wicala approach and stand quietly before me. She held my gaze for a long while before finally, she spoke.

"All in our herd knew you to be dead, great one, but somehow, you have returned to us. How… how did you find us…. how did you know of our terrible plight?" she asked.

"Beneath a mysterious storm of light, I lay sleeping near the canyon of the yellow rocks," I said. "An enormous messenger appeared suddenly from the flashing sky. The great winged one was sent to tell of the peril of my herd. He talked with words that had no sound, but I heard them plainly in my heart. Because of this, I knew his words were true. I had to come."

Wicala stared at me for a long time, her eyes brimming with emotion, then said finally, "Your heart is huge and filled with caring, Tateh. The steps with which you walk, are fearless. The courage and knowing with which you lead our kind is incredible. Thank you, great one, for returning, you have saved our lives," she said. "Thank you."

The cows turned then, their eyes filled with respect as they each passed slowly by. The herd walked toward the open hillside where they spread out in the sun with nervous calves beneath them, and began to graze.

I spent the remainder of the *season of renewal* with the cows and calves of my herd. My wounds from the wolf attack quickly healed as I rested on the ridge above the herd at night, and after grazing through the early part of each day, lay among them in the warming sun. Often, when I walked through their midst, terrified calves would jump from my path. Mirthfully, I realized, the little ones had no way to know that within the great bull that walked before them, was a calf that looked at the world with much the same awe and amazement as did they.

As the *season of renewal* wore on, the days became warmer and the snow line crept upward on the mountain above us. No longer did we hear the wailing howls of wolves echo through the mountains at night. As the warming days passed, my herd worked peacefully upward on the mountain toward the huge basin above.

I stood one day at the edge of the basin with Wicala and her young calf as we looked across the huge expanse. The snow was gone from the great opening, and the rolling hills shone with greenness in the midday light. No words needed saying as she turned from my gaze and walked away from me into the basin with her young calf trailing behind her. I watched proudly as the cow and calf disappeared from view. The hills around me in the basin were dotted with the cows and calves of my herd as each began their solitary journey, a rite that each year filled our mountains with new life. I knew that soon the young ones that trustfully followed their expectant mothers, would be pushed away to form small herds of their own.

I spent most of the season of *growing grass* roaming through the small plateaus and valleys of the great basin. As the time of *ripening berries* grew closer, I dropped into the canyon of the healing water. Near the pond, I again entered the secret ritual of bulls, as I readied myself once more for the coming season of mating.

Many seasons came and went, and never again did I doubt my strength or relentless will to lead. During each season of mating, I led my herd fearlessly, and without hesitation I dealt punishment to those bulls that challenged me. I spent the *seasons of renewal* with the shaggy ones near the sacred canyon of the yellow rocks. I was always excited when the season of *ducks returning* came at last, and I could begin my journey toward the great basin where I would spend the season of *growing grass.* When the time of *ripening berries* grew near, I descended again into my beloved canyon of the healing water where I would prepare myself once more for the challenges of the season of mating.

A great peace it seemed, had settled over the wonderful mountain home of my kind. Though we still shared our mountains with the wolves, Kasota's death had somehow changed them. No longer in the *season of renewal* did they ruthlessly kill great numbers of my kind as they once had. The killing two-legged ones who carried their terrible thunder to our mountains had somehow lost their way, it seemed. They came no more. Many seasons had passed since the thundering sounds of their lightning sticks had last echoed through our land. The long-haired ones though, came often, but always upon seeing us, sat cross legged on the ground and quietly watched our passage. The numbers of my kind grew, and many bulls now lived to grow as old and large as Ksapa had once told me all bulls did.

In this, the eighteenth year of my life, the *season of renewal* had been an easy one. The snows near the canyon of the yellow rocks had not grown deep, and the grass around the ponds of bubbling water had been abundant. As I once had long ago with Ksapa, I began my yearly journey toward the great basin very early in the season of *ducks returning*. During the *season of growing grass,* the rains did not fall. The grass grew only in short clumps in meadows where in years past, it had stood tall and flowing. The sun shone each day from a cloudless sky, sending me in search of shade in the dense forest on the cool north-facing sides of my canyon. The once chaotic creeks in my mountain home now crept quietly through the forest with little water in them. In many, lay only rocks and dry moss. Late in the day when I stood looking from high ridges, I often saw towering columns of dark smoke that boiled into the sky at the far side of the valley as they once had here, long ago.

When the time of *ripening berries* arrived at last, I readied myself as I had for years, for the coming season of mating. I had led the great herd here for many years, and the bulls with which I shared my mountain home had come to know me well. Though they sought constantly to steal my cows, seldom was I ever challenged for leadership, for it had become well known that any bull that challenged me would suffer my terrible wrath.

To the canyons and meadows of my mountains now came many of my kind to whom I was unknown. They had been driven from their faraway mountains by terrible fires that had begun burning in them during the *season of growing grass*. Enormous bulls that I had not seen or heard before, now bellowed their challenging calls from the canyons and ridges around my herd.

Through the days of the season of mating, I was challenged many times by the huge newcomers, and each time, I met their angry challenge and defeated them, often in terrible battle. As the end of the season of mating drew slowly closer, the fatigue that had grown within me was far greater than any I had ever known. I reached deep inside now for strength each time I was forced to defend my herd.

To my mountains slowly came the season of *falling leaves.* It was rare now, that I heard the thundering challenge of other bulls echo from the trees around my herd as I moved my cows and calves closer each day, to the healing water.

Late one day, I circled my herd in the shade of a large meadow high in the canyon above the healing pond. A soft breeze flowed gently down the steep canyon's side, gently stroking the grass in the meadow before us as it moved silently on. A reverberating bugle thundered suddenly from the canyon below us. Anger boiled within me, as I glared indignantly toward the unseen maker of this call that challenged me now, when the bulls of the season of mating should be at rest.

The bellowing call echoed again from the trees below our meadow, and I knew that a great bull now quickly approached. The enormous one burst from the trees at the edge of the meadow and stood broadside, glaring upward toward where I stood. The bull had wide, towering antlers that were as thick, it seemed, as were his front legs. Muscles rippled beneath the light tan hide of his shoulders and hips as he began moving slowly upward.

I stood quietly in the center of the meadow, my nervous cows watching from the edge, as the immense bull, grunting and moaning fiercely, moved toward me. When but a few paces away, the bull sprang forward, and we met with a deafening crash of antlers. I lunged and twisted, grinding my antlers powerfully against his great horns, as I pushed him backward across the meadow. Shaking free from him, I raised my head glaring with rage, and sprang forward once more to collide furiously with him. The air was filled with the wrenching sounds of our terrible struggle

444

as I drove the bull backward through the meadow. Twisting my head with all my strength, I drove him straining and grunting, to the ground. As I tore free from the antlers of the bull, he sprang immediately to his feet and lunged forward once more, striking me with all the strength he had.

Again, and again, we crashed violently together, huffing and heaving, shrouded in a rising cloud of dust. With each shocking collision I drove him groaning to the ground, only to see him struggle boldly to his feet and attack me once more. As our battle raged on, we crashed from the meadow into the surrounding forest, sending frightened cows and calves bolting in all directions. From deep within us came shuddering grunts and moans as we collided, grinding our great antlers violently together, twisting and turning, destroying all that was around us. We powerfully forced one another through clumps of small trees and stumbled and crashed over brushy, fallen logs.

As I lunged once more, pushing the immense bull backward with all my might, we crashed awkwardly over yet another downfallen tree. I felt my foot sink deeply into an unseen foxhole hidden beneath its brushy limbs. With a resounding crack, the old bullet wound in my front shoulder gave way. In searing pain, I twisted awkwardly to the ground as my opponent's mighty antlers sank deep into my ribs. I sprang to my feet in a fit of rage with blood pouring from my side. Dragging my front leg that hung uselessly from my broken shoulder, I hit the great bull with all my strength.

445

My frightened cows and calves watched in disbelief as the bull drove me again to the earth. Fighting desperately to gain my feet and barely able to stand, I lowered my antlers and faced him.

"Finish your work, huge one!" I bellowed with rage as he glared angrily back. As the bull lowered his head for his final attack, Wicala jumped suddenly from the timber and stood between us.

"Leave us, Wicala, we must finish!" I shouted angrily.

"No, great one," said Wicala, "I will not go. I will stand between you and death as you have done for me many times. I will gladly give my life for you," she said, as she turned and faced the enormous bull.

The confused bull slowly raised his head and watched in awe as cows and calves poured from the forest and gathered around Wicala and me.

"Go with him," I gasped painfully to the cows and calves that now stood around me. "He has earned the right to lead. You must go."

But they remained at my sides and would not leave. Even when the frustrated victor knocked the cows from their feet as he tried angrily to push them from the meadow, they would rise from the ground and glare at him in defiance, then stand once again near me in their herd.

Frustrated by their unyielding refusal of his attempts to herd them, the bull realized finally that even though I stood crippled and dying before him, he had somehow lost. Angrily, he walked stiffly past my rebellious herd of cows and disappeared into the trees at the meadow's edge.

As he walked from the meadow, the world around me began to grow dark. I sank weakly to the ground and lay staring blankly upward in the midst of my shaken cows. Curiously, my eyes focused on a tiny object far above me in the sky. As it drew steadily closer, I realized it was a great winged one. The eagle circled closely above me in the meadow, bathing me in comforting gusts of wind as it pumped its mighty wings. Then with a loud, screeching call, the great bird flew downward in the canyon toward the healing water.

Remembering the mysterious strength of the secret pond, I rolled and kicked and struggled somehow to my feet. With my bewildered herd following quietly behind, I stumbled downward in the canyon toward the healing water. My journey through the trees and meadows of the canyon was agonizing, but somehow, I staggered on. As I looked behind me at the loyal cows and calves that had refused to leave, I realized that my herd was growing steadily as others joined us on our strange, downward passage.

The great winged one flew from the top of a tree at my side as I entered the meadow that lay above the healing water and circled above me as I struggled painfully forward toward the pond at its lower end.

My bleary eyes were drawn somehow to a strangely familiar figure as I neared the steaming water. A cow and calf watched silently from the edge of the pond as I approached. I felt suddenly as if I walked in both the present and the past. It was as though I was suspended between two worlds, torn between two places and times as I remembered years ago, watching quietly from my mother's side as the enormous wounded leader staggered painfully toward us.

As I neared the pond, the eagle landed in a tree at its edge and watched as I stumbled down the bank and splashed painfully into the warm water.

"Thank you, Ksapa, you have brought me home," I breathed, as I watched the huge bird spring from the tree in a flurry of wings and fly silently from view.

The cows and calves of my herd spread throughout the meadow around the pond and began feeding nervously as I lay soaking in the healing water. Wicala stood quietly on the bank at my side.

The water soothed the terrible pain in my shoulder, and I soon entered a dazed restfulness.

In my mind, I saw my mother again at the pond's edge as she rolled and kicked in the yellow mud when first she had showed me how to wallow. I remembered the terrible fire that had roared through the trees around me here, when as a calf I had stood terrified in these waters, hoping somehow to survive the twisting flames. I could see again the great silver bear as he stared quietly at me from across the water, as together, we endured the terrible firestorm. I remembered the wrathful warning I had given Kasota when staring into his wild eyes from the pond's edge, long ago. "Indeed," I muttered quietly, "we did meet again."

As I lay in the water in a strange half-sleep, lost in the memories of my life's journey, the words that Woslolkia had so often shared with me in the shadowy haze of my dreams, echoed softly from the darkness. I clearly heard the words he had spoken to me long ago, when as a calf I had turned anxiously from him in a blinding fog to begin my first journey. Finally, I understood this second journey of the two he had said I must walk alone in life. I knew, as Woslolkia had promised, that I would soon understand the endless circle of life. I remembered the great bull's calming words when I had once stood before him overwhelmed with fear, and afraid to walk forward. As he had predicted on that foggy mountain long ago, I had indeed faced the most fearsome predator of all. I had shown the two-legged ones the path upon which they would find their way home. My life had been as my mother had said, when at the end of my first journey she had given me my name.

"Yes, mother," I whispered into the darkness, "Like the wind after which you named me, I have touched all corners of this great land." 'Indeed,' I realized, 'I had walked with the wind.'

I lay in the healing water until far into the night. The terrible pain in my shoulder and my dizzying sickness slowly eased, replaced by a strange calmness that began to settle over me.

When the first streaks of light began to show in the sky, I struggled to my feet and staggered from the water. With Wicala walking beside me, I stumbled through the meadow toward the trees. As I neared the meadow's edge, I saw the silhouette of the cow and calf I had seen earlier, lying beneath the trees where my mother and I had lain so many times. I remembered when long ago, the enormous wounded herd bull had struggled past us in the darkness. As I moved past them, I thought of the protective warmth of my mother, and I wished that she were with me now.

Lightning flashed above the meadow and thunder echoed through the canyon when daylight at last came. As the day became fully light, I lay in the grass beneath a steady rain with Wicala standing silently at my side. I watched through weakening eyes as the cows and calves of my herd passed respectfully before me. As they spread out through the grassy opening and began to feed, my eyes were drawn to a large cow with a young calf standing nervously beneath her. They watched me in silence, nearly hidden in the mist at the edge of the meadow. "Mother…." I whispered.

Suddenly, from in the canyon below the healing water came a thunderous bugle.

All heads shot from the grass, and ears strained forward as the cows and calves of my herd watched intently. Two huge bulls crashed suddenly from the trees below the pond, grunting and bellowing as they battled one another angrily. An enormous bull, much larger than the first two, pushed a small herd of anxious cows and calves from the trees behind the fighting pair. With nostrils flared and eyes wide with intensity, he stood quietly breathing the scent of the many cows and calves in the meadow before him. The bull that had defeated me finally in our violent battle for the right to lead, had followed me here to the healing water. A wave of anger boiled suddenly within me, but I was unable even to raise my head.

The enormous bull ran excitedly through my herd, angrily horning and prodding as he gathered the nervous cows that had just a day before denied his leadership. As the new leader anxiously pressed my frightened herd rumbling past where I lay, a great flash of lightning filled the sky and as thunder rolled through the canyon, I struggled once more from my growing darkness. I raised my head from the grass and watched with dignity as my great herd thundered by.

As the churning bodies rumbled past me, I saw through my growing haze, a beautiful cow behind which desperately ran a young bull calf. Our eyes locked for a moment as the wide-eyed young one lunged fearfully by. I saw in his frightened eyes the beginning of the journey that had been mine. I understood suddenly that this little one's path and mine were one. I knew that his great circle of life would end here, where I now lay.

"Go fearlessly, young one," I whispered.

As darkness descended upon me, a brilliant flash of light filled the canyon....

My head shot from the grass in fright as a mighty crash of thunder shook the canyon around me. I struggled into wakefulness torn suddenly from my fitful dream. I became slowly aware of a soft warmth against which I lay as I fought to clear my mind from the troubling fog that had filled my sleep. Fully awake, I sprang from my bed in bewilderment. I stared in shock at my small, spotted, tan body and the short, frail legs upon which I stood.

"I...I am a calf, again!" I screamed in disbelief, as I whirled and stared in astonishment at the wondrous form of my mother who lay watching me sleepily from our grassy bed.

"Mother," I cried excitedly, "You are here! ...You have returned to me!"

Unable to contain the terrible excitement that pounded through every fiber of my being, I spun away from my bewildered mother. Across the meadow I bound, darting crazily this way and that, in a frenzy of indescribable joy. My jubilance was instantly contagious, and my curious mother ran excitedly behind me, following my headlong rush through the rain.

Overcome suddenly by the incredible reality that had befallen me, I came to a sliding halt and spun wildly to stare into her perplexed eyes.

"The wolves!... Ksapa!... the great fire!... it was a dream!... a dream!" I blurted breathlessly to her.

Beyond my mother, a movement at the edge of the meadow caught my eye. The old cow that had stayed faithfully beside the great wounded leader rose feebly from the grass at his side. The mysterious bull lay motionless beneath her in the grass as if asleep.

As I studied the old cow, I was suddenly over-come by a strange knowing. "It was not a dream," I muttered aloud.

I stood for a moment shuddering at the enormity of what I suddenly knew to be so.

"Wicala," I whispered, as I looked breathlessly back to my mother.

"Yes, it is Wicala" she said, as she held my pleading stare with timeless, knowing eyes.

Then, she said quietly, "now, Tateh, my brave young son….fearless leader of our kind, you know at last, the great bull's name."

Made in United States
Orlando, FL
17 December 2021

12032418R00248